Microsoft®
COMBAT FLIGHT SIMULATOR
WWII EUROPE SERIES

Ben Chiu

Microsoft *Press*

PUBLISHED BY
Microsoft Press
A Division of Microsoft Corporation
One Microsoft Way
Redmond, Washington 98052-6399

Copyright © 1998 by The PC Press, Inc.

Library of Congress Cataloging-in-Publication Data
Chiu, Ben, 1963-
     Microsoft Combat Flight Simulator: Inside Moves / Ben Chiu.
          p. cm.
     Includes index.
     ISBN 1-57231-592-X
     1. Microsoft Combat Flight Simulator.   2. Computer war games.
3. Fighter plane combat--Computer simulation.   4. Computer flight
games. 5. World War, 1939-1945--Aerial operations--Computer
simulation. I. Title.
     U310.C42   1998
     793.9'2'0285--dc21   98-38263
                                                           CIP

Printed and bound in the United States of America.

2 3 4 5 6 7 8 9   MLML   3 2 1 0 9 8

Distributed in Canada by ITP Nelson, a division of Thomson Canada Limited.

A CIP catalogue record for this book is available from the British Library.

Microsoft Press books are available through booksellers and distributors worldwide. For further information about international editions, contact your local Microsoft Corporation office or contact Microsoft Press International directly at fax (425) 936-7329. Visit our Web site at mspress.microsoft.com.

Acquisitions Editor: Kim Fryer
Project Editor: Saul Candib

Dedication

This book is dedicated to the men and women
of the armed services past, present, and future
for putting their lives on the line
so the rest of us can play games on our computers.
Honor those who have fallen by teaching your children—
those who forget history are doomed to repeat it.

And to Uncle Jimmy, who taught me the lessons of honor,
responsibility, respect, and compassion
through his example.

Ben Chiu

Acknowledgments

I would like to thank Ben Chiu for the hundreds of hours
he has spent researching, studying, writing and—in general—relentlessly
pursuing the information found in this book.
I would also like to thank Mary for putting up with both of us,
but mostly for putting up with Ben.
Thanks are also due Kathleen Ingram, Kim Davis,
Lance Elko, and Phill Powell at The PC Press, Inc.
and Kim Fryer and Saul Candib at Microsoft Press.,
Numerous people at Microsoft Games were involved
in kindly providing us with help and patient assistance,
even during their own work crunches.
On the Combat Flight Simulator Team: Christina Chen, Kris Shankar,
Mike Schroeter, Michael Ahn, and Todd Laney.
Our thanks also to Carl E. Hellerich, John Mooney, Joseph Favors,
the entire CFS Beta testing team, and especially Steve Coutches
for his hands-on insights into the fabulous Mustang.

Robert C. Lock
President and Editor-in-Chief
The PC Press, Inc.

Contents

Introduction

So Ya Wanna Be a Fighter Pilot...

Microsoft Combat Flight Simulator: Inside Moves is the comprehensive guide for hints, tips, and strategies to the combat version of world's most popular flight simulator—Microsoft Flight Simulator 98. This book was designed as an enhancement to the Pilot's Manual and the extensive online help system that comes with Combat Flight Simulator—not to replace them. Air combat is an extremely complex subject. This book covers the essential skills you should know and learn while providing some historical and tactical insights into air combat during WWII. Armed with these critical details, you'll be able rule the virtual skies of Combat Flight Simulator!

Every effort has been made not to duplicate information found in Combat Flight Simulator's resources, so if you see something you think is missing here, the chances are good you'll find it in Combat Flight Simulator's Pilot's Manual, Combat Flight Simulator's online help system, or in the Training Missions.

The Pilot's Manual and Combat Flight Simulator's help system tell you what things are, and provide some general information on how to use them. This book takes you to the next level and discusses the little details and tips on how things are used, *when* they should be used, and perhaps—most valuable of all—*why* things are done the way they're done. For example the combination of knowing a maneuver, *and* where it could be used within a battle can mean the difference between becoming an Ace or becoming a virtual statistic. Microsoft Combat Flight Simulator: Inside Moves will help transform even the greenest flight cadet into a skilled fighter pilot because it contains tips and strategies found nowhere else—straight from the source.

If you're new to aviation, as you probably imagine, flying is a complex subject all by itself. When you add other airplanes and air combat it really complicates matters. Becoming a successful combat pilot is in some ways is like becoming a musician. You need to study and practice to become really good at it (in air combat the idea is to shoot down other airplanes while not getting shot down yourself). To quote General Chuck Yeager, "there ain't no such thing as a natural pilot." Training is everything. Take that to heart if you

ever feel overwhelmed while learning the concepts discussed in this book. Another thing you should remember is everyone (even the best combat pilots) were beginners at some time, and everyone encounters one problem or another during their flight and combat training.

Statistically, the chances are pretty good that many of you are Flight Simulator veterans. While what you've learned in Flight Simulator will serve you well, flying combat is a whole other ball of wax. When it comes to aviation (real or simulated) it takes knowledge AND skill to become a truly great aviator and combat pilot. So it really helps to be open-minded and learn from as many sources as you have at your disposal. Fortunately for everyone, with Combat Flight Simulator you potentially get the best of both worlds.

It has been said that air combat isn't fought like a chess match—move and countermove—because it's a "fluid" event. As a consequence of this belief many believe it shouldn't be taught like the ancient strategic board game either. During my years of martial arts training, the business of hand-to-hand combat was taught exactly by move and countermove. After years of repetition, learning variations and options, your fighting style becomes fluid. When it does it enables you to perform through instinct rather than through a conscious thought process. I believe air combat could be taught roughly the same way. I've had great success in passing along air combat theory using this method throughout my career.

Few of us can afford to dedicate years to studying the art of air combat, and our priority is to get you up flying and fighting in the shortest time possible. That's why instead of just throwing maneuvers at you as many other books and manuals tend to do, we'll discuss concepts within the context of an air battle. I've found this to be the best way to impart exact examples of how and when maneuvers are performed, but more importantly, it'll help you understand why they work. Not only has this helped newer pilots comprehend this subject, it makes it infinitely easier to see the "big picture" of an air battle and the roles of each of the various elements.

Whether you're serious or just curious, no matter what your preference, this book has something to offer flight simulation and air combat fans of all levels. As a multi-engine and instrument rated pilot who works as a computer flight simulation analyst specializing in air combat, I hope to introduce the important concepts and tactics you'll need to fight this war while providing some engaging perspectives on why things went the way they did. So if you're ready, let's get started. There're bandits out there and we need good pilots! Welcome to the squadron and good hunting!

—Ben Chiu

Chapter One

SCRAMBLE—QUICK START

"Combat is the ultimate flying experience."

—Brig. General (ret.) Chuck Yeager, USAF, 13 kills.

Welcome to Microsoft Combat Flight Simulator! Microsoft Flight Simulator has always pushed the limits of existing technologies, and Combat Flight Simulator continues the tradition.

Installing Combat Flight Simulator

To Install Combat Flight Simulator, insert the Combat Flight Simulator CD into your CD-ROM drive. If Autoplay is enabled (the feature that automatically runs a CD when its inserted in your drive), the Combat Flight Simulator Setup Screen will launch automatically. If Autoplay is disabled and the Combat Flight Simulator Setup Screen does not automatically launch, go to My Computer and double-click your CD-ROM drive's icon. Next double-click the file named SETUP.EXE. Click the Install button in the Combat Flight Simulator welcome screen, and follow the directions as they're presented to you by the installation routine.

Welcome to Microsoft Combat Flight Simulator!

Once installation is complete, you'll then be asked whether you'd like to Restart your computer. Although you can exit Setup without restarting your computer, note that you won't be able to play Combat Flight Simulator until you do restart.

Starting Combat Flight Simulator for the First Time

Once Combat Flight Simulator is installed (if you have Autoplay enabled on your system), the next time you insert the Combat Flight Simulator CD into your CD-ROM drive, you will now see a Play button, as well as two new buttons named Reinstall and Uninstall.

As you'd expect, clicking the Play button will start Combat Flight Simulator. The first time you run Combat Flight Simulator and any time you add new scenery files, a message box will appear indicating that a database for new scenery files is being built. There's nothing to do here but sit back and get ready to fly!

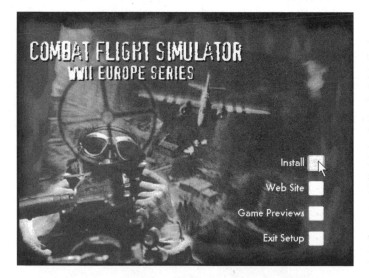

The Setup screen appears when you insert the Combat Flight Simulator CD—if you have Autoplay enabled.

The Main Menu

When you start up Combat Flight Simulator, the Microsoft logo movie and Combat Flight Simulator movie will play. Next you're be introduced to Combat Flight Simulator's Main Menu, which is often referred to in the game as Home.

From the Main Menu you can access Combat Flight Simulator's main activities with just a click of your mouse. On the right side of this screen are six options: Free Flight, Quick

Combat, Single Missions, Campaigns, Multiplayer, and Training Missions. Along the bottom of the screen are three more options named Settings, Help, and Exit.

Go ahead and click the Free Flight button and then click Fly Now! We'll come back to the other activities in a minute. Let's discuss some of the more basic features of Combat Flight Simulator before moving on.

You can access Combat Flight Simulator's main activities from this screen.

Navigating the Combat Flight Simulator Interface

Because Combat Flight Simulator is based on Microsoft Flight Simulator technology, most everything in Combat Flight Simulator is point and click—you literally point to what you want to do with your mouse pointer and click it. In addition to all of the general Windows 95 and Windows 98 conventions such as resizing a window by dragging a window border (achieved by clicking and holding the mouse button as you move the mouse) or closing a window (achieved by clicking on the Close Control Box), many of the dials and switches on the cockpit instrument panels also work by clicking or dragging them with your mouse.

For instance you can engage the engine starter by clicking it. Next click the flap control handle, for example, to adjust flap settings.

To learn how to operate control knobs and levers that don't simply toggle on and off with your mouse, first note that when you position the mouse pointer over a control, the pointer changes from the usual arrow symbol to a hand symbol. The

There are six main options on the Home screen.

Combat Flight Simulator supports all of the general Windows 95 conventions such as clicking on the Close Control Box to close a window.

Clicking the starter switch will engage the engine's starter.

You can adjust control settings by strategically placing the pointer and clicking the control.

hand has a plus sign or a minus sign superimposed on it; a plus sign means that control will increase its current setting with each mouse click, while a minus sign will decrease the current setting with each mouse click. Pointing to the top or bottom (or right side or left side depending on its orientation) of each knob will change the pointer's polarity or sign. But generally pointing above or to the right side of a control will change the pointer to a plus sign, and pointing below or to the left of a control will change the pointer to a minus sign.

Other features associated with Combat Flight Simulator's mouse are drop-down menus and Quicktips.

Drop-down menus are called up by a right-click and they provide quick access to often used features and settings. Drop-down menus are window sensitive. In other words, right-clicking another window (which sometimes just look like another area of the screen) may bring up additional menu choices.

Quicktips are little reminders that appear when you point at a hotspot. Combat Flight Simulator's hotspots are all located on instrument panels—so if you forget what an instrument is, just point your pointer at it. A second later, a little window with the name of the instrument will appear.

The last two Windows conventions you should be aware of are the Fullscreen toggle and the Cool Switch (also known as the task switch). Pressing the Alt + Enter combination on the keyboard will cycle Combat Flight Simulator between Fullscreen and Windows mode.

The Cool Switch keys Alt + Tab will allow you to switch between Combat Flight Simulator and other Windows programs. To achieve the best performance, you shouldn't be running other programs in the background while running Combat Flight Simulator, although sometimes it's unavoidable (for example, when playing against other pilots over the Internet).

Main Activities in Combat Flight Simulator

As we mentioned earlier, you can access all of Combat Flight Simulator's activities from the main Home screen. Let's discuss the activities offered here.

Free Flight

The Free Flight activity can be very handy if you want to get to know your airplane without having to worry about someone shooting at you. Just getting into the air and flying can be a daunting task all by itself—so if you're a beginner, you'd naturally want to spend some time here. But even if you're a combat hardened veteran, this area can help you hone your flying skills as well as help you lean the intricacies of extracting maximum performance from a fighter.

Clicking the Free Flight selection causes the Free Flight window to appear. In this window you are able to select and configure the aircraft that you'll fly, select the time of day and weather conditions, and select where you'll begin your flight.

Player Aircraft: This allows you to select any of the Combat Flight Simulator user-flyable aircraft you have installed on your system, and then configure its fuel and weapons loadout. You can use your mouse to manipulate the model of the selected airplane that appears in the window and read up on some of the vital specifications of the aircraft.

Time and Weather Stats: From the Time and Weather dialogue box you can adjust the Time of day, Clouds, and Wind that you'll encounter during your flight. You can select any time of the day (night is not an option), any of three cloud types (clear is not an option), and one of four wind conditions. Once these variables are set, they'll remain constant throughout your flight.

Start Location: Allows you to choose the location where you'll begin your flight and the starting altitude. There are two ways to set the starting location for your flight. The simplest is by selecting an airport from the drop-down menu on the upper right hand side of the screen. By selecting the Exact location radio button and entering the coordinates and altitude in the appropriate boxes, you can be even more specific.

Quick Combat

Just as it sounds, Quick Combat is the fastest way to get into action. In addition to being a great way to blow off steam, this activity can also be used for combat training and honing your air combat skills. The Quick Combat selection on the Home screen will take you to the Quick Combat window. From here you can access the same configuration items found on the Free Flight screen, as well as two new configuration areas.

Enemies: Here you can select the number and type of enemy aircraft you'll face, and the tactical situation you'll be placed in when you enter combat. The number of aircraft you select will also dictate the number of aircraft that will make up a wave. In other words if you select 5 aircraft waves, a new set of five aircraft will appear when you destroy all of the previous five.

Aircraft can be selected by type (fighters, bombers, or both), aircraft model, or war affiliation. Tactical situations are referenced to your selected tactical situation. If you select Offensive, you'll be in no danger of being shot when you first enter the activity. If you select Neutral or Defensive, watch out!

Enemy level: You can select one of three enemy skill levels you'll face. All enemy pilots will be the same—based on your selection. As you'd expect, Rookie will be the dumbest, Ace will be the smartest, and Veteran will fall somewhere in between.

Single Missions

The difference between Single Missions and a Campaign are two-fold—you can play single missions in any order you choose, and there is no "career" or pilot being tracked for performance. This means you can't earn medals and your success or failure has no bearing on anything other than your pride.

From the Single Mission window you can select the Enemy level. The radio buttons next to the Fly For text will mask all but the selected choice. For example, selecting the RAF button will keep all of the missions—except those flown from the Royal Air Force perspective—from appearing in the main window in the center of the screen.

Clicking the Next button will take you to the Mission Briefing screen. From there you'll have access to the Change Aircraft window—but more importantly, this is where you'll receive your mission briefing. We'll discuss missions and how Mission Briefings fit into the big picture later on in the book.

Campaigns

We'll also discuss Combat Flight Simulator's Campaigns more later on—but briefly, the Campaigns screen is where you select the campaign you'll fight in, which side you'll fight for, and the pilot you'll fly as. As we hinted earlier, the

main differences between Single Missions and Campaigns are mission sequencing and your career as a pilot.

Multiplayer

In addition to simple multiplayer activities (modem, LAN, and direct connect gameplay), another one of Combat Flight Simulator's features is the ability to fly Combat Flight Simulator with other desktop pilots on the Internet. Clicking Multiplayer brings up the Multiplayer screen, which allows you to connect with other players. We'll talk more about this activity later on in this book.

Training Missions

As you might imagine, Training Missions contain just that—missions designed to help you learn the business of air combat. From this window you can select the Training Mission you want to study and watch training videos. The main difference between Training Missions and other missions is that you receive instruction as you fly the mission.

Getting Help

There are three Combat Flight Simulator help resources available to you. Just like the concept behind open book tests—knowing everything isn't always possible, but knowing where to look for the right answers is the next best thing. Let's look at each of Combat Flight Simulator's help resources and talk a little about what kind of information they contain and how to access each of them.

Pilot's Manual

The first obvious place to look for help is the printed Pilot's Manual that's included in the Combat Flight Simulator package. It includes background information about the new features in Combat Flight Simulator, the airplanes modeled, and basic flight theory. If you are seeking information other than this—you'll need to check one of the other sources.

Microsoft Combat Flight Simulator Help

The next obvious place to look for help is in the aptly named Microsoft Combat Flight Simulator Help system. Microsoft Combat Flight Simulator's Help

Note: *Custom key assignments will not be reflected in the Keyboard Quick Reference.*

system is further broken down into other sections.

Game Controllers Overview: This section includes information about using the joystick, mouse, or keyboard in Combat Flight Simulator—including procedures for using and customizing these controllers.

Maximizing Performance: This section contains suggestions on how to maximize Combat Flight Simulator's performance on your computer.

Keyboard Quick Reference: Can be accessed any time you're in an airplane by pressing F2. This command brings up an overlay that contains many of the most common key commands.

Help Contents and Index: Places all of the information in Combat Flight Simulator's Help system at your fingertips. From here you can directly search for the answers you're after.

Glossary: This is where you'll find the meanings to the terms and acronyms you'll encounter in Combat Flight Simulator.

There are three ways to start Microsoft Combat Flight Simulator's Help system: click the Help selection on the menu bar in Combat Flight Simulator's main window, click on any of the Help buttons or ? buttons from any of the other screens, or press F1 on your keyboard.

What's This?

Combat Flight Simulator's help system also has a context-sensitive help feature. Right-clicking an instrument or control in a cockpit and selecting What's This? from the drop-down menu will bring up a quick help text box.

Microsoft on the Web

The last, but always most current, source for help and information about Combat Flight Simulator is on the Internet. Combat Flight Simulator provides links to Web pages in the Help menu of the main Flight Simulator 98 window.

Chapter Two

PREFLIGHT

In the real world, an aircraft preflight is a safety check. Only a pilot wishing to tempt death jumps into an airplane and takes off without some sort of preflight check. That's because an airplane is a complex machine and you're bound to run into trouble if you forget or neglect to preflight your aircraft.

Although Microsoft Combat Flight Simulator is merely a simulation played on your computer (so the only thing at risk is your virtual life—although the pride of some overanxious pilots has been known to take a little dent or two), there are several things that must be setup or checked *before* takeoff. Otherwise your flight may end up being unexpectedly short. A couple of minutes spent here can spare you a lot of aggravation in the long run. This chapter covers the little hardware and software details that can make or break your flight before you ever get a chance to see a bandit.

Controllers

Just as medieval knights had to become a fighting unit with their trusty mounts, you need to develop a similar relationship with your aircraft. At the risk of sounding like a Zen master, you need to become "one with your aircraft"—and the way you're "interfacing" with your aircraft is through some kind of control input device. We're talking about

Neglecting to preflight your virtual aircraft can lead to shorter than expected flights.

CH Products' Virtual Pilot Pro is a good example of a quality flight yoke. But be aware that all of the user-flyable aircraft in Combat Flight Simulator use joysticks for control in real life.

A joystick with a view hat like this X-Fighter from ThrustMaster should be a main priority.

the keyboard, mouse, joystick or other controller. So let's contemplate some of the considerations and recommendations for controller choices, as well as installation and configuration instructions.

Recommended Joystick

Although there are those who can fly well by keyboard alone (or by mouse and keyboard), for the rest of us *mere mortals*, a good quality joystick (one that centers fairly well and won't snap off in your hands) can mean the difference between life and death in air combat. In addition, beginning desktop pilots usually find a joystick or flight yoke (a kind of steering wheel setup for airplanes) easier to adjust to.

The reasoning behind this is easy to understand when you consider that all of the real aircraft modeled in Combat Flight Simulator use either a flight stick or flight yoke, rather than a mouse or keyboard for flight control. (Note that all of the real versions of the aircraft modeled in Combat Flight Simulator—that you're allowed to fly—are controlled by joystick.) If flying by a keyboard or mouse offered any advantages, these peripherals would have been adopted by the aviation world by now. So if you're after realism, the controller choice will be obvious.

If you're shopping for a new joystick, look for one that feels good and sturdy. Some sticks are better suited for big hands, and some are good for people with smaller hands.

The best advice is to go to a store and check them out in person.

Another thing to consider is that in the heat of battle (depending on how cool you are in the cockpit) your joystick may have to take a lot of abuse, so only consider buying one from an established company. The chances are greater that they'll be around to support you in the future should you have any problems. ThrustMaster, CH Products, and of course, Microsoft all make quality products worthy of your consideration.

Next, choosing a stick with a view hat should be a main priority. As you'll see later on, staying alive during an air combat sortie will require you to be able to see the enemy before they can get the jump on you. It's been estimated that about 90 percent of all air-to-air losses recorded in all wars were a result of the victim not even seeing their attacker. Because we're playing on a computer and our view of the simulated world is limited to looking at a monitor, anything that can assist your viewing duties will greatly increase your chances of survival.

The flexibility of a programmable stick like this F-22 Pro from ThrustMaster will justify the increased cost over a standard joystick.

While it may be tough to get used to, a view hat will reduce your viewing effort because of its convenience. Eventually its use will become second nature and you'll know where you are looking based on tactile feel (for example, the direction you push the hat). Anything you can do to decrease your cockpit workload will help you in the long run.

Finally, even though you can map Combat Flight Simulator's commands to use joystick inputs, a joystick with programmability features like the ThrustMaster F-22 Pro can still be handy. The flexibility of programmable sticks will justify the increase in cost if you're serious about your sim'ing. Other features such as a throttle slider and rotational capabilities (twisting action) are good if you don't plan on buying separate throttle rudder controllers.

The CH F-16 Combatstick features a throttle wheel at its base.

Controller Placement

One aspect of controller configuration that usually goes un-addressed when discussing flight sims is the physical placement of the controllers. What we're talking about is the physical location of each controller in relation to where you sit, and what you sit on.

Because your aircraft is moving in flight when you sit inside the cockpit of an airplane—and possibly bouncing around quite a bit—the only way to maintain precise control of your aircraft is to have steady hands. The way you help keep your hands steady under such conditions is to brace your arms (or more precisely your elbows) on something. When your elbows are supported against something solid, it helps your hands maintain the stability required for good aircraft control—and ultimately good aircraft control is the main component of good marksmanship and extracting maximum flight performance.

Naturally you don't need to worry about G forces, turbulence, or other jarring movements while sitting in front of your computer, but the technique used in real airplanes can be beneficial to computer pilots just the same. Moving your controls to an exact position is really difficult to do without bracing yourself against something. What you can use to brace yourself ranges from pressing your back into a sturdy chair, to resting the edge of your palm or wrist against the base of your joystick as you move it.

The control stick in a typical WWII fighter usually extends from the floor up between the pilot's legs. While you're seated in the cockpit seat you can generally rely on your body to be a fairly stable place to brace your elbow (because you're strapped in your seat pretty firmly). Pressing your elbow against your rib cage or resting your forearm on your leg can give you the support you desire. Unfortunately, the vast majority of computer flight controllers are designed for desktop use, so these traditional, real-world bracing points become less useful.

Popular alternatives for desktop controllers include using the arm of a chair or the edge of your computer table as substitutes. Using the "arm in the rib cage" method isn't recommended because it can become tiresome after a while. Of course such decisions are a matter of personal preference, but the armrest works the best for many pilots.

If you use rudder pedals, their placement and what you sit on also deserves some attention. First, you want to sit close enough to not only reach the rudder pedals, but to be able to operate them throughout their complete range of motion.

Next, because you'll be losing much of the stability normally gained from having your feet firmly planted on the floor, the kind of chair you sit on is equally important. The first time you do a little dance on your rudder pedals and your nifty, super-ergonomic computer chair rolls or tilts backwards, you'll quickly realize that you need to develop a more stable seating arrangement.

Now that you know what to look for, try anything you can think of to meet your requirements and see what works best for you. Again, even though you aren't faced with outside forces affecting your controller stability, bracing your hands and sitting on something stable will increase the precision of your controller movements greatly. Try it, you'll like it!

> **Note:** *Unless you disable auto rudder by un-checking the Enable auto rudder box in the Settings window, your rudder controller won't work when you're up in the air.*

Recommended Rudder Pedals

If you have rudder pedals, use them. If you don't, consider purchasing a quality set of pedals like the ThrustMaster Elite Rudder Pedals or a joystick with rotational capabilities such as the Microsoft SideWinder 3D Pro. (You can calibrate the rotational axis on those types of joysticks to act as rudder pedals.)

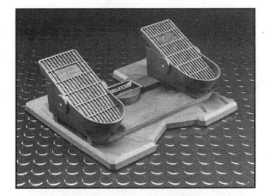

Consider purchasing a quality set of rudder pedals like the ThrustMaster Elite Rudder Pedals—if you're going to fly at the Hard and Medium Aircraft Flight Realism Levels.

The Pro Pedals from CH Products work well for both driving sims and racing sims.

Which one you'll be happier with is a matter of personal preference. Using rudder pedals in real airplanes is all part of the experience of flying, and for some people, using a twisting joystick instead of a set of pedals just may not seem realistic enough. So that's one consideration you may want to grapple with.

The other consideration is that a joystick and a set of pedals will usually cost more than a multi-axis joystick—but not always. So if cost is factor (and when isn't it for anyone?)—it pays to shop around.

Anyway, the ultimate reason for geting a set of rudder pedals or other rudder controller is that the lack of precision rudder control will hamper your marksmanship skills and can even make you an easier target to shoot down. One of the main reasons rudder pedals are more critical in Combat Flight Simulator—as opposed to simulations such as Flight Simulator 98—is that the relative sizes of bullets compared to an enemy airplane is much greater than the relative sizes of your aircraft to a runway. So any extra help you can get to assist lining up your aircraft will only help make your job easier.

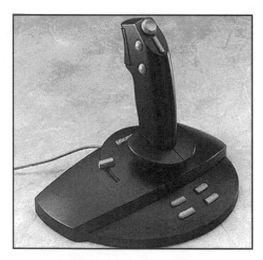

A joystick such as the Microsoft SideWinder 3D Pro has rotational capabilities and a throttle slider all in one neatly arranged package.

Throttle—Neat, But Not a "Must Have"

Combat Flight Simulator allows you to use the keyboard, mouse, or throttle controller (whether it's a dedicated throttle controller or the throttle wheel on a joystick) to control the throttle. But unlike rudder control, the keyboard is fine for throttle control. Despite the philosophical realism differences, a lack of precision throttle control won't get you killed. If you have to make a choice between a rudder controller or throttle controller,

you'd be better off getting the rudder controller. Then again, a joystick with a throttle wheel and a set of rudder pedals is a pretty good compromise.

Force Feedback Support

Combat Flight Simulator supports force feedback joysticks through DirectX 6.0. In addition to a force feedback joystick, you'll need the proper drivers to use it. Please see your force feedback joystick manufacturer's instructions for installation instructions.

A force feedback joystick can really add to the Combat Flight Simulator flight experience. In addition to being a pleasure to use and offering a whole new level of realism, it can also provide other advantages. Through the force feedback feature you'll be able to feel the shaking of oncoming stalls, the bumping of turbulence, the rumble of your wheels rolling on the ground, appropriate control stiffening when airspeeds increase, and the contrasting lightening as airspeed decreases.

Since you can't feel with your body what your virtual airplane is doing while you sit in front of your computer, force feedback technology can help remedy this deficiency. This will (as you'll see later when we talk about extracting maximum performance from

Note: *The Game Controllers control panel can be accessed from inside Combat Flight Simulator by clicking the Game Controllers button in the Settings window.*

The ThrustMaster WCS II is a programmable throttle controller that will work with most joysticks and will add programmability to them as well.

Although it's modeled after a modern F-16 jet fighter instead of a WWII aircraft, the TQS from ThrustMaster is the companion throttle controller that'll only work with their F-22Pro and FLCS programmable joysticks.

your aircraft) net you a big advantage. If you're after the ultimate that Combat Flight Simulator can offer, consider checking out force feedback technology.

Graphics and Hardware Issues

One of the oldest quandaries of computer games and simulations is what many call the "look and feel dilemma." Unless you're at the peak of the "bleeding edge" of computer technology or in the "hardware of the week upgrade club", we're all forced to make the decision to fly simulations that either look good and feel bad, or feel good and look bad.

Fortunately, Combat Flight Simulator features many configuration options to provide some middle ground for those of us who don't have the fastest computers on the planet. We'll discuss how that works and why you have to make such choices in a minute. But if you have some extra money burning a hole in your pocket, let's look at some of the hardware options available to you.

You can't have too much computing power for Combat Flight Simulator. Any additional computer processing power you may have (or dream of having) can be turned into higher resolution graphics.

Graphics Performance = Combat Performance

As mentioned earlier, Combat Flight Simulator offers a myriad of configuration options—and the most consequential of them are the graphics options. Graphics options not only affect what you see on your monitor, but they can also help compensate for hardware performance limitations. The trade off for graphics complexity is the speed with which graphics are redrawn to produce the illusion of movement (commonly referred to as *frame rate*). Combat Flight Simulator is no exception.

Frame rate refers to the number of times your screen (*frame*) is redrawn within a second. The faster your screen is re-drawn, the smoother the animation will appear to move. But when it comes to simulations, a low frame rate will affect how the simulation *feels* as well.

Everybody wants both super graphics and silky smooth frame rates. It's easy to understand the craving for eye-popping graphics, but the frame rate issue may not be so obvious. When you're engaged in a real-time game (where action happens as you play it) like Combat Flight Simulator, any interruptions like graphics stuttering or slow updates can devastate your combat

performance. You're looking for a fluid motion in what you see on your screen—however, what's considered acceptable varies from person to person.

> **Note:** *If you use a programmable joystick, note that the calibration routine may not work if you've programmed the joystick buttons as key presses. See the joystick's manufacturer instructions for information on restoring your buttons to act as a standard joystick.*

Unfortunately there's currently no substitute for state-of-the-art hardware, so choosing between high-resolution graphics and frame rate is a never-ending dilemma for both simulation fans and developers. While everyone can usually find an acceptable balance between scenery and game feel, when you're engaged in air combat, there can be significant advantages or penalties for some graphics choices—so you must choose carefully. Although we can do a little tweaking with the Display options to speed things up, don't expect miracles.

When you get down to it, this is another subjective area that ultimately is left to personal preferences. What's comfortable for one person may not be comfortable to another. So the best we can do is offer some guidelines.

Anything you do to Combat Flight Simulator's display settings will affect your graphics performance. This includes the amount of detail set, screen resolution, flight traffic, weather, number of windows, and window sizes. Because you'll mainly be flying combat missions rather than sightseeing, you want a detail and resolution setting that makes your airplane feel instantly responsive and makes the motions of other aircraft seem smooth and predictable. If your system isn't able to keep up with your current detail and resolution settings, you'll always be playing catch up and you'll never fly well or shoot anyone down.

Although people have different opinions on the subject, (with the exception that faster is better), most people agree that frame rates under 15 frames per second are too choppy for serious combat and that 20 frames or better seems to be a good place to start. Combat Flight Simulator has a frame rate display that can help you determine what your tolerances are and assists you with your graphics detail balancing. Pressing Shift + Z on your keyboard will cycle through the coordinate displays and

> **Tip:** *You can enable the mouse for flight control and use it simultaneously with a joystick by clicking the right mouse button and selecting Mouse As Yoke while you're in the cockpit. You'll be able to use the mouse for flight control, but once you move the joystick, it will override any mouse control inputs.*

frame rate counter in the upper left corner of your current window. Now that you know what you want, let's take a look at what you can change to reach your goals.

Display Settings

Combat Flight Simulator allows you to adjust display settings two ways—though predetermined levels or as a user defined setting. The slide control in the upper left side of the Settings window will control the Display settings in a predetermined fashion—if you have the radio button next to the words "Best graphics" enabled. Sliding the bar toward Fastest will increase your frame rate, but at the cost of graphical detail. Conversely, sliding the bar toward Best graphics will increase graphics detail at the expense of frame rate.

Setting Image Complexity

Two lines below the graphics display setting slider is the Image complexity drop-down menu. This menu allows you to select one of five settings: Very Sparse, Sparse, Normal, Dense, and Very Dense. This setting determines how many ground objects are displayed in the Combat Flight Simulator world. As you'd expect, the denser the setting, the more processing power will be required.

The Settings window is accessed from this screen.

Enabling 3D Hardware

Combat Flight Simulator will automatically detect your 3D hardware if it was installed in your machine when you installed the Combat Flight Simulator software. But if you've

added or changed a 3D card after installing Combat Flight Simulator, you may need to enable or change the 3D card's driver.

At the bottom of the Display menu in the Settings window is the Enable hardware acceleration check box. Unless you have a 3D card, you won't be able to toggle this option on. It allows you to choose whether or not Combat Flight Simulator will use your 3D-accelerator card for graphics rendering.

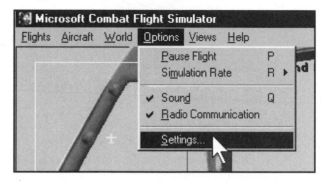

You can get to the Settings window from here also.

This box must be checked to enable 3D card support or to be able to select any 3D driver. Changes in your 3D driver and other 3D graphics options will be configured in the Advanced Display Settings window. So let's talk about that next.

Advanced Display Settings

The Advanced Display Settings window is accessed by clicking the Advanced Display Settings button in the Settings window. The Advanced Display Settings window is where you're able to "manually" set Aircraft, Scenery, and Hardware acceleration settings.

Clicking the Advanced Display Settings button and changing any of the Aircraft or Scenery settings will automatically switch the radio button on the Settings window to Player defined (in the Advanced Display Settings).

Aircraft Display Settings

As you'd expect, the Aircraft Display Settings choices affect how the aircraft in Combat Flight Simulator appear. Aircraft Display options are as follows:

Aircraft texture: If you have this option disabled, all aircraft will be devoid of any markings such as stripes or numbers, and while in Virtual cockpit mode you'll lose the cockpit interior as well.

Aircraft shadows: This only applies to your aircraft shadows. Other than looking a bit odd from external views, there's little reason to keep this on other than for aesthetics. But if you see a performance hit when shadows appear, just turn it off. Unless you fly using external views near the ground, or fly extreme banking maneuvers or dives near the ground, you probably won't miss aircraft shadows.

Your plane from cockpit: This option removes the interior and exterior of your airplane from all of your views in Cockpit view and Virtual Cockpit view. If you have this toggled off, you won't be able to see your propeller from inside the aircraft if you have the next option enabled.

Propeller: This option makes your propeller invisible in all fixed views—except for the forward view (Virtual Cockpit view), and in all external views. This option probably falls in the category of "eye candy", as it doesn't really add to the scenery and it doesn't help your performance as a pilot either. Then again, if you don't see a performance hit when your propeller is visible, there's little reason to turn this off.

Scenery Display Settings

Combat Flight Simulator's Scenery Display Settings control how the ground, sky, and ground objects such as buildings appear. The Scenery Display Settings offer the following options:

Textured ground: This option is a big CPU hog. Reducing terrain detail conserves memory, which in turn, facilitates faster game performance. While the ground textures are one of the coolest things about Combat Flight Simulator's spectacular graphics, you should know that ground details are secondary for air combat. Most of your fighting is done in the air. If you need to turn some details off to increase frame rate, these options are good candidates. Although the ground is really ugly without textures enabled, there are advantages to be had by turning them off. Not only will it speed up your graphics, but it can also help you to identify aircraft because they won't blend into the background clutter as easily.

On the other hand, some pilots like to keep ground textures enabled because it gives them a better sensation of speed—but more importantly it offers a point of reference for judging their altitude above the ground.

Textured buildings: Enabling this option adds textures to buildings and ground objects—trucks or other airplanes, for example. But the difference between ground object airplanes and the ones you'll fly with and against is that ground object airplanes do not move.

For example, turning this option off makes buildings look like colored boxes. You'll lose all window and door detail. Unless you're flying near a city, you won't gain much with this option turned off.

As with the Textured ground option, turning off Textured buildings conserves memory and increases game performance. You really won't have time to admire the details of ground objects, except when you're taking off or landing. So if you turn these off, you'll probably miss these the least.

Textured water: As the name suggests, this option enables water textures. By now you probably realize, unless there's water to be seen, this option will have no effect on your graphics performance.

Image smoothing: This option smoothes out the terrain texture maps and makes them look less blocky. Although the maps may be ugly, if you need to gain some additional frames, turn this off.

Gradient horizon: This option adds the *haze* out on the horizon, but only if there is no cloud cover to block your view. In other words, unless you have a clear sky, you'll never see the gradient. This effect makes the view look less artificial, and the frame rate penalty is pretty small. But even so, turning off the horizon gradient can make detecting enemy aircraft easier.

Ground scenery shadows: If you're sightseeing, this is a nice option to have enabled. But since we're flying air combat, there's no disadvantage to turning this off. If you need to gain some extra frames, turn this option off.

Textured sky: When you disable this option, you'll lose the ability to toggle the Wispy cloud effect option. Textured sky probably should have been named cloud textures. Turning this off can gain you a lot of extra frames if there are clouds in the area to be seen—but the penalty is that your clouds will now look like big sheets of color in the sky.

Wispy cloud effects: These are nice effects, but they don't add much more than a flashing effect as you fly through clouds. On the plus side, they don't require a lot of CPU power.

Hardware Acceleration Settings

You can configure the Hardware Acceleration Settings in the Advanced Display Settings menu. From there you can select the full screen device driver, full screen resolution, and two other related settings.

Combat Flight Simulator can be run inside Windows as a regular Windows application, or in "Full screen" mode. Full screen refers to the mode that Combat Flight Simulator runs in when there are no Windows borders around the screen. You can toggle between both modes using Alt + Enter.

Because some 3D-accelerators only do their magic in Full screen mode, this drop-down menu allows you to choose the device you'll use while in Full screen mode. If you don't have a 3D-accelerator, you won't need to change this option.

Full screen device driver: Select which device you want Combat Flight Simulator to use when it runs in Full screen mode from this drop-down menu. If you've got a 3D card, you'll want to select that. If you've got more than one 3D-capable card installed on your system, select the fastest one unless you've got a reason not to use it.

Filter texture maps: This option smoothes out ground and building textures. Most 3D cards can handle this with minimal degradation, but experimentation will tell you for sure what will happen on your system.

MIP mapping: MIP (Multim In Parvum) mapping is a method of enhancing the illusion of depth by using several different resolutions of an object's texture to represent the distance an object. MIP maps (pre-filtered multi-resolution texture maps) tend to increase the "locality" of memory access during texturing. That is, the lower-resolution version fits into a small area of memory, and as the graphics chip puts the texture on an object far from the viewpoint, it accesses that sub-sampled version of texture—all within a small memory region.

Without MIP mapping, the chip must skip over many bytes of the single-resolution larger texture to find the right texel for each pixel—so memory addresses jump in large increments, and the memory bandwidth is lowered.

Whether or not you want to enable this option depends on your 3D card's performance and capabilities. If performance degrades excessively when it's enabled, you'll probably want to turn it off.

Full screen resolution: This drop-down menu allows you to choose the screen resolution that Combat Flight Simulator uses when you run in Full screen

mode. Be aware that the higher the resolution you run, the slower your frame rate will be. Note that you don't need to have a 3D-accelerator card to take advantage of this feature.

Sound Settings

The volume setting for Combat Flight Simulator's sounds is also adjusted in the Settings window. As you'd expect, this is where you can adjust the sound levels. A slider control is used for changing each of Combat Flight Simulator's Sound categories. (Naturally the slider will only work when the game's Sound is enabled. Pressing the Q key will toggle it on and off.)

Adjustments made in Sound Setting won't affect your graphics performance as much as the adjustments made in Display Settings—so, depending on the speed of your computer, you may need to tinker with this. But there are certain air combat advantages to keeping some sounds enabled. Let's discuss what they are and why you might consider certain settings over others.

Cockpit: Cockpit sounds cover the sounds that landing gear and flap mechanisms make when they're operated. It also covers the sounds that are made when your aircraft's wheels touch the ground. Knowing when your wheels actually touch the ground during a landing with an audio cue will only help you with situational awareness.

Effects: Controls the volume of machine gun and cannon (including that belonging to all other aircraft), rockets, bombs, other aircraft engines, airplane hits, crashes, and explosions. While there is something to be said for loud explosions and crashes for enhancing gameplay (as twisted as that may sound), turning up the Effects volume isn't always as purely self-indulgent as it may seem.

Sounds such as airplane hits and enemy weapons fire all directly relate to your current situation. The audio cues can reveal things to you that your eyes may not be able to show you. That's why you should consider setting the Effects Setting to the highest level.

Communications: If you disable these sounds, you'll really be missing a treat. This option enables the voice radio communications with other pilots and ground control to be heard.

Engine: This only affects the sound of your engine, and can come in handy for a few reasons. Besides instantly making you aware when your engine ceases running, audio engine cues can generally tell you your engine setting without you having to look at the instrument panel. For example, the sound that an engine makes when WEP (War Emergency Power) is enabled is distinctly different than that of an engine that isn't running it.

Realism Settings

The Realism Settings window is accessed from the Settings window by clicking the Realism Settings button. There are four areas of realism that you can control in Combat Flight Simulator—Aircraft, Visual, Stores, and Combat.

Just as we saw in our discussion of Display Settings, Realism Settings are adjusted in predetermined increments or custom tailored to meet your needs. The predetermined increments are Easy, Medium, and Hard.

Realism Settings

	Easy	Medium	Hard
Flight model	Easy	Medium	Hard
Unlimited fuel	X		
Unlimited ammo	X		
Sun glare			X
G effects			X
Weapon effectiveness	Strongest	Strong	Normal

Aircraft

Combat Flight Simulator's Aircraft Realism Settings control two aspects of the aircraft that you fly. Let's take a look at what they are.

Flight Model Realism Setting: This drop-down menu has three settings: Easy, Medium, and Hard (as discussed above). With decreased realism, you gain increased stability, scaled down left-turning tendencies, scaled down pitch over on the ground due to braking, and reduced negative G cutout on Spit I and Hurricane engines scaled at 100% at HARD, 50% at MED, and 0% at EASY. In addition, the airplanes tend to be more difficult to stall at the lower settings. For now just consider using the setting based on your preferences and goals.

Indicated Air Speed: This option selects the type of air speed displayed by your airspeed indicator. If you have it disabled, your airspeed indicator (ASI) will display TAS (True Air Speed). If you enable it, your ASI will display IAS (Indicated Air Speed) instead. We'll discuss the differences between the two in Chapter Four. For now, your best bet is to enable this option.

Aircraft, Visual, Stores, and Combat Realism Settings are set in this window.

Visuals

The Visuals Realism Settings determine whether what you see is affected by your actions in Combat Flight Simulator.

Sun glare: As you'll see later on in the book, the sun has been used to mask attacks for as long as man has used aircraft as a weapon. Enabling this setting will cause the screen to go white—mimicking the glare of the sun when you look into it.

G effects: This setting determines whether the physiological effects of gravity will affect your virtual persona. These effects are known as *blackouts* and *redouts*. We'll discuss what these mean later, but for now consider enabling this setting to avoid learning bad habits that'll be tougher for you to shake later on.

Stores

The Stores Settings are pretty obvious. Checking either of these boxes will provide you with unlimited fuel or ammo. Consider enabling both of these for training purposes. They also come in handy in Quick Combat mode when you play it like a video game (play until you're killed to try and achieve the highest score).

Combat

Two settings fall under the Combat realism settings area—Weapons effectiveness, and Player is invincible.

Weapons effectiveness: The three choices in the Weapons effectiveness selection menu are Normal, Strong, and Strongest. The names of these settings are a bit deceiving. This setting changes the size of the hit boxes (we'll cover them in Chapter Six) instead of the power of the weapons. At the highest level this means you essentially have a larger target to shoot at. So the likelihood of landing more hits on it increases proportionately.

Player is invincible: Select this mode during your training and it'll save you a lot of frustration. In addition to making you invincible to the attacks of the enemy, it'll also prevent you from being killed if you crash into something. This makes it especially handy when you're learning to take off and land. It's there, make use of it if you need it.

Windows, Windows, and More Windows

Although we've covered how the graphics and sound configurations affect system performance, there is still one aspect of the graphics *picture* we've yet to cover. By now we know that graphics performance is directly related to what is displayed, how much is displayed, and the quality of the displayed image. The last three graphics performance qualifiers we should discuss are the size of the display, the number of displays, and the view itself. Let's continue with displays first.

The term "window" can be easily confused with several things in Combat Flight Simulator. You may have to read through this several times before it makes sense, but see if you can follow this:

Combat Flight Simulator is a Windows (the operating system) program that runs either on the Windows desktop (operating system) in a window (a graphical bordered box—and in this instance with a title bar and menu bar), or Full screen. Regardless of whether Combat Flight Simulator is run Full screen or windowed (same graphical box), Combat Flight Simulator's views (Cockpit, Virtual Cockpit, Full, Padlock, Spot, and Chase views) and instrument panels run as separate windows (other graphical boxes), too. So, in essence, when you run Combat Flight Simulator in a window (on the Windows 95 or Windows 98 desktop), you are also running windows (instrument panels and views) inside the Combat Flight Simulator window.

Size matters

Each of the windows we've discussed (other than the operating system itself) conforms to general Windows conventions. You can move them to another position by dragging them with your mouse—or resize them by dragging the corner or side of the window. Okay, first concept: The size of every window will affect graphic performance—the larger the window, the lower your frame rate.

Window-Mania

The next concept concerns the number of windows being drawn. The physical number of windows will also decrease your frame rate. Naturally, the more windows you have to draw, the less computing power will be available to each individual window. So the rule of thumb is: keep graphic performance up by using as few windows as possible for your requirements.

A feature of Combat Flight Simulator that migrated over from Flight Simulator 98 is multiple *undockable* windows. What this means is windows (the view and control windows) can be undocked from the main Combat Flight Simulator window and placed elsewhere on your desktop.

To undock a window, right-click the view or control panel window you want to undock, and then click Undock Window from the pull-down menu that appears. To redock an undocked window, right-click the undocked window you want to redock and then re-select Undock Window from the pull-down menu to remove the check mark next to it. To close an undocked window, right-click the undocked window you want to close, and then select Close Window from the pull-down menu (or click the close box in the upper right corner of the window).

While undockable windows are a neat feature, don't get carried away creating too many windows. Not only can it become confusing, but your frame rate can drop to unacceptable levels very quickly.

More Tips for Improving Performance

Even though we've now setup and configured everything in Combat Flight Simulator, we shouldn't ignore the Windows operating system—as we're running the game inside Windows. Although you really can't gain any performance from tweaking Windows, you can sometimes improve a dismal

Combat Flight Simulator performance by reducing some of the overhead that Windows, Windows applications, and utilities introduce. But again, don't expect miracles—there's no substitute for state of the art hardware.

Close Non-Essential Utilities

There are several Windows utilities that either run in the background when you run Combat Flight Simulator or that use system resources when you have them loaded. These utilities can hamper performance, because they use CPU cycles or system memory or both.

The effects of these utilities on Combat Flight Simulator manifest themselves as slower frame rates or frequent pausing during flight or both. Although many things can cause such symptoms, the more common ones are networking, animated pointers, screen savers, and memory resident virus scanners. You may want to try shutting each or all of them to see if this helps improve Combat Flight Simulator's performance. (See the associated program or utility manual for instructions.) Here are some solutions for some of the more common ones.

Banish FindFast

Microsoft's FindFast comes as part of Microsoft Office 97 software. It indexes the contents of your entire hard disk at regular intervals. This can require quite a bit of valuable CPU processing time. Uninstall FindFast by running Office 97 Setup and deselecting the FindFast option, or by removing it from the STARTUP folder in the Start Menu. To do this right, click the Taskbar, and then select Properties. Next click the Start Menu Programs tab and click the Remove button. Find the STARTUP folder, highlight FindFast and then click the next Remove button.

Tip: *If you're installing a bunch of new hardware just to fly Combat Flight Simulator (of course no one publicly admits to that kind of thing), do yourself a favor and only install one device at a time. Make sure that it's working properly before installing the next piece of hardware. Adding too many things at once will just complicate troubleshooting things if a device doesn't work properly.*

Deactivate Active Desktop

If you run Windows 98 or Windows 95 with Internet Explorer 4.0 or greater, you know that Active Desktop offers a lot of neat features. Unfortunately, the luxury of being able to add Web content to your desktop can drain your system's resources. Although you can turn off

individual Active Desktop items by right-clicking on the desktop and selecting Properties and then selecting the Web tab to indicate the items you want to shut down—you may consider shutting down Active Desktop altogether when playing Combat Flight simulator. Overhead is overhead, and anything you can do to give Combat Flight Simulator more resources will help it run at its best.

To shut down Active Desktop completely, right-click your desktop, select Active Desktop, and then deselect View As Web Page (or, you can select Start, Settings, Active Desktop, and then deselect View As Web Page).

Remove Unused Network protocols

This is best left to your network administrator, but removing any unused network protocols can steal CPU cycles as Windows attempts to connect to networks that don't exist.

Defrag Your Hard Drive

It's generally known that one way to make your applications run faster is to "defragment" your hard drive. Over time, as you add and delete files to your computer (which includes installing and uninstalling programs), your computer will start placing files in the nearest "open" spot on your hard disk. This causes your files and data to fragment. This means that all of your data or files may not be located in the same physical area—causing your hard disk to have to search for the data and files it needs and increasing the amount of time it takes your hard disk to retrieve what it needs.

Defragmenting your hard disk places your files in continuous physical sectors on your hard disk. But users of Windows 98 are able to take this one step further. An option included in the Windows 98 defrag utility allows you to defrag your drive while keeping all of an application's files together. This allows them to load even faster for the same reasons—your drive doesn't have to search all over the place to retrieve the required files.

You can manually run the Disk Defragmenter by selecting Start, Programs, Accessories, System Tools, and then Disk Defragmenter. Windows 98 users can then click the Settings button and select "Rearrange program files so my files start faster."

Now that we've covered the preflighting duties, we're ready to move on to Air Combat Conventions we'll be using in Combat Flight Simulator!

Chapter Three

Air Combat Conventions

Simulators are meant to mimic the real world. That's why many of the conventions used in the real world directly apply to the simulation world. Before we can begin air combat discussions, it's important that we establish the basic conventions we'll be using.

These essentials are best established as early as possible—definitely before you're up in the wild blue, where you'll have other things to worry about. Flying and air combat are complicated enough without additional confusion over concepts and terminology. While that's what this chapter is about, we'll also discuss some of the *good to know* aviation conventions.

Forces of Flight

There are four forces that act upon an airplane in flight—thrust, drag, lift, and weight. Some of the ways that they all interact with each other are:

- Thrust provided by the engine acts against drag.
- Drag decreases lift.
- Lift provided by the wings counteracts the weight of the aircraft.
- Gravity (weight) acts against lift.
- Lift creates drag.
- Drag counteracts thrust.

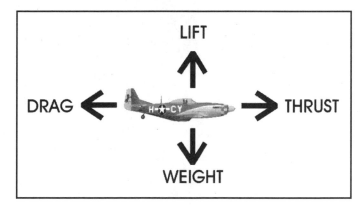

The four forces that act upon an airplane in flight are lift, drag, thrust, and weight.

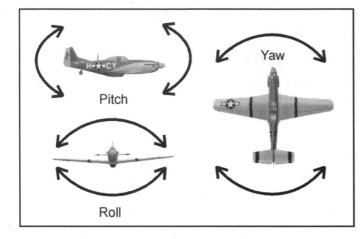

Aircraft maneuver along three axes—pitch, roll (bank), and yaw.

Flight Axes

All aircraft maneuver along three axes. These axes are known as pitch (turning about the lateral axis, with the front end rising and falling), roll (often referred to as bank, or turning on the axis extending from the nose of the aircraft through the tail), and yaw (turning about the vertical axis).

Spatial and Flight Relations

An understanding of spatial and flight relations is very important for several reasons—namely target tracking, collision avoidance, and for clarity and efficiency in our discussions. Although you can choose whether you are flying alone in the skies of the Combat Flight Simulator world (you have the choice of flying with other human pilots over the Internet, LAN, and direct connect, or sharing airspace with computer generated

Learning to recognize potential collision situations is important because colliding with another aircraft is just as lethal as getting shot down.

aircraft), learning to recognize potential collision situations is a valuable skill to develop. That's because colliding with another aircraft is just as lethal as getting shot down or flying into the ground.

The other reason for developing a common understanding of spatial and flight relations is so that when you read or hear things like *8 o'clock low* or *off the port wing*, you'll know exactly where we're talking about. We describe spatial relations in this manner because we can't say "hey, look over there" and point a finger in the appropriate direction. From a more practical standpoint, the *shout and point* method doesn't work very well during radio communications or when your hands are busy doing other things in the cockpit either. We'll have you walkin' and talkin' like genuine fighter pilots in no time!

Is This the Air Force or the Navy?

There are many theories as to why airplanes and boats have so much in common, but the one theory that seems to make the most sense is that back during the early development of the airplane, the only form of reliable long range navigation was nautical. Another strong argument is that many early aircraft were actually just flying boats. Whatever the real reason, aviation is still chock full of nautical terms.

Unless otherwise specified, relative positions are determined from the reference point of you sitting in the cockpit. Your left is known as *port*, your right is *starboard*, and the rear is *aft* when you're referring to the interior, and *stern* when you're referring to a positional external reference.

An easy way to remember which side is port and which is starboard is by recalling that the word right has more letters in it than the word left, and that the word starboard

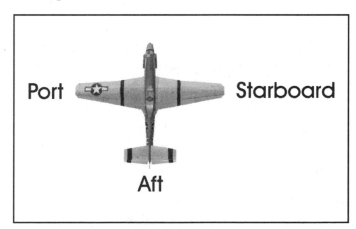

Left is known as port, right is starboard, and the rear is aft or stern when used for an exterior positional reference.

Note: *The terms "rear" and "tail" also describe the rear of the aircraft physically or directionally in combat circles.*

also has more letters in it than the word port. As for aft, just remember that aft comes *aft*-ter you.

The front of your aircraft is known as the *nose* (this is a purely an aviation term), and anything in front of the aircraft is known as *forward*. Other nautical terms such as bow and stem are not used in aviation.

Around the Clock

When flying combat, you must constantly consider the spatial relationship between yourself and enemy aircraft. While port, starboard, and aft work pretty well for slow moving ships, and lumbering aircraft—when it comes to air combat, spotting the enemy at the greatest distance has many advantages. Unfortunately, when objects are far away they appear very small and become proportionately harder to see. Because of this, a relatively higher precision directional convention eventually developed.

In military aviation the convention for external spatial relations is described using the metaphor of a clock. Imagine yourself sitting in your airplane directly in the center of a giant imaginary clock. Your nose faces the 12 o'clock position. Directly to your right (off your starboard wing) is 3 o'clock, directly aft is 6 o'clock, and directly off your port wing, is 9 o'clock.

An addition to the clock convention is fairly common in air combat circles. The term "extended six" for example, refer's to the relative direction of 6 o'clock *extended* out to indicate an external point, object, or in some instances, distance. For "extended six," imagine a line being drawn from the pilot's seat straight out the tail of the aircraft. The context in which the term is being used will indicate the subject being referenced.

Military convention names relative positions of other aircraft with numbers on a clock as if you were sitting in the middle of a giant imaginary clock.

High or Low, How Do You Know?

Air combat takes place in three-dimensional space—in addition to directional orientation, we need to consider altitude relationships. As you'll see when we discuss energy management, the relative altitude of other aircraft is extremely important. While the terms high, low, and level are straightforward, deciphering the relative altitude of an airplane isn't always so obvious. The rule of thumb is this: if an aircraft appears above the horizon, it's above you; if it's below the horizon, it's below you. If an aircraft is on the horizon, its altitude is comparable to yours (sometimes referred to as *co-alt*). So if an airplane appears to be level with the horizon—watch out! It's at the same altitude you are and thus at a greater risk of colliding with you.

In three-dimensional space, relative altitudes can be estimated by relation to the horizon.

Tip: *Keep the nose of your airplane above the horizon or any obstacle in front of you and you won't hit it—that is, provided your airplane can supply sufficient power and lift to maintain your new course.*

Which Way Can You Go?

Okay, we now know that air combat is fought on horizontal and vertical planes, but technically there is a third plane and it's a combination of the two called the *oblique*. When we say *plane*, we're not talking about an airplane but rather a planar (flat two-dimensional) maneuverable direction relative to the ground. For example, if you climb (gain altitude) in your airplane, you'll be maneuvering on the vertical plane.

Air combat is fought on horizontal planes (white), vertical planes (gray), and oblique planes (black).

Range to Target

Whether or not an aircraft at your altitude is really a problem depends on the third dimension we've yet to discuss—range or distance. If the distance between two aircraft at the same altitude is large enough, it makes the situation less urgent, but any aircraft within visual range should always remain high on your list of potential problems, regardless of its distance. (There are bandits out there that want to turn your spiffy new fighter back into airplane parts!)

Unfortunately, unless you have labels enabled (we'll get to that later), or have the tactical display enabled (press F9) you can only estimate the range of other aircraft. The rule of thumb for this is obvious—the bigger it is, the closer it is—but accuracy is something that only experience can develop. We'll talk about using gun sights for estimating range when we talk about marksmanship, but for now the best advice is to remain alert and keep track of any aircraft within visual range—regardless of direction, altitude, or apparent proximity.

Relative Flight Paths

Putting aside air-to-air weapons factors (guns, cannon, and rockets) for now, what changes a potential collision situation into an impending collision (or for combat tactical discussions, closing) situation is whether the aircraft in question increases its ability to collide with you. The only way this can happen is if your relative flight paths converge. Fighters move pretty fast, and the closer your two aircraft are to each other, the less time either of you will have to react. So how can you determine your relative flight paths?

The way that most people can tell which way an airplane is traveling is by watching where it moves in the sky. The other indicator is if you can visually make out the shape of the airplane. You know that airplanes fly forward so if you can distinguish which way the nose is pointed, you can pretty much figure out the airplane's direction of travel.

Unfortunately, if a bogey (unidentified aircraft) is far enough away, it only looks like a *dot* in the sky. The way you can tell whether another aircraft is heading directly for you under these conditions is by its relative motion in the sky. If you can visually see it moving in relation to your cockpit window, you're not in immediate danger of collision. But if the other aircraft remains in the same relative position, it's headed either directly towards you or directly away from you. When faced with such a situation, it's always best to assume the worst.

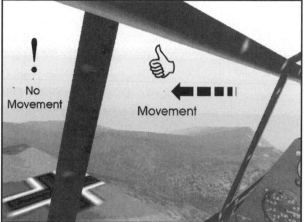

You can tell whether another aircraft is closing (heading directly for you) by its relative motion in the sky.

Pursuit Flight Paths

When an offensive fighter converges on a bandit (enemy aircraft), the flight paths or pursuit course options are lead pursuit, pure pursuit, or lag pursuit.

- When the nose of your aircraft points in front of the bandit, you're flying a lead pursuit course.
- When the nose of your aircraft points directly at the bandit, you're flying a pure pursuit course.
- When the nose of your aircraft points behind the bandit, you're flying a lag pursuit course.

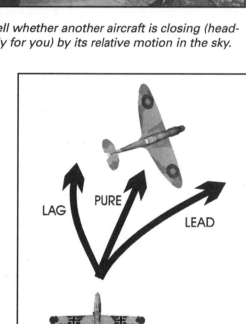

The three pursuit courses are lead, pure, and lag.

As we discussed in the last section, you can tell which pursuit course another aircraft is using to track you by the relative motion of the target aircraft. If it remains stationary in your cockpit window, it's on a lead pursuit course—and if it's close enough, the bandit is probably getting ready to fire on you. If it moves in the opposite direction of your flight path, it's moving on either a pure or lag pursuit course. Conversely, if it moves in the same direction as your flight path, it's on a large lead pursuit course or just flying in a relative direction that happens to be ahead of you at a faster speed. But given the fact that you're flying the unfriendly skies of WWII, the latter is highly unlikely—and as such, it's always best to assume the worst.

Deflection Angle

Unguided projectiles such as machine gun bullets and cannon shells will fire in a straight line (more or less—we'll explain later). The problem is that it takes time for the projectile to reach its target once it's been fired.

Although gun and cannon velocities are very fast compared to the speeds of WWII aircraft, a projectile's time of flight is long enough to allow a target to move out of the targeted area before the shell can reach it. The solution to this problem has been well known to hunters for centuries—in order to hit a moving target, one must aim ahead of the target's path of motion so the projectile and the target will meet at a future point in time. This technique is known as *pulling lead*, and the amount of lead angle is known as the angle of deflection or deflection angle.

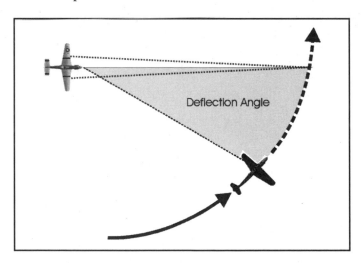

Deflection Angle

The deflection angle is the amount of angle you need to fire ahead of the flight path of your target (pull lead) in order to hit it.

Angle Off Tail

AOT (Angle Off Tail) is the angle of your flight path compared to that of the bandit. Realize that AOT applies even if both aircraft are not on the same dimensional plane (above or below versus left or right)— and the nose of your airplane doesn't need to point directly at the target to calculate AOT. Moreover, AOT remains constant because it's based on flight paths.

0 (zero) degrees is directly behind the bandit. This is the most desirable and easiest shot because no deflection shooting is required. As you might imagine, the higher your AOT, the higher the angle of deflection shot required to hit your target. Furthermore, in addition to AOT, the distance (separation) from your target will also affect the amount of deflection required to land your BB's (slang for machine gun rounds).

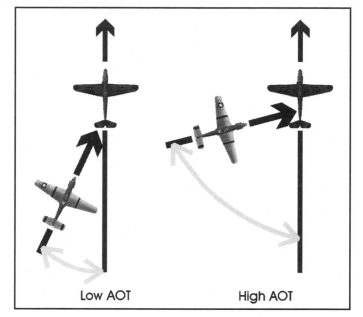

Low AOT   High AOT

AOT is the angle of your flight path compared to that of the other aircraft, and a lower AOT is preferable to a higher AOT because it doesn't require as high of a deflection angle to shoot the bandit.

Note: *Although deflection angles and AOT's can be described in hard numbers as degrees—they're usually not quoted because these angles are only used as points of reference to illustrate concepts.*

Heads You Win, Tails They Lose

At their most basic, fighters are just flying weapon platforms. They're designed to maneuver into position so they can dispatch their weapons with maximum lethality. Because the only air-to-air weapons modeled in Combat Flight Simulator are stationary guns, cannon, and unguided rockets, this makes the nose of a fighter the most dangerous end of the aircraft. All other areas on a fighter are vulnerable, but the most vulnerable is the tail for the reasons we just described. Although that's not the case with bombers (due to their tail gunners), for now let's stick to fighters.

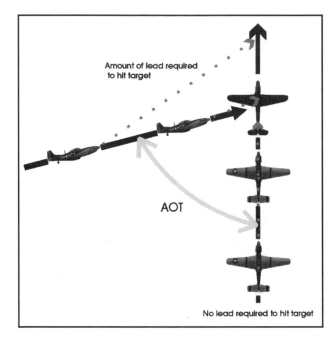

Amount of lead required
to hit target

AOT

No lead required to hit target

Use larger deflection angles to hit your target as AOT and the distance to target increase.

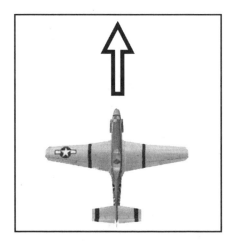

The nose of a fighter is the most dangerous point because machine guns (and cannon and rockets, if so equipped) all aim forward.

There are four possible situations when encountering an enemy fighter. From most desirable to least desirable we have Head to Tail (H2T), Tail to Tail (T2T), Head to Head (H2H), and Tail to Head (T2H). The convention is to indicate your airplane first in relation to the other airplane. For example, in an H2T situation, the *head* or nose of your airplane is facing any part of the other airplane other than its nose. Conversely, a T2H situation places the other aircraft facing your tail. While some pilots consider H2H more desirable than T2T, the importance is based on danger to you and not your offensive capability.

Next it's important to categorize each of these situations as offensive, defensive, or both. Some situations can be both offensive and defensive at the same time. While some tacticians categorize such situations as being neutral, they're actually both offensive *and* defensive. Anytime a bandit has its gun pointed at you, you're defensive. Conversely, anytime your nose is pointed at your opponent, you're offensive (and in air combat, that's good!). So, in the case of a H2H relationship, you are both offensive and defensive.

The T2T orientation is a neutral situation. Of course, all of these situations are based on the assumption that both parties have ammunition and all are within effective weapons range. That's because if you're both outside of weapons range, offensive or defensive categorization doesn't apply.

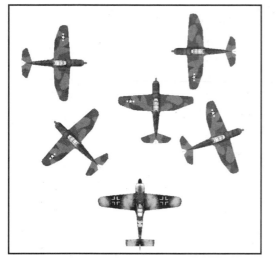

The H2T situation is most desirable because you can shoot at your enemy and he can't shoot at you.

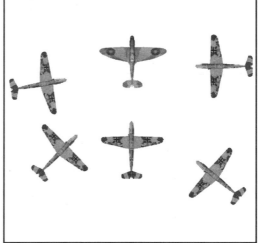

The T2H position is the least desirable because your enemy can shoot at you, but you can't return fire.

A H2H situation is both offensive and defensive—both you and the bandit can shoot at each other.

The T2T is a neutral situation because neither of you can shoot at the other. This makes it the second most desirable position.

Flights, Elements, Staffels, and Vics

In order to understand how multiple aircraft interact with each other, it's advantageous to understand how each country modeled in Combat Flight Simulator organized their Air Forces during World War II.

Organization of the Royal Air Force

The Royal Air Force (RAF) designated the Squadron as their basic unit. Each Squadron consisted of two flights (also referred to as a division), and each flight was comprised of two sections. During the early part of the war, RAF sections were made up of three planes which flew in "vics" (formations resembling the letter "V"). Later in 1941, the RAF switched to the adaptable "finger four" formation—increasing the section size to four airplanes. Typically sections were color coded with "A" Flight being named Red or Yellow, and "B" Flights named Blue or Green.

Before 1941, British Squadrons consisted of 12 to 16 aircraft, and 12 to 16 pilots. After 1941 Squadron sizes increased to 26 pilots and between 16 to 20 planes. Letter combinations on the side of the aircraft designated individual Squadrons and aircraft. The Squadron's two-letter designation was located forward of the "bulls eye" national insignia on the side of the fuselage, and the individual plane's designation was located on the rearward side.

An RAF Wing was comprised of three squadrons, but not all of the squadrons within a Wing had the same type aircraft—however fighters were grouped with fighters and bombers grouped with bombers.

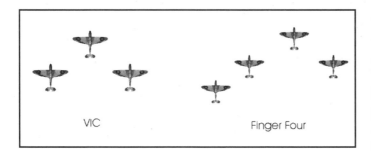

VIC   Finger Four

Three aircraft Vic formations later gave way to the Finger Four.

Organization of the United States Army Air Force

The United States Army Air Force (the forerunner of the present day United States Air Force) also based their fighter organization around the Squadron, but each Squadron consisted of 24

planes and 32 pilots. Missions were flown by four flights of four fighters (16 planes per Squadron) with each Flight flying in finger four formation. Flights were color-coded typically using Red, White, Blue, and Yellow as designations.

Tip: *In 1944 USAAF Fighter Groups began to color in the noses of their aircraft to aid in identification. This had the added benefit of boosting the morale of pilots.*

A Fighter Group consisted of three Squadrons for a total of 48 planes per Group, and each fighter Group operated the same type of aircraft in each of the three squadrons. In 1944 fighter Squadron sizes increased to 32 aircraft and 45 pilots, and Groups began to fly in two "A" and "B" formations consisting of three 12 plane Squadrons each.

Letter and numeric combinations on the side of the aircraft designated individual USAAF Squadrons and aircraft. The Squadron two letter or letter and numeral designation was located forward of the "stars and bars" national insignia on the side of the fuselage (some as far forward as the nose). Individual aircraft letter or letter and numeral designations were located behind the national insignia on the side of the fuselage or on the tail. When more than 26 aircraft were assigned to a Squadron a bar was placed under the individual plane designation.

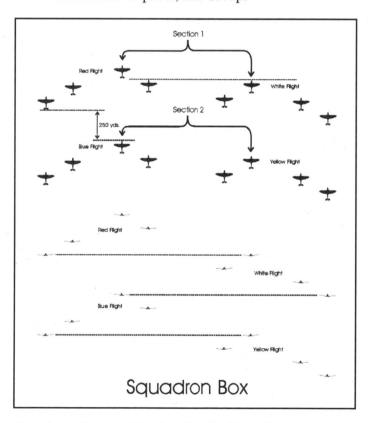

Squadrons flew missions in a "box" of four flights comprised of four aircraft each.

Organization of the Luftwaffe

The Luftwaffe basic unit was the *Staffel,* which was comprised of 12 aircraft. A *Gruppe* consisted of three Staffels for a total of 36 aircraft. "I Gruppe" consisted of number 1, number 2, and number 3 Staffels; "II Gruppe" consisted of numbers 4, 5, and 6 Staffels; "III Gruppe" consisted of numbers 7, 8, and 9 Staffels; and so on.

A *gerschwader* was made up of three Gruppen. A gerschwader of fighters was called a Jadg Geschwader (jager means hunter—single-seat day fighter wings, abbreviated as "JG"). In other words (using the American designations), a Jagd Geschwader consisted of three groups of three fighter squadrons. But unlike the Americans, the Luftwaffe Jadg Geschwader Gruppen did not all fly the same aircraft, nor did they always operate together or even in the same theater.

Two other Luftwaffe gerschwader classifications were Zerstorer Geschwaders ("zerstorer" means "destroyer"), heavy day fighter wings, abbreviated as "ZG", and Nachtjagd Geschwaders, night fighter wings, abbreviated as "NJG". German Gruppen were identified by Roman numerals as parts of their geschwader. For example the Fourth Gruppe of Jagd Geschwader 11 is denoted as "IV/JG11".

Gruppen were denoted by symbols or lack of them on the sides of the aircraft. No symbol designated I Gruppe, a horizontal bar designated II Gruppe, and a vertical bar designated III Gruppe. These symbols were located rearward of the "Swastika" or "iron cross" national insignia on the sides of the fuselage. Within each Gruppe, Staffels were denoted by color-coded numbers on the sides of the planes. These numbers were placed on the fuselage forward of the national insignia. Finally, chevrons, bars, and other markings placed forward of the national insignia denoted commanders and other high-ranking officers.

Numbers and Letters

If we're going to learn to fly by the numbers, we should talk a little about some aviation numbers. Okay, that probably sounds a bit odd, numbers are numbers right? Well, not always. Read ahead and you'll understand.

Navigation Numerals

Three methods of navigation are used in the aviation world of Combat Flight Simulator: *pilotage*, or flying by reference to landmarks; *dead (deduced) reckoning*, which relies on maps, headings, ground speed, wind and time; and *radio navigation*, which makes use of radio aids.

These methods use directional headings roughly based on the magnetic compass. Note the word *roughly*. Without going into any details about deviation error, turning errors, and acceleration or deceleration errors, it should suffice to say that magnetic North (where your compass points) and geographical true North are not the same in most places around the world. This is known as magnetic variation.

There are 360 degrees on a compass just as there are in a circle. When it comes to aviation navigation, North corresponds to 360 degrees, East is 090, South is 180, and West is 270. Notice that three digits are used for compass directions or *headings*, as they're more commonly referred to. When headings are spoken, they are recited as single digits rather than as a whole number. For instance, 360 would be *three-six-zero* rather than *three hundred and sixty*, and 090 would be pronounced *zero-nine-zero* instead of *ninety*.

Standard or Metric—Depends on What You Fly

During WWII, both British and U.S. aviation used the system of feet, miles, gallons (more on this in a minute), and pounds. On the other hand, German aviation used the metric system of meters, kilometers, liters, and kilograms. Here are some notes about each, as well as some handy conversion formulas to help you visualize each measurement.

Mile by Mile

A statute mile, the kind of mile that automobiles use in the United States, is 5280 feet. (From now on, when we refer to a "mile" we'll be referring to a statute mile, unless otherwise indicated.) A kilometer equals 0.62137 miles, and one mile equals 1.609344 kilometers.

- To convert miles into kilometers, multiply miles by 1.609344.
- To convert kilometer into miles, multiply kilometers by 0.62137.

A nautical mile is 6080 feet, and corresponds to 1 minute of latitude, or 1 minute of longitude at the equator (the earth is shaped like a sphere so longitude distances change as you move away from the equator). Although people in the U.S. use statute miles to *navigate* the highways on the ground, in the air and on the sea, nautical miles are used. This wasn't always the case. Statute miles were used in aviation back in WWII.

Although all aircraft manufactured after 1976 report airspeed in KIAS (Knots Indicated Airspeed), airspeeds in Combat Flight Simulator (as was done in WWII) are reported in MPH (Mile Per Hour, also known as IAS—Indicated Air Speed) or KPH (Kilometers Per Hour—also measured by "indicated" air speed using the metric system). Combat Flight Simulator has a feature that displays your aircraft's speed in TAS (True Airspeed in MPH or Kilometers for German aircraft) or just IAS (Indicated Airspeed in MPH or again Kilometers for German aircraft). We'll discuss the difference between the TAS and IAS in the next chapter.

It's a common misconception that the "K" in KIAS stands for kilometers—but it doesn't. One kilometer equals 3280.84 feet. So when you see KPH or KM, it's referring to kilometers. Thoroughly confused? Now you get a pretty good idea why aviation measurements became more or less standardized after WWII.

Altitude—Feet and Meters

Just as with anything else, a measurement of something must be in relation to something else. You're probably aware that altitude refers to an airplane's height in the air, but in relation to what can mean the difference between crossing over a mountain ridge or making a smoking hole in the ground.

Aviation uses two forms of altitude measurements; absolute altitude and true altitude. Absolute altitude is height above the surface or AGL (Above Ground Level), and true altitude is height above mean sea level (MSL). You should note that although the altimeter readings in Combat Flight Simulator's airplanes are supposed to be based on MSL, their *indicated* altitudes are not correct unless your altimeter has been adjusted for the current atmospheric conditions.

Finally, as we've seen before, depending on which side you fly for, altitude will be displayed in either feet or meters (or more precisely kilometers—which are *thousands* of meters). A meter equals 39.37 inches (3.28083 feet) and a foot equals .3048 meters.

- To convert feet into meters, multiply feet by 0.3048.
- To convert meters into feet, multiply meters by 3.28083.

- To convert miles into kilometers, multiply miles by 1.609344.
- To convert kilometers into miles, multiply kilometers by 0.62137.
- To convert yards into meters, multiply yards by 0.9144.
- To convert meters into yards, multiply meters by 1.0936.

> **Tip:** *If you can't be bothered with converting MPH to KPH or vice versa (and no one blames you) in your head, the HUD (press the W key to cycle through HUD modes) will digitally display your airspeed in MPH.*

When's a Gallon Not a Gallon?

Although the names are the same, all "gallons" are not created equal. A U.S. gallon equals 3.785 liters. A British (or Imperial) gallon equals 4.546 liters.

- To convert U.S. gallons into British gallons, multiply U.S. gallons by 0.83267.
- To convert British gallons into U.S. gallons, multiply British gallons by 1.2009.
- To convert U.S. gallons into liters multiply U.S. gallons by 3.7584.
- To convert British gallons into liters, multiply British gallons by 4.546.
- To convert liters into U.S. gallons, multiply liters by 0.26417.
- To convert liters into British gallons, multiply liters by 0.21997.

In aviation, fuel is one of the main factors that dictate total flight range and flight performance. Obviously, the more fuel you have on board, the longer your engine will run before you run out of fuel. But what many new pilots fail to recall is that fuel has weight (about 6 pounds per U.S. gallon) and weight will affect your fighter's combat performance. In most cases, having your aircraft as light as possible will allow it to fly at its best. Of course "as light as possible" should include enough fuel to make it home.

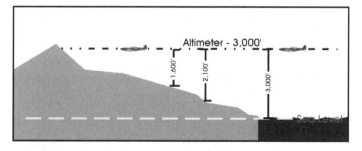

Absolute altitude is the height above the surface or AGL (Above Ground Level), and true altitude is your height above mean sea level (MSL).

Weighty Issues

Okay, now that we've said that weight affects your aircraft (we'll get into the details later in the book), this would probably be a good time to discuss weight measurements. We should make it clear that when we talk about "pounds," we're talking about weight and not British Pounds Sterling (currency). A pound equals 0.453592 kilograms, and a kilogram equals 2.2046 pounds.

- To convert kilograms into pounds, multiply kilograms by 2.20462.
- To convert pounds into kilograms, multiply pounds by 0.4536.

Chapter Four

GROUND SCHOOL

There's an old aviation saying that offers a truism: "takeoffs are optional, but landings are mandatory." This chapter is about those basic piloting concepts and skills best learned while you're on the ground. We'll discuss these topics before getting you airborne because we'll have more than enough to talk about when you're flying. It's best to get these basic concepts down now—you don't need to be dealing with overload while you're in the air.

Situational Awareness

Situational Awareness or SA is a term you hear many desktop pilots and real world pilots (if you know any) make references to. Although they'll generally use this term as an all-inclusive one, in reality SA in the air-combat world is really comprised of two focal points—enemy aircraft and flight conditions/performance (which includes the relative position with the ground). When experienced fighter sim jocks talk about SA, they are often referring to knowing where the bandits are around them. It is usually just taken for granted that the pilot knows his present flying attitude and where the ground is.

For rookie pilots, the loss of SA is just as deadly as a bandit shooting bullets at them because the ground is a very worthy and fatal adversary. Compared to non-combat aircraft like those found in Flight Simulator 98, Microsoft Combat Flight Simulator pilots naturally enjoy some advantages allowing them to ignore the ground for longer periods of time than their unarmed cousins. Fighters usually fly at higher altitudes, they rarely fly in bad weather, and their aircraft usually sport an excess of power and maneuverability. If fighter sim pilots get into trouble, they can usually maneuver quickly enough and get back to worrying about those bandits, but they still need to be aware of flight conditions.

Using Views

In real life, the best way to learn SA is to learn your instruments well, and the most in-depth way to learn your instruments is to learn to fly by reference to instruments only. While looking out the window for flight-orientation references (flying visually) is very natural when windows (the real things you look out of—not the operating system) surround you, you don't have the same luxury wtih flight sims. So in addition to introducing the flight instruments at your disposal, we also need to look at Combat Flight Simulator's viewing systems. We'll start with viewing system basics now, but we'll leave viewing strategies for later on when we'll be able to add some context to their usage.

There are two main view perspectives offered in most flight simulations—internal and external. Internal refers to views that are positioned as if you were actually sitting in the pilot's seat in the aircraft, and external views are shown from outside the aircraft. Although Combat Flight Simulator's exterior views, such as the Bomb or Rocket view (the A key), are good for seeing explosions, and the Chase view (the C key) is similar to the perspective seen in many arcade games, neither of these views is of much use for realistic air combat.

Combat Flight Simulator has three internal viewing systems (Fixed, Virtual Cockpit, and Padlock) that we could categorize as combat viewing systems due to their suitability for this task. Given the limitations of current computer monitor display technology, each of these viewing systems has its drawbacks. Let's talk about what they are and how to use them.

The Cockpit View includes the interior of the cockpit and instruments.

Fixed Views

The term Fixed views refers to views set at specific perspectives not adjustable by the user. Combat Flight Simulator comes with 18

fixed views and the option of using them with the instrument panel visible and the aircraft structure visible, with only the instrument panel visible, or with a HUD (Head Up Display) or both.

You access Fixed views using the Num Pad number keys with the Num Lock enabled or by pressing Shift with the appropriate view key. If you're using a joystick, you access fixed views with your joystick hat switch by default if it's working in analog mode. Access the 18 fixed views as follows:

Fixed View Key Commands

View	Key Command	View	Key Command
Look ahead	Shift + Num 8	Look Up 90 degrees	Shift + Num 5
Look ahead/right	Shift + Num 9	Look Forward, Up 45	Shift + Num 8 + 5
Look right	Shift + Num 6	Look Rear, Up 45 degrees	Shift + Num 2 + 5
Look back/right	Shift + Num 3	Look Left 45, Up 45 degrees	Shift + Num 7 + 5
Look back	Shift + Num 2	Look Left 90, Up 45 degrees	Shift + Num 4 + 5
Look back/left	Shift + Num 1	Look left 135, Up 45 degrees	Shift + Num 1 + 5
Look left	Shift + Num 4	Look Right 45, Up 45 degrees	Shift + Num 9 + 5
Look ahead/left	Shift + Num 7	Look Right 90, Up 45 degrees	Shift + Num 6 + 5
Look down	Ctrl + Shift + Num 5	Look Right 135, Up 45 degrees	Shift + Num 3 + 5

Many pilots find the fixed views easiest to use because of the basic system of pressing the appropriate key (or moving the joystick's view hat in the appropriate direction) to get the desired view. An additional benefit (and most important to some): Once you've become comfortable with these controls, you'll "know" what you're viewing from the position you're holding the view hat.

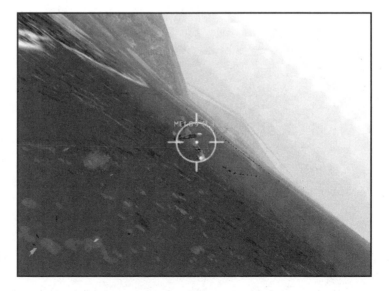

Pressing the W key will remove the cockpit and provide an unobstructed view of the airspace.

Tip: *Some joysticks like those in the Microsoft SideWinder line feature 8-way hats enabling use of additional views.*

If you use a ThrustMaster FLCS or F-22 Pro, Hat 1 (as well as the other hats on your stick) are really 8-way hats. (But it doesn't work on all systems due to game card and other hardware variations.) This means in addition to the regular up, right, down, and left positions, there are top right, bottom right, bottom left, and top left positions as well. Of course you'll need to program these views in your .B50 and .F22 files by using H1UL, H1DL, H1DR, and H1UR. (See your ThrustMaster manuals for more programming details.)

When accessing these diagonal views, do so in a clockwise motion. For instance, when accessing the down right view, push the hat toward right, hold it, and then slide it down. When accessing the down left view, push the hat down, hold it, and then slide it towards the left. Every motion must start from the adjacent counterclockwise position and then move clockwise toward the final destination view, but accessing the top right view has been known to be a little flaky in early models. ThrustMaster has eliminated this operational ritual with ROM version 1.17 and greater for the F22 Pro. Contact ThrustMaster for more information.

To give you an example of how this works, let's say you know you're checking six (looking directly aft) instinctively when you pull the view hat backwards. Although it may not seem like it when you first start using a view hat, using the fixed views will eventually become second nature and your brain will automatically correlate where you're looking simply from the position of joystick view hat.

Even though view perspectives are fixed by nature, you have some flexibility in adjusting just how much of your aircraft you want to be visible. The default forward view features a realistic rendering of your fighter's instrument panel—which provides maximum information about the aircraft's flight status and its orientation. You can toggle the instrument panel on and off by pressing the W key.

While Combat Flight Simulator is more realistic with the instrument panel visible, it's easier to see the action with it disabled. That's because without an instrument panel to block your view, you'll be treated to an unobstructed view (without the instrument panel and canopy frame) of the airspace in front of you. Also disabling the instrument panel view requires less computing power to render. So if your computer hardware is struggling to run Combat Flight Simulator, hiding the instrument panel can help.

The information provided on the HUD is pretty straightforward. Across the top center of the HUD is the local time. Below that are your orientation instruments—a compass rose that indicates the magnetic heading

that you're facing, as well as altitude and airspeed. Below those are your condition indicators—fuel, throttle, flaps and landing gear. At the bottom are your weapon stores and score.

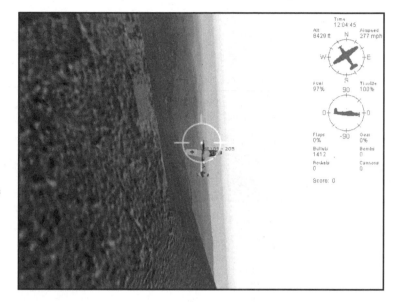

With additional presses of the W key, you can toggle the HUD flight data.

The only part of the HUD that may require some explaining is a pitch indicator dial located on the lower center of the HUD. When the nose of the airplane picture points at 0, your pitch is level with the horizon. Positive and negative pitch angles are indicated by degrees. Although no real world instrument works like this, what it means when the little aircraft points to the 0 on the left is your aircraft is inverted. It doesn't matter whether you got into that position by pitch or roll or whether your heading has changed. The device only indicates your pitch angle.

Finally, if you disable the Advanced Graphics option named Your Plane From Cockpit, you will see areas around the airplane that are normally obstructed by the aircraft structure itself. However, the forward

Tip: *To change the color of the HUD text and HUD graphics, press Shift + W. Although a HUD isn't exactly historically accurate (but neither is flying with an unobstructed view of the airspace in front of you) and it doesn't display all of the information that the instrument panel does, it can be used for combat and most flight operations. As a matter of fact, historical accuracy aside, many pilots prefer the HUD because by design, information is easier to absorb (the text is larger and in the color of your choice, and the readouts are digital). Plus you can toggle the HUD to display altitude and airspeed in feet and MPH, or in meters and km/h by pressing Ctrl + W.*

Virtual Cockpit mode is the most realistic because it allows you to pan around so you can look out on all sides of the airplane—but it can be awkward to use.

view remains the same as when you remove the instrument panel from view, but you also have the option of keeping the instrument panel visible in the Forward view regardless of the Your Plane From Cockpit Setting.

Virtual Cockpit

Press the S key to cycle through to the Virtual Cockpit mode. This view is similar to the Cockpit View but it allows you to pan around and look out on all sides of the airplane. You scroll your view around by using the following Panning View commands or by using the view hat on your joystick.

Planning View Key Commands

Panning View	Key Command
Pan left	Ctrl + Shift + Backspace
Pan right	Ctrl + Shift + Enter
Pan up	Shift + Backspace
Pan down	Shift + Enter
Pan view reset (snap to front view)	Ctrl + Spacebar

While the Virtual Cockpit mode arguably provides the most realistic viewing experience of actually sitting in the cockpit of the airplane, the multiple key presses required for panning the view can be awkward. Virtual Cockpit mode works very well for visual Detection stage duties (we'll get to that in Chapter Six), but due to

Tip: *Although no banking information is presented through the HUD, or HUD pitch indicator dial, the heading ribbon will indicate whether you're turning.*

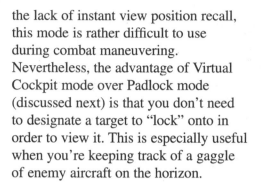

the lack of instant view position recall, this mode is rather difficult to use during combat maneuvering. Nevertheless, the advantage of Virtual Cockpit mode over Padlock mode (discussed next) is that you don't need to designate a target to "lock" onto in order to view it. This is especially useful when you're keeping track of a gaggle of enemy aircraft on the horizon.

> **Tip:** *Press the Backspace key first and then use the + (Plus) and - (Minus) keys to change the zoom factor of your view. (To reset zoom back to normal, press the Backspace key.) Zooming your view is quite advantageous if enemy aircraft appear too small, but note that the cockpit instrument panel and gunsight will only scale with the view in Virtual Cockpit mode and Padlock mode.*

Padlock View

One variation of the 3D Cockpit View is the Padlocked 3D Cockpit View. Padlock roughly translates into "locked on enemy view." Pressing lower case tildé on the keyboard brings up this view, which naturally is only available when enemy airplanes are in the vicinity. This view allows you to find out the location of the enemy. It automatically pans the cockpit around and locks the view on the first enemy on the target list or the target you've selected by

cycling the Tab key. (Shift + Tab will cycle through the current target list in reverse, and pressing Shift + Lower Case ~ will cancel target selection).

The Padlocked 3D view sounds like a great idea—and in theory it is—but in practice it can be disorienting when flying airplanes without claustrophobic cockpit interiors or canopy rails (the P-51D's bubble canopy is a good example) to help you keep your bearings

Padlock mode locks the view on your selected enemy, and the view scrolls around as your enemy moves around you.

straight. This is because once you lose reference to where you're looking (when you see nothing but blue sky, for example) it becomes extremely difficult to figure out which way you need to move your aircraft's controls. One strategy to remedy this situation is to use the padlock view only to locate targets, and then switch to the fixed views for combat.

The Enemy Indicator

To call up the Enemy Indicator, press the U key. The Enemy Indicator is a 3D pointer that directs you towards the currently selected target. Of course real combat aircraft don't have a handy feature like this, but it can be very helpful for beginning fighter pilots, since it allows you to fight (more or less) using only one view. In fact it's possible to fly and win air-combat engagements in Combat Flight Simulator using only the forward view as long as you've got the Enemy Indicator and Tactical Display enabled. (We'll cover the Tactical Display in Chapter Six.) Now let's talk about how to use the Enemy Indicator.

Because the Enemy Indicator will always point to the target you select (press the Tab key to cycle through targets just as in Padlock mode), all you

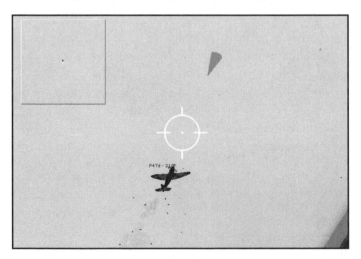

need to do is turn towards where the "cone" is pointing. If you can keep your turn rate up, you'll eventually maneuver so the bandit ends up in front of you.

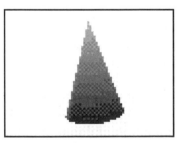

Locking the Enemy Indicator on a second bandit while you're engaged with another bandit can help you stay on top of the fight.

The Enemy Indicator is a 3D pointer that directs you to the currently selected target.

The Enemy Indicator may disappear when the bandit can be seen in your current view, or when no enemies are in the area. (You can use the Tactical Display to cross check whether any threats exist in the area—again.)

> **Tip:** *Flying with the Instrument Panel removed, HUD, Enemy Indicator, and Tactical Display enabled is the easiest configuration for new pilots to fight with, but consider that using these "handicaps" may make learning the other viewing systems more difficult later.*

Attitude Flying

The term *attitude flying* refers to the instrument known as the *attitude indicator* or *artificial horizon*. We'll talk about the instruments in detail in a minute, but let's continue with what attitude flying means.

In modern real-world aviation you use the attitude indicator (or Artificial Horizon as it was called in the 1940s) as the reference for every conscious movement of the flight controls (changing pitch or bank). This is exactly what *attitude flying*, or more descriptively, flying by the attitude indicator means.

The attitude indicator (AI) is the only instrument that gives direct information about the aircraft's attitude. The operative word here is direct. You can interpolate your

Multiple Monitors

One of the new features in Windows 98 is the ability to use up to nine monitors simultaneously. Of course not many of us own that many (or have that many unoccupied) bus slots in our computers to accommodate those video graphics cards, but the support is there.

The advantage of multiple monitors: The size of your Windows desktop is increased so it extends across multiple monitor screens for viewing multiple applications or windows simultaneously. For Combat Flight Simulator, the ideal situation would be to create multiple view windows for each monitor in a multiple-monitor setup. This way you could theoretically have monitors placed around you and never have to switch views to look around—all you'd have to do is turn you head—just like in a real airplane! Unfortunately, there's a frame rate hit (decrease in performance) involved.

All of the information you'll need to set up multiple monitors in Windows 98 is in the Display.txt file found in the Windows folder. Within this file you'll find information on the Required Hardware for Multiple Monitors (supported by certain PCI-based cards—the file contains a list of supported video chipsets) and how to set up multiple monitors as well as a troubleshooting guide.

aircraft's attitude from indications of other instruments, but the attitude indicator requires no additional thought analysis. What you see is what you get.

Flight Instruments

There are six basic flight instruments on all modern airplanes that comprise what is known as a standard instrument cluster. Although, as you'll see, not all aircraft were equipped with each of the six and they seem to be strewn randomly on each aircraft's instrument panel, you'll begin to understand why the modern standard instrument cluster is specifically arranged in two rows of three instruments each.

A standard instrument cluster consists of:

- Attitude Indicator (AI)
- Airspeed Indicator (ASI)
- Altimeter (ALT)
- Vertical Speed Indicator (VSI)
- Turn Instrument (either a Slip Indicator or Turn and Slip Indictor)
- Directional Gyro

Attitude Indicator

In our previous discussion, we noted that the Attitude Indicator was commonly referred to many years ago as the Artificial Horizon. We also noted that the AI provides pitch and bank information. It's important to understand that a bank indication on the AI doesn't necessarily indicate a turn, and a nose high attitude doesn't necessarily mean you're climbing. For example, during slow flight or landing descents, you can have a nose high attitude even though you are not climbing.

Every AI works on a gyroscopic property known as gyroscopic inertia, sometimes referred to as "rigidity in space." AI readings are based on the inertial frame of reference provided by a spinning gyroscope. As the aircraft maneuvers, this frame of reference remains constant so it can indicate the change between the two.

Understanding the AI

Each of the user-flyable aircraft in Combat Flight Simulator has an AI on its instrument panel except for the Bf 109E. Furthermore, Combat Flight Simulator models four different AIs—one German, one American, and two British. However different they may appear, they all work on the same principle, and they all present the same information (except the German AI also features a built-in slip indicator).

Every AI has a symbol at the center representing your aircraft. The German AI features a depiction of an airplane. The British AI's use inverted triangles, and the American version uses a straight white line.

Just as the name artificial horizon suggests, what's depicted in the AI corresponds with the horizon outside your cockpit windshield. The thick

This is the German AI found on the Bf 109G and Fw 190A.

Both the Spitfire Mk I and the Spitfire Mk IX use this AI.

horizontal white line stretching across the center of the instrument represents the horizon on all of the AI's except the one found on the Hurricane. It uses two thin white lines.

Across the top of the British Hurricane AI and American AI, and across the bottom of the British Spitfire AI are index marks positioned in an arc pointing towards the center. This configuration is known as the bank index. Each numeral or line (depending on the AI) represents a certain amount of bank attitude. The index mark in the 12:00 position (clock position—not spatial positioning discussed in Chapter Three) on all of the AIs (including the German version) except on the Spitfire represents zero degrees of bank. (Remember the Spitfire's AI bank index is along the bottom of the instrument)

Directly below the bank index (or above it on the Spit's AI) is the bank index pointer. This will always point up (or down in the case of the AI on the Spits). On the American AI, the shorter bank index lines represent 30-degree increments of bank, and the longer lines at the 3:00 and 9:00 positions indicate 90 degrees of bank. As you'd expect if your bank index pointer points to the first short line on the left, you'd be in a 30-degree bank to the right (note the relationship of the airplane in the center of the AI with the AI's horizon). Naturally if your bank index pointer points to the horizon line, it would indicate a 90-degree bank.

This is the Hurricane's AI.

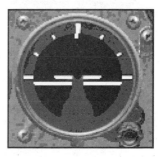

The P-51D and the P-47D are both equipped with this AI.

The Hurricane's AI has two short index lines on the bank index to the left and right of the zero degree mark that represent 10 degrees of bank for each line. The numerals 3 and 6 indicate 30-degree and 60-degree index marks. The 90-degree marks on this AI are indicated by small loops. When these loops line up with the two thin horizon lines, you are flying level (level pitch and bank).

Despite having inverted bank index marks, the Spitfire AIs use the same numerical convention for 30-degree and 60-degree index marks. However, like the German AIs, the Spitfire AIs use lines for their 90-degree index marks.

Pitch information on a modern AI is indicated via a pitch index or *pitch ladder*. Unfortunately the AIs from this era do not relate this information (the modern "ball" style AI wasn't invented yet). Therefore the only useful pitch information you can gather from all of the modeled AIs in Combat Flight Simulator is when your pitch is level. This of course is indicated when the horizon line matches the 90-degree bank index marks.

Airspeed Indicator

As the name suggests, the airspeed indicator (ASI) indicates the speed of the air around your aircraft. It doesn't indicate the speed of your airplane in relation to the ground. When it comes to flying, we're mostly interested in IAS (Indicated Airspeed). That's because all performance specs are given in indicated airspeed terms. Also, performance based on the IAS indicator doesn't vary as much numerically as when using the TAS (True Airspeed) indicator option.

Many desktop pilots try and explain the difference between IAS and TAS this way: "TAS shows your plane's speed in relation to the ground." Well, this statement is a little misleading. The air pressure exerted on the airspeed indicator, which is channeled from a pickup/sensor called a *pitot tube*, measures IAS. This mechanism doesn't know that the atmosphere gets thinner the higher you fly or as temperature increases. It only knows how much air pressure it receives.

Note: *Although modern airspeed indicators represent both indicated and true airspeeds in nautical miles per hour (knots), the abbreviations IAS and TAS normally refer to airspeed in statute (ground) miles.*

TAS, just as its name suggests, is true speed of air—specifically airspeed corrected for pressure, altitude, and temperature. Even though Combat Flight Simulator, like Flight Simulator 98, models weather, TAS is automatically calculated for you and the

results are the same as ground speed in level flight. But bear in mind that this conversion can't always be absolutely relied upon as ground speed. They really aren't the same things.

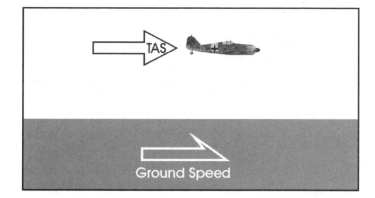

TAS will equal ground speed in level flight and zero wind.

To illustrate this point, let's say you dive straight down. Your TAS indicator will increase, but your ground speed will drop to nearly zero. The truth is TAS is just another way to measure the air flowing around an aircraft. These are just different *scales* or references used to do the same thing.

None of the aircraft in Combat Flight Simulator will care whether you use IAS or TAS. All they know is how much airflow they need to perform their maneuvers.

Understanding the ASI

Combat Flight Simulator models six ASIs, and interestingly enough, all of them are located on the left side of the instrument panel. Surprisingly, only one ASI

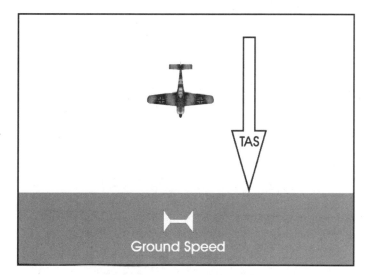

It's important to understand that TAS doesn't automatically equal ground speed. After all, it's possible to have a high TAS and very little ground speed.

(the P-47's) has any ASI limitation markings on it at all. Airspeed Indicator Limitation Markings are color-coded marks on the ASI that indicate the performance limitations of the particular aircraft. The concept behind ASI limitation markings is to provide quick visual reference to potential dangerous

The ASI of the P-47D.

Like the ASI of the P-47D, the P-51D's ASI has a variable index scale.

The Hurricane's ASI's outer scale goes up to 240 MPH.

airspeed situations. In the case of the P-47D's, the 500 MPH index mark indicates the aircraft's Vne (Never Exceed - Maximum speed all operations).

But the biggest differences between Combat Flight Simulator's ASIs are the scales each plane uses. Beyond the fact that Allied aircraft (British and American) ASIs indicate airspeed in MPH, and Axis aircraft (German in our case) indicate airspeed in km/h, the scales (the index marks' spacing rather than units) vary from ASI to ASI modeled in Combat Flight Simulator.

The ASIs on the American airplanes (the P-47D and P-51D) have scales indicating 0 in the 12:00 position and feature a variable index mark layout. Up to 250 IAS on the P-51, and 300 IAS on the P-47, each index line represents 10 MPH. Beyond the aforementioned limits, each index line then represents 50 MPH. But notice that the actual spacing between major increments such as 100-MPH marks decreases as airspeed increases.

Although it may not seem important, the most notable feature of the American ASIs is that its entire airspeed range is represented by a single revolution of the ASI needle. By contrast the German and British ASIs outer index marks are used for the ASI needle's first revolution and then continue on the inner index scale for the needle's second revolution.

For example, the Hurricane's ASI indicates 240 MPH on the outer scale. Beyond that speed, when the needle makes a 360-degree rotation, airspeed is indicated using the inner scale which begins at 260 MPH.

The Hurricane's ASI short index marks on the outer ring represent 2-MPH increments. The longer lines represent 10-MPH increments both on the inner and outer scales.

The ASIs on the Spitfires have three index line sizes. On the outer scale the shortest lines indicate 5-MPH increments, the medium and long sized lines indicate 10-MPH increments. On the inner scale, short lines represent 10-MPH increments and the longer index lines represent 20-MPH increments.

The short index marks on the German ASIs outer scales represent 10-km/h increments and the longer lines 50-km/h increments. The longest line on the Fw 190's ASI represents 750 km/h. Each line on the inner scale also represents 50 km/h. While the Bf 109 ASI is similar in design, note that while the Fw's 800-km/h index mark is aligned with the 100-km/h index mark on the outer scale, the Bf's 800-km/h index lines up with the 80-km/h index mark instead.

The ASIs of the Spitfires have three index line sizes, but their airspeed value depends on which scale they're located.

The ASIs of the Bf 109's display speed in km/h.

Similar to the British and Bf-109s, the Fw 190's ASIs have an inner and outer index.

Altimeter

The altimeter (ALT) is arguably the most important instrument for flying. In the simplest terms, it indicates your height above sea level (in most cases). Basically, an altimeter is a mercury-based barometer that's calibrated in feet (or meters on German aircraft) instead of inches. The altimeter receives access to the atmosphere through the pitot-static system static source. This is in contrast to the pitot tube *ram air* source that powers the ASI.

Understanding the ALT

Like the ASI, the ALTs on all user-flyable aircraft in Combat Flight Simulator are located on the left side of the instrument panel. There are five versions of analogue ALTs modeled in Combat Flight Simulator. As you may have inferred by now, the British and American versions display altitude in feet, and the German versions display altitude in meters.

Although the various ALTs in British and American planes have different pointer/indictor needle shapes, they're read essentially the same way. The faces of these ALTs look like

The longest pointer on the P-51's ALT indicates hundreds of feet.

The longest pointer (with the triangle on the end) on the P-47's ALT indicates tens of thousands of feet.

The ALT on the Hurricane is nearly identical to those found on the Spitfires.

The Spitfire ALTs have three indicators, and the one with the circle near the tip indicates thousands of feet.

This is the ALT found on all user-flyable German fighters in Combat Flight Simulator.

the face of a clock, but if you look closely, you'll see 10, not 12, main divisions. Each small index line between each of the main divisions on the American ALTs represent 20 units. On the British versions the small index lines represents 50 units.

Also like a clock, there are three pointers or hands on the British and American ALTs. On the P-51D, the longest hand indicates hundreds of feet and the medium-sized hand, indicates thousands of feet. The thin white hand indicates tens of thousands of feet. But on the P-47D, the longest hand (with the triangle on the end) indicates tens of thousands of feet while the medium and short hands indicate hundreds and thousands of feet, respectively.

The ALTs on the Hurricane and on the Spitfires also have three hands—one long, one short, and one with a circle near the tip. The long pointers indicate hundreds of feet, and the hand with the circle near the tip indicates thousands of feet, and the short hand indicates tens of thousands of feet.

All user-flyable German airplanes in Combat Flight Simulator are equipped with the same ALT. German ALTs, as already noted, are calibrated in kilometers. But there's an even bigger difference between these ALTs and their Allied counterparts—there's only one indicator needle. These ALTs are read in meters (displayed as "fractions" of kilometers—recall there are 1000 meters in a kilometer, so 0.1 kilometers equals 100 meters) indicated by the needle, and

kilometers (thousands of meters) are indicated by the numeral in the little window at the bottom of the ALT.

There are three sizes of index marks around the circumference of the ALT. The shortest index lines represent 10 meters, the medium length index lines represent 50 meters each, and the longest index lines represent 100 meters.

Vertical Speed Indicator

The final static air source fed, pitot-static instrument is the vertical speed indicator (VSI) which was known as the Rate-of-Climb Indicator back in WWII. Like the ALT, the VSI is also a barometer, but this barometer has what is often called a "calibrated leak."

During level flight, the pressure inside and outside the VSI is equal, so your VSI will read zero. When you climb or descend, the pressure differential causes the VSI hand to indicate the trend. The pressure differential exists only as long as your airplane climbs or descends because the air cannot move through the calibrated leak as fast as it can though its static air source.

> **Note:** *Although it may seem simple enough reading kilometers as a number on the German ALTs, be aware that just reading the number being pointed to doesn't mean you're at that altitude. Being an analogue instrument, the relative position of that number within the window makes a difference. For example, if the number 2 is positioned to the right of center (use the index mark in the 6:00 position for a reference), it means you are below 2 kilometers. Conversely, if it's to the left of the center index, you're above 2 kilometers.*

> **Tip:** *Because the VSI reacts to your airplane, many new pilots make the mistake of trying to fly (moving aircraft controls) by the VSI instead using it as a reference to their control inputs. In other words if you try and match the movements on the VSI with your controls, you'll never catch up because what you see on the VSI actually lags behind your control movements.*

Understanding the VSI

None of the user-flyable German fighters in Combat Flight Simulator are equipped with VSIs. But all of the VSIs modeled in Combat Flight Simulator are located on the right side of their instrument panels.

There are basically two types of VSIs in Combat Flight Simulator—one British and the other American. (Although the colors of the index marks and indicator needle are different on the P-51's VSI from the P-47's, they're essentially identical.) The only differences between the Allied counterparts are the respective index scales and markings.

Despite the different color of the index marks and indicator needle on this P-51D VSI, it's essentially identical to the one on the P-47D.

The P-47D's VSI features four sizes of index lines.

Combat Flight Simulator's Hurricane and Spitfire VSI's are 0-4000 fpm units.

The American VSIs are 0-6000 fpm (feet per minute) units and the British version 0-4000 fpm. The British VSI features two sizes of index lines and the American VSI has four. On the British VSIs, each of the small index lines represents 200-foot increments and the long index lines represent 1000-foot increments.

On the American VSIs, each of the smallest index lines represents 100-foot increments. The medium length index lines found between the 1000-2000 fpm marks represent 200-foot increments. The next larger size index line represents 500-foot increments, and the longest index lines represent 1000-foot increments.

When the VSI needle is pointing above 0, you are climbing, and when it points below that mark, you are descending. For example, if the needle points to the .5 mark above the 0 on an American VSI, you're climbing at the rate of 500 fpm. Conversely, if the VSI needle is pointing to the .5 mark below the 0 reference, you're descending at the rate of 500 fpm.

Power Management

While energy management (the process of maintaining airspeed and altitude through the use of gravity and momentum) is critical for air-combat success, the management of power is critical for flying. That's because powered aircraft's first design goal is to fly with power. (Besides, gliders don't make very good fighters!)

For our discussions, we need to be aware that internal-combustion piston engines use propellers to produce thrust. We'll cover some of the basics of how they produce power and thrust as we talk about their relative controls, systems, and effects.

Throttle Control

The throttle controls engine power. To display your airplane's engine controls press Shift + 2. You "push" forward (or what looks like "up" on your screen if it is displayed) to increase power, and pull it back to decrease power.

Depending on which aircraft you're flying and which view you're using to fly in, there are up to three ways to control the throttle in Combat Flight Simulator:

> **Note:** *To control the throttle by mouse, be sure to first open the engine controls window.*

- To control the throttle by keyboard, press F4 or 9 on the keypad to increase throttle, and press F3 or 3 on the keypad to decrease throttle. You can also set the throttle using the 5-0 keys. Pressing 5 will set the throttle at 50 percent, pressing 6 will set the throttle at 60 percent, and so on, with the 0 key setting the throttle at 100 percent.

These control knobs manipulate the engine of the P-51D.

- To control the throttle by a throttle controller, push the throttle controller (or slider) forward to increase throttle, and pull it back to decrease throttle.
- To control the throttle by mouse, click and hold the throttle control on the instrument panel, then move your mouse upward to increase throttle or downward to decrease.

Manifold Pressure Gauge

A manifold pressure gauge (or *boost gauge* as it's called by the British) reports vacuum pressure inside the engine's manifold. In simple terms, the manifold is the *plumbing* that guides the air/fuel mixture into the engine. The amount of vacuum pressure in this area is a direct indication of how hard the engine is working.

Understanding the Manifold Pressure Gauge

In the most basics terms, when you increase throttle, you increase the fuel flow into the engine. With more fuel to burn, this increases the engines rpm (revolutions per minute) and its hunger for air to maintain the rpm. Manifold pressure is measured in inches of mercury below atmospheric pressure in

The manifold pressure gauge of the Fw 190A displays limitation markings.

Except for the lack of limitation markings, the Bf 109's manifold pressure gauge is essentially identical to the Fw's.

British and American airplanes, and in ATA in German airplanes. ATA stands for Atmosphere Absolut. 1 ATA = 1 kg/sq. cm. = 28.957 in. Hg (inches of mercury).

Because the atmosphere thins as you increase altitude, your maximum obtainable manifold pressure decreases the higher you fly. Supercharged and turbocharged engines still suffer from the same thin air problem, but they're able to make gains on the thinning atmosphere by pressurizing their engine's air intake. (That's what superchargers and turbochargers do.)

Combat Flight Simulator models six different manifold pressure gauges, and each is located on the right side of the instrument panel of every user-flyable aircraft. The differences between all of these gauges is their capacity ranges and limitation markings. The manifold pressure gauges in Combat Flight Simulator's Bf 109's and the Fw 190 are basically identical except that the Fw's version features limitation markings.

Both German manifold pressure gauges have long index marks that represent 0.1 ATA increments, and shorter index marks that represent 0.02 ATA increments. However as we just mentioned, the Fw's version has limitation markings that indicate Normal operating range (1.05 ATA -1.45 ATA), Cautionary range (1.45-1.6 ATA), and the Never Exceed limit (1.6 ATA).

At first glance, the American manifold pressure gauges on the P-47D and the P-51D appear like their VSIs—essentially identical except for the colors used on the markings and indicator needles. While their index markings are identical (the shorter index lines represent 1-inch increments and the longer index lines represent 10-inch increments), upon closer inspection you'll notice that the P-47's version has a Never Exceed redline and the P-51's does not.

> **Tip:** *Even though the manifold pressure gauges of the Bf 109s don't display limitation markings, the limitations and ranges are identical to the Fw's.*

Regardless, the Normal operation range on the P-47D is 31-52 inches Hg with maximum takeoff pressure 52-inches Hg. On the P-51, the Normal operation range is 26-54 inches Hg with the maximum takeoff pressure being 61-inches Hg.

Finally, although the British manifold pressure gauges look identical except for the colors used on the index and limitation marks, they are different. While the limitation markings and index lines are the same—short index lines represent 1-inch increments (they're dark green and hard to see against the black face on the Spitfires), and the longer lines represent 2-inch increments—the total capacities are different. The maximum manifold pressure for the Hurricane's gauge is 20-inches Hg, and the Spitfire's is 24-inches Hg.

Fixed vs. Constant Speed Prop

The term *constant speed propeller*, while descriptive of the way it does its job, doesn't really explain what it does. The other term used for this device—variable pitch propellers—is a little more descriptive if you're

The manifold pressure gauge on the P-47D is virtually identical to the P-51D's except for the Never Exceed redline limitation marking.

Just because the P-51D's manifold pressure gauge lacks a Never Exceed limitation index mark does not mean that the engine has no maximum limit.

Nearly identical to the Spitfire, this is the Hurricane's manifold pressure gauge.

The Spitfire's manifold pressure gauge tops out at 24-inches Hg.

Note: *Maximum manifold pressure gauge capacity has little to do with the maximum amount of manifold pressure the attached engine can produce. Although the Spitfire's gauge has a higher capacity, it's Never Exceed range is exactly the same as the Hurricane's.*

unfamiliar with these devices. At the most basic level, when compared to fixed pitch propellers, variable pitch propellers can change their blade pitch (angle) in relation to the oncoming airflow. Fixed pitch propellers cannot change their pitch. Its pitch is *fixed* at one angle.

The reason why you'd even want to mess with a propeller's pitch has to do with efficiency on two levels—aerodynamic and power. If you were to cut off a section of propeller and look at it, the cross-section shape of the blade would look just like an airfoil. That's because a propeller is an airfoil. It generates lift in the direction you want to go.

Airfoils, whether they're airplane wings or a prop blade, generate more lift when there are more air molecules to create lift. If there aren't enough, you can compensate either by increasing airspeed (which brings more air molecules around) or increasing the airfoil's angle of attack (AOA). (Angle of attack is the angle of the wing chord line in relation to the oncoming airflow.)

So how does this relate to your prop? When you start climbing high into the thinning air, there are less air molecules for a prop to bite into. You can increase your prop's "bite" by increasing power (which in turn would increase prop rpm), or you can increase the pitch (which would increase the prop's AOA).

You're probably now wondering why you need to go through all the trouble with a variable speed prop if all you need to do is increase engine rpm to maintain thrust. This leads us to the engine efficiency part of the puzzle. As we know already, engines produce continually less power as they climb higher due to thinning air. If you're already at maximum manifold pressure at high altitude, there's no more power to provide additional rpm.

Engines produce power in a way that if mapped out on graph paper, more or less looks like a curve. If you're no stranger to autosports or high-performance sports cars, you'll know this as a power curve. Engines produce more power or are more efficient at a certain rpm. A variable pitch prop allows you to adjust your propeller rpm to take advantage of an engine's power curve.

So why not design airplanes that match engine power curves with propellers? It goes back to propeller efficiency. To use our car analogy once again, you can design a car for good power or good highway mileage. You can design to have a little of each, but one or the other (or both most likely) will suffer from some degree of reduced performance. Airplane props and engines

Despite the different bezels that encase them, the American tachs are identical. They can read from 0-4500 rpm, each short radial index line representing 100 rpm and each longer line representing 500 rpm increments. Also worthy of note are the American tachs, the only ones modeled in Combat Flight Simulator with redline limitation marks. The normal operation rpm

The Bf 109 tachs can read from 600-3600 rpm.

A 500-3500 rpm tach is found on the Fw 190A.

range for both the P-47D and P-51D is from 1600-2700, and redline is 3000 rpm.

The two remaining tachs are found on the German aircraft. Although the index mark increments are the same on both (short index line represents 100 rpm and each long index represents increments of 500 rpm), the Bf 109 tachs can read from 600-3600, and the Fw 190 from 500-3500 rpm. Normal operating rpm ranges for either German aircraft is from 2000-2700 and maximum rpm for the Bf 109 is 3000. Neither tach has operation limitation markings.

Mixture Control

Combustion requires a certain amount of air to mix with fuel. If fuel exceeds the optimum air/fuel combustion mixture, the excess fuel goes either unburned or only partially burned. The result is known as a rich condition. (An easy truism to remember: Fuel costs money and air is free.) The consequences of a rich mixture are poor power and bad fuel economy.

Conversely, when air exceeds the optimum air/fuel combustion mixture ratio (a lean condition) there are more serious consequences. A lean air/fuel mixture causes the mixture to burn hotter and consequently raises engine temperatures overall. More specifically, cylinder head and exhaust gas temperatures are elevated. To simplify a more technical matter, the reason a lean mixture will burn hotter is because the physical density of a lean mixture is too thin for optimum combustion. The relatively higher density of an optimum air/fuel mixture will control the combustion explosion inside the piston cylinder.

In the simplest of terms, a lean mixture ratio burns too quickly. A good analogy for this condition is the saying "a light bulb that burns twice as bright will only burn half as long." The big problem with lean mixtures is the increased heat they produce from burning "twice as bright." If the heat in the combustion chamber rises too high, the incoming air/fuel mixture will ignite prematurely (before the spark plug is supposed to ignite the mixture) causing pre-ignition. In milder cases, pre-ignition will severely reduce power, and in the worst scenario it can physically damage the engine. You want neither result.

So what does this have to do with airplanes and mixture controls? On piston-driven aircraft the mixture control allows you to adjust the air/fuel mixture. The reason you want to be able to adjust your mixture is because air thins as you increase altitude. The higher you fly, the richer your mixture will become without your intervention. Alternately, if you have an optimized mixture ratio at high altitude, you'll get a lean condition when you descend into the thicker air below.

The only piston aircraft in Combat Flight Simulator without mixture control are the German ones. Like the prop control levers, the mixture control levers vary from aircraft to aircraft. The mixture control lever on the P-51D and the Spitfires are located on the left side of the throttle quadrant. The Hurricane on the other hand has its mixture control located between the throttle and prop control levers. The P-47D has its mixture control located on the right side of the throttle quadrant.

- To operate mixture control by keyboard, press Ctrl + Shift + F3 on the keyboard to enrich the air/fuel mixture, and Ctrl + Shift + F2 on the keyboard to lean it up. To quickly move the mixture control to full rich press Ctrl + Shift + F4, and to instantly cut off fuel to your engine press Ctrl + Shift + F1.
- To operate mixture control by mouse, click and hold the mixture control on the instrument panel, and then move your mouse upward to enrich the mixture or downward to lean the mixture.

Engine Gauges

Every user-flyable aircraft in Combat Flight Simulator has a number of engine monitoring gauges. Basically, engine monitoring gauges report temperatures, pressures, capacities, and anything else critical for performance and for maintaining operational status. There isn't a lot to understand about their operation other than if they indicate *green* (meaning within normal operation ranges), you're okay. You don't control gauges—they're used only as references for performance and for troubleshooting problems.

Engine gauges can be categorized into three groups—performance monitoring, fluid monitoring, and system monitoring. Combat Flight Simulator models the first two, so let's take a quick look at them.

The P-47D's CHT gauge is located on the lower right corner of the instrument panel.

Performance Gauges

The two performance gauges modeled in Combat Flight Simulator are the Cylinder Head Temperature Gauge, and the Radiator Outlet Temperature Gauge.

Cylinder Head Temperature (CHT) Gauge: Only the P-47D is equipped with a CHT gauge and it's located on the lower right corner of the instrument panel. The CHT is useful for checking for lean mixtures, ensuring that the engine is at operating temperature, and to help the pilot guard against *shock cooling* the engine. (Shock cooling is allowing a hot engine to cool too quickly. This can warp cylinder heads). The normal operating CHT range is 232-260 degrees Celsius. Each short index line represents 10 degrees centigrade, and each longer line represents 50-degree increments. The CHT redline index mark is at 260 degrees C.

Radiator Outlet Temperature (ROT) Gauge: Despite its fancy name, the ROT Gauge for all intents and purposes is a coolant temperature gauge. Although you'd think that this gauge should be listed under Fluid Gauges, engine coolant isn't a fluid consumed by the engine.

Just as on your automobile, coolant temperature is an indicator of engine performance. It can indicate when you're asking too much from the engine or when an engine failure is impending or both. (Heat is the enemy of all mechanical devices.)

Every user-flyable fighter in Combat Flight Simulator, except for the P-47D and the Fw 190A, has Radiator Outlet Temperature gauges. These two exceptions have air-cooled radial engines. Like the CHT gauges, these gauges are calibrated in centigrade and all but the P-51's are located on the left side of their respective instrument panels. (The P-51D's is located on the upper right of its instrument panel.)

The ROT gauges on the Spitfires lack the last digit zeros.

The Hurricane's ROT gauge reports in degrees centigrade.

The ROT gauges on the Bf 109s read from 40 to 140 degrees centigrade.

The P-51D's ROT can read up to 150 degrees centigrade.

All of the ROT gauges read from 40 to 140 degrees C except for the P-51's, which reads up to 150 degrees C. The British ROT gauges are virtually identical except for the Spitfire's, whose numerals lack last digit zeros. Nevertheless both the Spitfire's and Hurricane's normal maximum continuous operation temperature is105 degrees C, but for as long as five minutes the engine can withstand a temperature of 135 degrees C. (This last spec is what's commonly referred to as maximum combat performance.)

The Bf 109's normal maximum continuous operation temperature is 115 degrees C, and its maximum combat performance temperature (up to five minutes) is 120 degrees C. The P-51D's normal ROT operating temperature range is 60-110 degrees C, and the maximum combat performance temperature is 121 degrees C.

Fluid Gauges

Besides any War Emergency Power (WEP—we'll get to it later) consumables, there are only two other kinds of fluids consumed by the user-flyable fighter engines modeled in Combat Flight Simulator. They are fuel and oil.

Combat Flight Simulator's fuel gauges monitor fuel quantity and fuel pressure. (Note that fuel capacity and useable fuel are two different numbers.) As covered in the last chapter, depending on the origin of the aircraft, fuel is monitored in gallons (Imperial or U.S.) or in liters.

The simplest fuel gauges in Combat Flight Simulator's are found on the German airplanes. On both the Bf 109 and Fw 190, there's a single gauge for their sole onboard fuel tanks. The 109's fuel gauge is located just right of center on the lower half of the instrument panel and the 190's in the upper right corner of its instrument panel.

When your fuel level drops below 80 liters in these airplanes, the red fuel warning light will light up. (The Bf 109's is directly to the left of the fuel gauge, and the Fw 190's is directly to the right of the gauge.) Both gauges display fuel quantities in liters with 50-liter increment index marks, but the 190's has two scales. The upper scale is used for the onboard tank.

The British user-flyable aircraft and the P-51D have multiple fuel tanks but only single indicator needle fuel gauges. With these configurations, the fuel gauge will display the quantity of fuel remaining on the selected tank. (Select Tanks by using the fuel selector switch, which is activated by your mouse.)

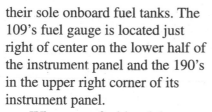

The fuel quantity in the single tank of the Bf 109 is indicated on this gauge.

The Fw 190's fuel quantity gauge has two scales.

The fuel level in the selected tank is displayed on the Spitfire's fuel quantity gauge.

Like the Spitfire's fuel gauge, the P-51 displays the fuel level of the selected tank.

Like the 190's fuel gauge, the Hurricane's has two scales. The upper scale is used for reserve tank readings, and the lower is used for reading levels of the main tanks. Only the P-47 has an indicator needle for each tank (a main and auxiliary tank to be exact). The auxiliary tank is read on the left, and the main tank is read on the right.

By monitoring fuel pressure, you can diagnose fuel leaks. The main hazard of fuel leaks (other than the obvious one of running out of fuel) is fire. Combat Flight Simulator models fuel pressure gauges for the American and German airplanes, and they're part of multiple indicator gauges.

The upper scale on the Hurricane's fuel quantity gauge is used to indicate the fuel level in its reserve tank.

The fuel quantity gauge on the P-47 has a separate indicator needle for each tank.

The fuel pressure gauge on the P-47 is found on the lower right side of the Engine T (3-way) gauge.

The Bf 109's fuel pressure gauge is found on the left side of this combination fuel pressure and oil pressure gauge.

The American fuel pressure gauge is in the lower right corner of what's known as the Engine T (3-way) gauge (located on the far right side of the instrument panels). In addition to fuel pressure, this gauge displays oil temperature and oil pressure. These fuel pressure gauges are marked in PSI (Pounds per Square Inch) increments and the normal fuel pressure range on the P-51 is 16-18 PSI with the maximum being 20 PSI. On the P-47, normal operating fuel pressure range is 16-17 PSI, and redline is 19 PSI.

The German version of the multi-gauge includes displays for both fuel and oil pressure. Fuel pressure is read on the left, yellow-colored side (marked in kilograms per square centimeter increments), and oil pressure is read on the right, brown-colored side. The only differences between the 109's and 190's gauges are in the limitation marks. The 109's normal fuel pressure operating range is 0-2 kg/sq. cm. and the 190's is 0-3 kg/sq. cm.

Oil gauges monitor oil pressure, temperature, and on some aircraft oil capacity (the latter isn't modeled in Combat Flight Simulator). Oil lubricates the moving parts of an engine and it also helps cool it as well. That's why it's so important to monitor. A loss of oil pressure will warn you of an oil leak or pump failure—either of which will lead to less oil reaching the engine. Finally, oil can burn. This means oil leaks can lead to fires.

Keeping with the conventions used with the fuel pressure gauges, every oil pressure indicator in the Allied aircraft displays oil pressure in PSI and

German aircraft indicate oil pressure in kg/sq. cm.

The user-flyable British aircraft have separate, rectangular-shaped oil pressure gauges. Both are marked in 30 PSI increments. Aside from the color of their bezels and their locations (on the upper far right of the instrument panel on the Hurricane and on the lower left side on the Spitfire), they're identical. 60-80 PSI is the normal operational oil pressure range in the Hurricane, and 45 PSI is the minimum to avoid damage. On the Spitfire's, 50-60 PSI is normal, and 30 PSI is the minimum.

On the user-flyable German aircraft, the oil pressure and fuel pressure readouts are housed within one physical gauge. The right side, brown color-coded side displays oil pressure. The gauges on the 109 and 190 are identical except for their limitation markings. Normal operational oil pressure ranges for the 109 and 190 are 0-10, and 0-15 kg/sq. cm. respectively.

Combat Flight Simulator's user-flyable American aircraft uses a combination fuel pressure, oil pressure, and oil temperature gauge called a "Engine T (3-way) gauge." Oil pressure is displayed on the lower left side of the gauge. Increment marks represent 10 PSI each. Normal operation range for the P-51D is 70-80 PSI with 50 PSI being the absolute tolerable minimum, and for the P-47D, the normal operation range is 60-90 PSI with best operation range being 75-85 PSI. Minimum oil pressure during idle is 25 PSI.

High oil temperatures can indicate a loss of lubrication or may lead to the breakdown of the lubricating properties of the oil. If an engine goes without lubrication long enough, it may seize and quit running altogether.

Aside from the color of its bezel and its location, this oil pressure gauge on the Spitfire is identical to the Hurricane's.

Identical to the one on the Bf 109, the Fw 190's combination oil-pressure and fuel-pressure gauge displays oil pressure on the right side.

The oil pressure display on the P-51D is found on the lower left side of the Engine T (3-way) gauge.

The Hurricane's oil temperature gauge is located on the lower far left side of the instrument panel.

The Spitfire's oil temperature gauge lacks last digit zeros.

The oil temperature gauge on the Bf 109's read from 0-160 degrees C, but normal operating range is 0-120 degrees C.

The Fw 190A's oil temperature gauge reads its entire normal operation range (0-200 degrees C).

Oil temperature is measured in Celsius in all airplanes in Combat Flight Simulator. The modeled British aircraft use separate oil temperature gauges. Furthermore, like their pressure-driven counterparts they're essentially identical to each other (and they're marked in 5-degree C increments).

Aside from their locations (on the lower far right of the instrument panel on the Hurricane and on the left side on the Spitfire), the only difference between them is the Spitfire's version lacks the last digit zeros. Both the Hurricane's and Spitfire's normal oil temperature is 105 degrees C in climbs, but they can handle 115 degrees C for up to five minutes.

Modeled German aircraft also use separate gauges for oil temperature. Aside from their mounting locations (on the right side of the instrument panel of the Bf 109 and on the far left side on the Fw 190A), the maximum temperature range of the 109 is 0-160 degrees C, and 0-200 degrees C on the 190. However normal operation oil temperature ranges are 0-120 degrees C and 0-200 degrees C for the 109 and 190, respectively.

The oil temperature gauges on the P-47D and the P-51D are found on the upper half of their respective Engine T (3-way) gauges. (Indexes are marked in 10-degrees C increments.) The P-47's normal oil temperature limits are 40-95 degrees C (redline is 95 degrees C), and best operation oil temperature range is 50-70 degrees C. On the P-51D, 70-80 degrees C is considered a normal oil temperature range, and 90 degrees C is redline.

Throttle vs. Airspeed vs. Lift

Now that we know all about power management, let's investigate how power affects flight. We know that lift increases with airspeed because more air molecules pass under (and over) the wing. So when you add power, you'll increase airspeed, which in turn increases lift. The result: You climb. Essentially, throttle controls altitude, correct? No way, throttle controls airspeed, right? Read on.

Elevator Trim

Using elevator trim is a very simple process, but inexperienced desktop pilots invariably have a hard time using it. Part of the problem is that without a force feedback joystick it's difficult to know when elevator pressure is easing off. A much bigger problem comes from the fact that most of the time no one has ever told these young pilots that a trim tab setting works only for the particular airspeed for which it was set.

Back to our wing and airspeed example. We know that an airplane's horizontal stabilizer (the little wing in back of the airplane to which the elevator is attached) helps maintain the airplane's pitch by either producing positive lift (raising the tail) or, more commonly, producing negative lift (downward force pushing the tail downward) to counteract the lift being generated from the main wing. As airspeed increases or decreases, the amount of lift generated by the main wing and the horizontal stabilizer (which remember is also a wing) does not increase or decrease at the same rate. This causes the pitch changes that require elevator control input.

An elevator trim tab acts like (and sometime is, literally) a small version of the main wing flaps. It increases or decreases the amount of lift on the elevator control surface. This helps the elevator maintain its position, which is in turn providing the proper amount of lift to counteract the lift from the main wing. So here's the bottom line: You can trim an airplane for any attitude, airspeed, or altitude as long as your airspeed remains constant.

Let's see how to use the elevator trim:

1. To trim your airplane to fly level, hold the joystick exactly where it has to be to remain flying level.

2. Wait a few seconds until the airplane has finished accelerating or de-accelerating (reached equilibrium).

Note: *Elevator trim isn't necessary when using the keyboard or mouse for flight control.*

3. Now press the 7 key on the keypad or press 1 on the keypad to trim the elevator. Use the 7 key if your controller is pushed forward to fly level or use the 1 key if your controller is pulled backwards for level flight. With each consecutive trim keypress, you should be able to return the controller further back to the neutral position. If not, you're pressing the wrong trim key. (Note that the Num Lock key must be disabled for trim keys to work.)

After following this process you'll eventually be flying level with your controller in the neutral position. Your trim will remain steady until you change your power setting, flight attitude, or bank—all of which will affect your airspeed. See how that works? Now you're gettin' it.

Elevator vs. Airspeed vs. Lift

We know that the elevator controls airplane pitch. You pull back on the elevator, the nose of the airplane pitches upward, and you gain altitude. You push forward on the elevator, the nose pitches downward, and you lose altitude. (As some pilots put it, "pull back on the stick and the houses get smaller, push forward and the houses get bigger.") This makes it very easy to conclude (incorrectly) that the elevator controls altitude. But wait a second! Didn't we just say that throttle controls altitude?

Here's a little way to prove what's what. You can try this after you get some flight time in and feel comfortable trimming your airplane for level flight. In the meantime, let's go over how it works now and you can try it on your own when you feel you're ready.

First trim your airplane for level flight. Next pull back on the elevator and watch your ASI. Your airspeed will drop and your altitude increases. Level out and trim up your airplane again. This time push forward on the elevator and watch the ASI. You airspeed will change (increase), but again so will your altitude—so you're probably still not convinced. Fair enough. Try this next.

Trim your airplane for level flight again, but this time at less than full throttle. Once you're set up, go ahead and give it full throttle. Watch the ASI and ALT. You'll notice that your altitude will increase, but your airspeed will remain more or less constant. Okay, bring the airplane back to level flight and trim it up at less than full throttle again. This time decrease throttle and watch what happens. You'll find that you're descending (losing altitude) but your airspeed will again remain more or less at a constant speed.

So there you have it. Elevator controls airspeed under constant power, and throttle controls altitude, or more precisely, rate of climb and rate of descent. Remember these principles—we'll rely on them later.

Stalls

Amidst all of this talk about climbing and descending, we should say a few words about stalls. Stalls are categorized as either elementary or advanced stalls. Elementary stalls consist of power on (also known as takeoff or departure stalls), power off (also known as approach to landing stalls), and turning stalls (turning with power on and turning with power off stalls). Advanced stalls include cross-control, accelerated, and top and bottom rudder stalls.

Contrary to what many believe, stalls are not caused by flying too slow. Stalls occur when your wings exceed the critical angle of attack (AOA). This means you can stall your airplane at any airspeed, any pitch attitude, any altitude, and any power setting.

This warning message will appear when you enter a stall.

People believe that stalls are caused by flying too slow because slower airspeeds create less lift. But, what usually happens is that when pilots realize that they're losing altitude, instead of applying power, they just add up elevator to make up for the lost lift. The theory is that increasing AOA will increase lift, which is true, but the problem is slow airspeeds require higher AOAs to generate the same lift that is produced at a higher airspeed. This makes it very easy to exceed the critical AOA because you're at a higher AOA to begin with when you fly at a very slow airspeed.

> **Tip:** *The way to avoid stalls is to be smooth and easy on the controls. Use precise, deliberate movements. If you find that you're still stalling all over the place, you may have a joystick/controller problem. Try adjusting your elevator axis controller sensitivity setting in Options.*

If the pilot leaves the airplane alone, it compensates for flying too slow by lowering its nose all by itself. In other words, the pilot causes the stall, not the lack of airspeed.

Regardless of the type of stall you're in or what caused it, the recovery for all stalls is the same. When you *feel* the stall buffet (especially noticeable with a Force Feedback joystick) or see the STALL warning message on the right side of the screen (whichever you recognize first), reduce elevator backpressure. If you're in a bank, neutralize your ailerons as well. If your power setting is less than full, smoothly increase power in addition to the other steps.

Spins

In order for an airplane to spin, it must first, and always, be stalled. What causes an airplane to spin is one wing creating lift while the other is stalled.

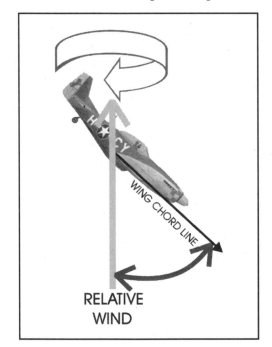

WING CHORD LINE

RELATIVE WIND

In order for an airplane to spin, it must first, and always, be stalled.

What this means is that if you never stall your airplane, you'll never have to worry about getting into spins.

Recovering from spins in modern aircraft is similar to stall recovery—which isn't really a surprise since one causes the other. First neutralize your ailerons, then instead of relaxing elevator backpressure, apply full down elevator. Next apply full rudder in the opposite direction of the spin. In other words, if you're in a counter-clockwise spin, apply full right rudder to counteract the spin. Keep correcting with your rudder to keep the nose steady.

Even though you may be tempted to apply opposite aileron to counteract the spin, resist the urge. It'll only make recovery take longer in most cases. Hold full down elevator until the spin stops, then slowly ease the elevator back to neutral. Your airplane will raise its nose by itself as your airspeed rises again. Hopefully you'll have enough altitude to recover.

Tip: *Sometimes it's difficult to decipher which direction the spin is going in. It's important to get the direction of spin right: If you apply rudder in the wrong direction, it will only increase your spin. If you need to, use the side views to help you determine which direction the spin is moving.*

If you spin with your flaps extended, be sure to retract your flaps first. Then follow the recommended spin recovery procedure. The reason for retracting your flaps is that extended flaps may disturb the airflow over the tail of your aircraft, rendering your elevators ineffective. This is known as tail blanking.

The only aspect of standard spin recovery that isn't an exact science is the application of power. Sometimes the application of power helps spin recovery, sometimes it doesn't. The benefits of pulling back the throttle when attempting spin recovery is that you'll tend to lose less altitude with the power off because of the resulting slower airspeed. On the other hand, if you don't recover, the altitude you saved can only help you when you try applying power for spin recovery.

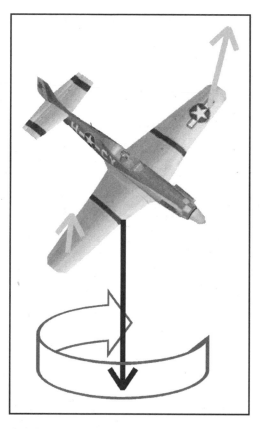

A spin rotation is caused by one wing creating lift while the other wing is stalled.

So, in that light, the recommendation is to first pull power off, but if you don't recover within one or two turns max, hit the power. You've got nothing to lose and everything to gain at that point.

Turns

Now that we've got the up and down stuff figured out, let's take a look at turning. First, lift is very important when turning an airplane. Although rudder turns are possible, the airplane must bank in order to turn regardless of the control surface that created the bank.

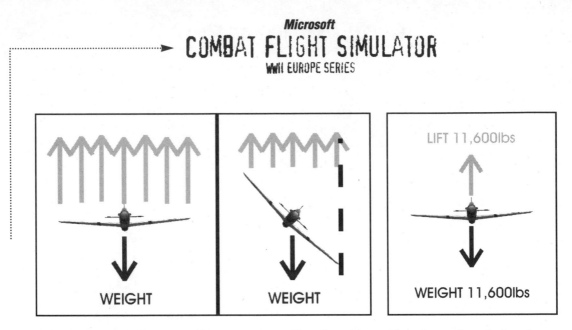

A banked airplane has a smaller percentage of its wing able to generate the lift in the right direction required to offset its weight.

The wings of an airplane in level flight must generate the same amount of lift as the weight of the airplane.

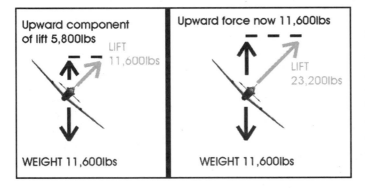

An airplane with its wings banked at 60 degrees requires twice the lift to maintain altitude because the upward component of lift is not now being used to counteract gravity (shown on left). This is why it's necessary to add up elevator in a turn to maintain altitude (shown on right).

When your airplane is banked, a smaller percentage of the wing is able to generate the lift in the right direction required to offset the weight of the airplane. This causes a loss in altitude. To counter this, increase lift. The easiest way to do that is to increase AOA by pulling back on the elevator.

Let's take a look at what's happening here. In order for an airplane to fly in level flight, the wings must generate the same amount of lift as the weight of the airplane. But when an airplane with its wings banked is at 60 degrees, it requires twice the lift to maintain altitude. (The cosine of 60 degrees is 0.500, or 50 percent.) This is because your upward component of lift is not now being totally used to counteract gravity. So it becomes necessary to add up elevator in a turn to maintain altitude.

Turn Coordination

Turn coordination is something you only need to concern yourself with if you have Enable auto rudder disabled in the Settings menu. (See Chapter Two for more information on how to do this.)

Turn rate is the number of degrees the nose of an airplane can move within a certain amount of time. The higher the number of degrees it can move, the higher the turn rate. Generally, the faster you fly, the faster you can move the nose of you airplane. (This only continues to a point where centrifugal force exceeds the lift being generated to keep the airplane in the turn. We'll get into turn performance concepts in detail in another chapter.)

A coordinated turn is a turn that neither slips nor skids. An airplane slips in a turn when its turn rate is less than the amount of bank it should bear. Conversely an airplane skids in a turn when the turn rate is too high for the amount of bank being used. This basically boils down to a coordinated turn in which the combined force of gravity and centrifugal force is directed straight through the floor of the airplane.

One analogy used to illustrate slipping and skidding errors is a racecar racing down a banked turn. If your speed is very high (which corresponds with a high turn rate), your car will skid towards the outside of the track. If you drove this same turn very slowly (a slow turn rate), your car would slide (slip) towards the inside of the track.

Okay, slide, skid, what's the big deal? From a flight performance point of view, uncoordinated turns at low airspeeds lead to stalls and spins. So let's talk about how to recognize and deal with uncoordinated turns.

There are two types of turn instruments used in Combat Flight Simulator to help you recognize uncoordinated turns:

Slip Indicator: The slip indicator (SI) is a liquid-filled, curved glass tube with an agate or steel ball inside of it. The liquid inside the slip indicator acts as a shock damper. (A slip indicator looks very similar to the little bubble level indicators found on a carpenter's level.)

The slip indicators on the Fw 190A and Bf 109G are located on the lower half of their respective AIs.

In a coordinated turn the ball will remain in the center of the indicator because centrifugal force offsets the pull of gravity. This unpowered device is found in one form or another on all the aircraft in Combat Flight Simulator except the British aircraft, which use a needle-based version. But the

This turn and slip indicator (like this one found on the P-47D) is often referred to as the old ball and needle.

The Bf 109E's T/S has L and R index marks that signify slips and skids to the left and right.

slip indicator in its stand-alone form is found only on the Fw 190A and Bf 109E where it's found on the lower half of their respective AIs.

Turn and Slip indicator: In the realm of gyro-operated turn instruments (turn and slip indicator and turn coordinator), the turn and slip indicator (T/S) is older of the two. The classic *ball and needle* turn instrument with a slip indicator at the bottom and a needle at the top is found on the Bf 109G, P-47D, and P-51D. You should be familiar with the slip indicator because it functions identically to the stand-alone version just discussed.

The needle on the T/S indicates the direction and rate of your turn. The needle points to the left (an "L" index mark is on the face of the Bf 109G) on the display when you make a left turn and to the right ("R" on the Bf 109G) when you make a right turn. The amount of needle deflection indicates the rate of turn. A larger deflection indicates a higher turn rate.

Although they may look different, all of the user-flyable British aircraft have T/S indicators as well. The only differences between them (the British called them Turn Indicators) and the ball-and-needle style T/Ss are that the SIs are needles. Look for the needle on top of the instrument instead of the bottom, where the "ball" is normally located. Also, turn rate is displayed in degrees (on the bottom index).

Now that we know what the turn instruments do, let's see how to use them. There are two ways to correct for slips and skids. One way is to increase or decrease bank. But in the real world this isn't done. It's much easier and safer to use the second method—apply the appropriate amount of rudder correction.

Tip: *The reaction of the T/S in a turn is exaggerated until you reach a steady angle of bank. Like we saw with the VSI, if you try and chase these instruments, you'll lose.*

Adding rudder will yaw the airplane to line up the resulting force of the combination of centrifugal force and gravity. In a slipping turn, you add inside rudder (rudder in the direction of the turn). In a skidding turn, you add outside rudder (rudder in the opposite direction of the turn). The easiest way to remember this is to remember the phrase *step on the ball*. This means to *step* on the rudder (apply rudder) on the side where the ball (or upper needle on the British Turn Indicator) is riding.

The amount of rudder you need to apply depends on how far the ball has deviated from center. You only need to apply enough rudder to re-center the ball.

The Hurricane's Turn Indicator (as the British called it) is a turn and slip indicator—it uses a needle instead of a ball.

Directional Gyro

This instrument has gone by many names over the years. It was known as a Gyro-Compass, Direction Indicator (British), and as it's known today, the Directional Gyro. The Directional Gyro (DG) is essentially a better version of the old magnetic compass. While it can't find North by itself, it can remember where you set it better than a magnetic compass under certain conditions.

A magnetic compass can suffer from an instrument error called deviation. This error is caused by the ferrous metal parts of the aircraft. Magnetic compasses are also subject to what is known as magnetic dip errors. These are errors that occur during turning and acceleration/deceleration maneuvers. Because of these inherent problems, the only time a properly calibrated (for deviation) magnetic compass is accurate is during straight and level unaccelerated flight.

So in addition to not being subject to magnetic dip and deviation errors, the main advantage that a DG has over a compass is that it won't bounce around like a standard fluid-dampened magnetic compass will in rough conditions. The DG also will not fluctuate its heading as wildly during a turn either.

Understanding the DG

There are two types of DGs modeled in Combat Flight Simulator. The first DG display is shaped like a circle and rotates like a wheel (only modeled on the Fw 190A and Bf 109G), and the other scrolling-style DGs (headings scroll from right to left or left to right) are found on the rest of the user-flyable aircraft. In either case, the operation of the DG is the same, but their locations vary from aircraft to aircraft.

The heading display of the DGs on the Fw 190A and Bf 109G rotates like a wheel.

This DG from the P-47D is representative of all of the side-scrolling DGs modeled in Combat Flight Simulator.

Tip: *The heading display on the scrolling style DG rotates against (opposite) the direction of your turn.*

The numbers on the DG and the outside of the wheel style DG correspond to the directions on a compass with the last digit removed. In other words 36 is 360 degrees, and 19 is 190 degrees. The DG number in the 12:00 position under the pointer indicates your current heading.

Reading the headings on the side-scrolling DG is as you might think—the number in the center of the display (under the index line/pointer) indicates your heading. In other words, if the number 24 shows up under the white line in the center of the display, you're facing (or flying) a heading of 240.

The Instrument Scan

Although you won't be making any IFR (Instrument Flight Rules) flights in Combat Flight Simulator due to mission and combat requirements, chances are pretty good that you eventually end up in a cloud. The problem of course with flying inside a cloud is (and why the skill of flying solely by reference to instruments is so valuable) that you can't see the horizon, ground, or sky.

The fundamental skill and key to good SA and instrument flying is learning a good instrument scan pattern. When you're flying IFR with nothing to see outside except white, you'll only need to scan your instruments. While there are no ideal scan patterns for all pilots or all situations, there are recommended patterns But most pilots develop their own habits to maximize their efficiency. We'll describe a typical basic scan pattern, but keep in mind that you'll probably have to discover your own.

The idea behind the instrument scan is to keep your eyes moving so that they can continuously read every gauge on your instrument panel. A common mistake is fixating on one gauge. Another is omitting or skipping some instruments. You have to constantly read, compare, and analyze what you see.

There he goes
Me262a destroyed.
P51D: Need help

A typical basic scan pattern is based around the AI (if your aircraft has one). This is because most pilots feel they can learn the most about their present situation from this device. In most cases, the AI is almost as good as (or better than depending on who you ask) as looking out the window. You can tell if your wings are level and if your nose is pointed at the horizon.

Developing an instrument scan pattern will increase greatly increase your situational awareness skills.

Next, scan down to the DG to see if you're flying your intended heading. Then scan back to the AI for a quick glimpse and then move over to the VSI to see if you're climbing or descending. Once you finish this, start over again back at the AI.

That's a basic scan pattern. Between the basic pattern cycle, mix in what we'll call (due to a lack of a better term) "sub scans." These sub scans involve quick scans to the ALT, the ASI, and then the turn instrument. When you maneuver, your scan pattern should alter a bit. For example, during a turn, your pattern should alter to include scanning the turn instrument more often. Other gauges get scanned occasionally, but *every* gauge does get scanned regularly.

The instrument scan is a tough skill to learn and you won't grasp what each instrument is displaying the first time you scan it. Just keep scanning and the *blind spots* will become apparent after a couple of cycles. Finally, keep practicing and don't give up. It's really pretty awkward at first, but if you stick with it and get acclimated, the rewards will be well worth your efforts.

Visualize!

Okay, the word *visualize* probably sounds like the mantra of a self-help seminar, but bear with me. If you try and visualize in your mind where you are and where you're going, it can help tremendously. Obviously, you won't "see" everything, especially if you're flying against multiple bandits, but visualizing the situation can help you keep up on what needs to be done. Flying and air combat requires you to think ahead. This isn't only so you're not caught off guard, but also because the workload becomes so demanding when there's a bandit in the area. If you can get as many of the various cockpit duties and mental calculations out of the way before you're in the thick of things, it will make everything that much easier.

Chapter Five

PRIMARY FLIGHT TRAINING

Fighter aircraft are flying gun platforms. You maneuver your aircraft into a position where you can effectively deploy your weapons. Learning to make gun kills is really all about learning to fly.

Getting airborne and staying there is really about learning and implementing flying procedures. If you've ever been in a real cockpit during a flight, you know why there are so many checklists and placards found everywhere. This chapter will teach you to *fly by the numbers*. This is the way it's done in real life, and Microsoft Combat Flight Simulator requires you to learn these same basic fundamentals.

Flying by the numbers means that by using specific settings (pitch, power, and bank) on your aircraft, its performance will be repeatable. This concept is summarized by an expression used in aviation: ATTITUDE + POWER = PERFORMANCE.

Although this phrase sounds like a slogan hammered into your head by a late-night TV motivational speaker, it means that given a specific pitch attitude and power setting, you can expect the exact airspeed, climb, or descent. As you might imagine, knowing exactly how your airplane will perform will go a long way to helping you maintain precision control of your aircraft.

If you're a veteran of Flight Simulator 98 or familiar with aviation, you may have noticed that the AIs in the aircraft modeled in Combat Flight Simulator don't include pitch index marks. If you look closely, there are no index lines on, above, or below the AI's horizon to provide precise pitch information—but fear not!

If you recall basic algebra, the equation Attitude + Power = Performance can also be expressed as Performance - Power = Attitude. In other words, with a certain power setting, the desired Performance can be met through adjustment of the aircraft's Attitude. It's really the same equation, and although not as precise as if you had precise attitude information—it'll still get the job done.

Note *There are items contained in our amplified lists that aren't modeled in Combat Flight Simulator, but we'll cover them anyway to give you a sense of what it was like to fly the real thing. If you'd like to cut to the chase and get into the air fast, skip to the Starting Engine section.*

In this chapter we'll walk you though the procedures associated with a normal flight in what many consider to the best fighter in WWII—the North American P-51D Mustang. We'll cover the configuration settings you'll need to fly by the numbers. The way we'll do this is by running through checklists. The *amplified* checklists we'll be using here are a little more detailed than the ones you'll find in Combat Flight Simulator—so as you we go through them, you may want to pause the simulation by pressing the P key on your keyboard between steps.

There are six normal flight configurations used on a modern airplane. They are:

- Climb
- Cruise
- Descent
- Approach
- Approach Descent
- Non-precision Approach Descent

Of course since we're flying a fighter, a combat configuration would be a logical addition to the list. We discuss that later, but for now we're only going to worry about the first four configurations. They're enough to get you off the ground and back again safely. The other two configurations are generally used for IFR flight.

While learning to fly IFR has its advantages, the main focus of Combat Flight Simulator is air combat, and radio navigation wasn't modeled to the extent that it is in Flight Simulator 98. In this case, it's probably fortunate. Besides being counterproductive (bogging you down with too many topics at once), new pilots in the real world don't instantly jump into flying IFR.

Note: *While we're about to cover may seem like a true flight, it's presented only to illustrate procedures. A true simulated mission would have a navigation plan.*

Starting Out

We're going to fly in Free Flight mode today to illustrate normal flight procedures. Specifically, we're going to take off from Interlaken Airfield in the

P-51D during a day flight. When you first start up Combat Flight Simulator, click Free Flight on the main screen. Click the Change/Modify button and select North American P-51D from the Change Aircraft window.

We'll fly with the default time and weather stats. When you've got everything selected for our flight, click Fly Now! Next you'll find yourself on the runway with your engine shut down.

All of the procedures listed in this book are based on the assumption that certain aircraft Realism and Controls Settings are enabled. Some of the specific configuration settings we'll be using are as follows:

- Aircraft Flight model realism slider—Hard.
- Enable auto rudder —unchecked.
- Enable auto mixture— unchecked (more on this later).

To access these settings, click Settings from the main screen or from the menu bar, click Options, and then select Settings. For anyone who's a

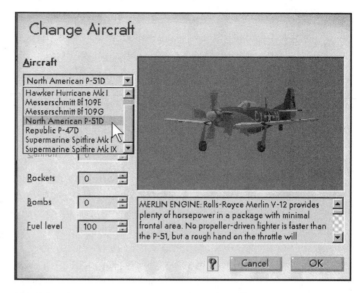

We'll be flying the North American P-51D.

When you've got everything ready, click Fly Now! to begin the flight.

Flight Simulator 98 veteran, flying the P-51D Mustang is a completely different experience from flying the Cessna 182S. Like any other high-performance, complex aircraft, the P-51D requires that you think way ahead of the aircraft. The P-51D requires you to think 450 MPH *ahead*! Anyway, just as when you were learning to fly that trusty old trainer, checklists are the key to learning procedures and staying ahead of the plane. So let's talk about that next.

Checklists

One of the features for Flight Simulator 98 that's crossed over to Combat Flight Simulator is the checklist feature. Combat Flight Simulator presents simplified aircraft flight checklists on your cockpit screen by default. These cockpit checklists offer tips for basic situations such as takeoff and landing. For our procedural flights you won't need these, so you can close them up and gain back some instrument panel real estate.

Pressing Shift + C will cycle through the checklists for the airplane you're flying. You can also close or display the checklists using this same key combination or by selecting Checklists from the Aircraft selection on the menu bar and then clicking the name of the specific checklist you want to see. To close the simplified checklists with your mouse, click the close button at the bottom-right corner of the list.

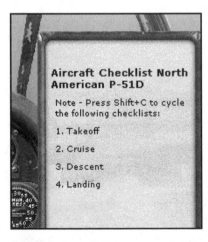

Simplified checklists are available on your cockpit screen by default.

Interior Check

Since we can't really walk around the aircraft to perform a proper preflight inspection, we'll begin here.

1. Fasten safety belt and shoulder harness. Check operation of shoulder-harness lock. Okay, this one's a little hokey for desktop piloting. But unless you have seat belts on your computer chair (don't laugh, I know guys that do), you can skip this one. Just say "check" and move on to the next step.

2. Adjust seat level to obtain full travel of rudder pedals in extreme position.

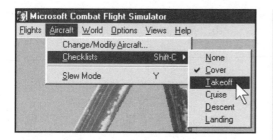

You can directly access the checklists by selecting Checklists from the Aircraft selection on the menu bar, and then clicking the specific one you want to see.

3. Adjust rudder pedals for proper leg length to obtain full brake control. Press foot against lever on inner side of each pedal.

4. Unlock control lock at base and just forward of control stick by pulling plunger on side of lock.

This isn't modeled in Combat Flight Simulator, but the control stick on the P-51D could be locked down to prevent it and the connected control surfaces from being damaged by wind.

5. Check controls for free and proper movement, watching control surfaces for correct response.

Tip: *Using a text editor such as Notepad, you can alter the default checklists or create your own by editing the *CHECK.CFG files (where * is the name of the aircraft) found in the specific aircraft's folder. Here are some tips:*

- *The first heading [lists] contains the text displayed on the menu checklist selection.*
- *The text in the [lists] section that follows a comma (,) will be displayed as the text title on the checklist itself.*
- *Each number followed by an = (Equal Sign) designates which list will be called up under the text title.*
- *The & (ampersand) sign will add an underscore to the next letter that follows it on the menu, enabling it to be selectable via that keyboard shortcut.*
- *Each numbered section, such as [0], designates and separates the individual checklist text.*
- *Each line of text in the checklist must be numbered followed by an = (Equal Sign). This will add a blank line between lines of text.*
- *Text will automatically wrap if it's too long for the width of the checklist.*

In a real airplane, checking your flight controls entails moving each of them to their limit. This usually isn't possible with the rudder because the nose wheel— or in the case of the user-flyable aircraft, tailwheel, is stationary. You're basically looking to make sure that your ailerons and elevator controls aren't binding and

NOTE: *Control reversing in the real world is rare, but I've been told it's happened on cable-controlled aircraft after major servicing, for example.*

that the control surfaces are moving in the right directions. As a desktop pilot you may believe you're immune from such things—but the truth is if you're using a joystick, rudder pedals, or flight yoke, you might want to pay attention here.

Although the control surfaces do actually move on the aircraft you're able to fly, seeing them from inside the cockpit is a bit difficult. But there are several ways to check to see whether the control surface movements match the control inputs.

The only way to check for correct control movement while on the ground is to switch to Spot Plane view by pressing the S key twice. The control surfaces on your airplane will actually move when viewed from external views. You are looking for ailerons that go up on the same side as the direction that you move the stick; a rudder that swings in the direction as the foot you push forward with rudder pedals (or rotate the control); and an elevator that goes up when you pull the stick back and that goes down when you push the stick forward. If you have a problem here, you may have the Reverse Joystick box enabled in Custom Controls.

6. Wing flap handle UP.

Check the flap control lever on the left side of the instrument panel. Flaps are raised in increments using the F6 key and fully raised with the F5 key. They're lowered incrementally with the F7 key and fully deployed with the F8 key. You can also operate the flaps with your mouse. Click the upper half of the flap control lever to retract the flaps or click the lower half of the flap control to lower the flaps.

The idea at this point is to make sure that your flap control lever is in the up or 0 degrees position. Lowering the flaps on a real P-51 facilitates re-fueling and access to the gun bays, so this step ensures that your flaps will be retracted when you perform the engine checks. Note that the hydraulically operated flaps like those on the P-51 will only start moving once you start the engine (which will start the hydraulic pump and thus make your flaps move).

You can see the control surfaces on your airplane move from any exterior view.

7. Carburetor ram-air control lever at UNRAMMED FILTERED AIR for all ground operations.

This is handled automatically for you in Combat Flight Simulator. Just like a 1960's-era American muscle car, the P-51D had a ram-air scoop that forces air into the engine, which allowed it to produce more power. Pushing clean, unrestricted, cool air from the outside of the vehicle into the engine produces more power.

The Mustang's carburetor ram-air scoop is located directly under the prop, and the reason you set it to UNRAMMED FILTERED AIR for ground operations is twofold: The Unrammed Filtered Setting keeps garbage from being sucked into the engine, and maximum performance isn't necessary while on the ground.

Every user-flyable aircraft has a flaps lever that can double as a position indicator (when the flaps are working). The P-51D's is located on the left side of the instrument panel.

8. Carburetor hot-air control lever NORMAL (late airplanes).

This refers to what is now commonly known as carburetor heat. Under certain atmospheric conditions, ice can form in the carburetor throat and clog it. Although Combat Flight Simulator doesn't currently model humidity or precipitation (making carb ice impossible), the quick answer to why ice can form on the carb even though the ambient air temperature is well above the freezing level (cases of carb icing have been recorded on days as high as 100 degrees F) is that carburetors are very effective refrigerators. The temperature of air entering the carburetor is lowered by the drop in pressure as air passes the venturi (narrowest part of the throat), and by the quick evaporation of fuel. The temperatures can get so low that if

Note: *Incremental full flap extension and retract keys may be redundant on airplanes with only two flaps settings. For example, the Spitfires have only two flaps settings—full up and full down. Therefore the F6 and F5 keys will operate the same way (retract flaps fully).*

there's moisture in the air, it may freeze on the carburetor throat as it enters.

Carburetor heat is an alternate air intake system comprised of a diverter and a separate set of intake ducting that draws air from inside the engine compartment (sometimes straight off the outside of an exhaust manifold). By raising the ambient air temperature, ice can't form. Normally, feeding an engine hot air reduces power output, but it's far better to have an engine running off its peak than an engine not running at all.

Note: *Although carburetor ice is an impossibility in this version of Combat Flight Simulator, carburetor heat is modeled (a carryover from Flight Simulator 98). But other than recognizing a slight drop in RPM when you enable it (press H) none of the aircraft currently modeled provide any indicator light or switch to visually verify its operation.*

9. Landing light switch OFF.

Although landing lights are thought of as the big bright headlight style light on the front of the airplane, the landing light on the P-51D swings out from under the left wheel well when the landing gear is extended. Nevertheless, landing lights are not currently modeled on any of the aircraft in Combat Flight Simulator.

For other aircraft, Ctrl + L toggles the landing lights on and off. Even if there isn't an indicator in the cockpit to tell you whether the landing lights are on or off you can tell by using an outside Spot views (press the S key to cycle, and then press the 8 key on the Num Pad to shift to a forward perspective). So, when you enter the airplane, the default position for the light switch is in the OFF position—and you won't have to mess with it at this time.

10. Windshield defroster and hot-air control knobs OFF.

It can get cold at 30,000 feet. Chuck Yeager once described flying high-altitude missions as akin to being in front of a window on a cold day with your shirt off and with your feet in a bucket of ice water while sitting on the hardest book you can find for six hours.

11. Check fuel quantity gauges.

You're not looking to make sure the ground crew filled-'er-up like they were supposed to (you most likely visually checked that during your walkaround before entering the airplane). But you're making sure that your fuel gauges are working (reflecting what you've seen in the tanks).

12. Throttle one inch open.

The notion behind setting the throttle so low is so that the engine just doesn't scream to life when it starts. A runaway engine at full power can cause a lot of damage—especially when you're still on the ground.

Because of the different monitor sizes, one inch would be difficult to judge by looking at the throttle control. The throw of the throttle lever on a real

P-51D is about 3.5 inches, excluding the WEP (War Emergency Power—we'll get to this later) detent gate. So, move the throttle forward about 1/5 of the way up from idle. To do this press Shift + 2 to bring up the throttle quadrant window and press F3 to bring the throttle all the way back (down from your viewpoint), and then press F4 about nine times.

13. Mixture control at IDLE CUTOFF.

IDLE CUTOFF is all the way back (down from your viewpoint). Press Ctrl + Shift + F1 to bring the mixture control lever all the way back, or move the mixture control (red knob) fully rearward with your mouse.

14. Propeller full INCREASE.

Full INCREASE is all the way forward, the default position, but you can press Ctrl + F1 to double-check it or move the prop control (center knob) full forward with your mouse. The reason you want full RPM on startup is because you don't want to make the strain of starting the engine harder on it than it has to be. If the prop pitch is set to a low RPM, it will produce unnecessary strain on the engine when we increase manifold pressure.

15. Friction locks on throttle quadrant adjusted for friction.

This is a hardware or controller issue (so naturally it isn't modeled in the sim). These friction locks are a mechanical means of tightening the throttle quadrant levers so that they'll stay in the position where they're left.

16. Gun sight gyro motor switch ON.

Combat Flight Simulator handles this for you automatically.

17. Gun sight selector switch at FIXED.

To toggle between fixed and lead calculating (gyro) guns sight mode, press the \ (backslash) key. We'll talk more about gunsights in the next chapter.

18. Parking brakes set.

Applying the parking brake is a precaution to keep your aircraft from rolling away when you start it and to also keep from getting into trouble while you're performing the ground check. Your parking brakes are not set by default

This message will appear when you set the parking brake.

when you first enter the flight. To set your brakes in the locked position (parking brakes) press Ctrl + . (period). You'll know they're set when you see the text message flash on the left side of the screen.

19. Supercharger control switch AUTO.

All aircraft with superchargers in Combat Flight Simulator are set to AUTO. In other words, Combat Flight Simulator handles all supercharger control for you and doesn't allow you to manually change the setting. The real P-51 has a two-stage, two-speed, engine-driven supercharger. In auto mode, it would automatically change speeds from low to high at altitude for best performance. On the V-1650-7 engine modeled in the plane we're flying, the blower (as superchargers are also known) would switch speeds between altitudes of 15,700 and 19,700 feet.

20. Clock set.

The system does this, so there's no need to do anything here. In real life, some pilots doing instrument scans find using the clock on the instrument panel easier to use than their wristwatch.

21. Gyro instruments uncaged.

Gyro-operated instruments (AI, DG, and T/S, but especially the AI) not designed for aerobatics/combat (they weren't invented yet in WWII) can tumble and lose their bearings, causing them to be useless if subjected to pitch attitudes of +/- 70 degrees or if bank exceeds 100 degrees. So some of these instruments (the AI specifically) were designed to be locked ("caged") into position to keep them from tumbling while performing combat flight maneuvers. Unlocking them before engine startup allows them to spin up and acquire proper reference orientations.

22. Altimeter set to field elevation.

Combat Flight Simulator automatically handles this for you.

23. Note manifold pressure reading (field barometric pressure) for subsequent use during preflight engine check.

Look over to the manifold pressure gauge. It should read 29.61 in. Hg. Remember this number—you'll need it again during the Preflight Engine Check.

24. Fuel shutoff lever ON T.

This isn't modeled in Combat Flight Simulator. It acts as a main fuel shut-off valve that cuts the flow of fuel to the engine regardless of the tanks selected.

The fuel selector on the P-51D is on the lower far right of the instrument panel.

25. Fuel tank selector handle to FUS. TANK. If fuselage tank is not serviced, selector handle to MAIN TANK L.H.

The P-51D was notorious for dangerous handling, ranging from untrimmable flight to reverse elevator control while its fuselage tank contained more than 40 gallons of fuel. Although the fuselage tank could hold 85 gallons, it was restricted to a maximum load of 65 gallons due to the adverse effects caused by the aft CG (center of gravity) that it produced. If you've got a fuselage tank full of fuel, your best bet is to burn that fuel first—which is why that tank is specified first.

> **Note:** *The designation L.H. on the fuel tank selector stands for Left Hand. As you would surmise, R.H. stands for Right Hand.*

To select fuel tanks, click the fuel selector switch on the far lower right of the instrument panel. Multiple mouse clicks will toggle the selector through available settings. On the P-51D, the center selection (pointing straight down) is the fuselage tank.

26. Ignition Switch OFF.

This is known as the magneto switch. A magneto (mag) is a type of generator that operates like the alternator on an automobile. When your engine is running, an alternator (and magneto in our case) generates electricity. A magneto's job is to keep the engine's ignition system going (powering the spark plugs), and an alternator usually charges systems to charge vehicle batteries. Batteries, in turn, power the vehicle's electrical systems.

The P-51D's mag switch is on the far-left side of the instrument panel.

Note: *Magnetos are found only on aircraft with internal combustion engines.*

The P-51D (and all of the internal combustion aircraft modeled in Combat Flight Simulator) is equipped with a double redundant magneto system and a generator. If you have a battery and generator failure from a run-in with an aggressive bandit, for example, it will not affect your engine's operation. We'll talk more about what the mag switches on another checklist. For now, simply know where the magneto controls are and how to operate them.

The mag switch on the P-51D is on the lower left side of the instrument panel. It has four positions: BOTH, L (Left), R (Right), and OFF. To operate the mags, press M on the keyboard and then press the - (Hyphen) key to rotate the mag switch counter clockwise or the = (Equal Sign) key to rotate the mag switch in a clockwise direction. You can also operate the mags by clicking the switch with the mouse when the appropriate Plus or Minus pointer icon appears. However beware that if you press the - (Minus Sign) key or click one time too many once the mag switch reaches B, it will trigger the engine starter.

When you entered this flight, the default for the mag switch was Off, so now the mags should be set to Off. But if you want to double-check it, press the M key followed by the - (Hyphen) key three times.

27. Landing gear fairing door emergency release handle in.

Not modeled in Combat Flight Simulator, this handle releases the hydraulic pressure for the landing gear and disengages the landing gear fairing doors (which releases the gear uplocks—mechanisms to keep the landing gear retracted even with a loss of hydraulic pressure). You would use this in a hydraulic pump failure to try and lower the landing gear. By releasing the pressure and the uplocks, combined with a little airplane wiggling and a little luck, the landing gear will drop and lock into place.

Note: *Although the recommendation during a hydraulic failure in Combat Flight Simulator is to manually pump pressure into the hydraulic system by pressing Ctrl+G to lower the landing gear, it isn't the way it's handled in the real P-51D. This was a design decision made to add procedural uniformity to the user-flyable aircraft.*

28. Oxygen gauge pressure 400 PSI. Test oxygen equipment operation.

Obviously this isn't modeled in Combat Flight Simulator. The P-51D, like most fighters, doesn't have a pressurized cockpit. That's why there was a need

for oxygen. Although the use of oxygen isn't considered necessary for flight below 12,500 feet, many fighter pilots wore their oxygen masks anyway. Although some radio microphones were located inside the oxygen mask, many pilots would keep them on as a matter of course to be "battle ready" at all times. Oxygen masks offered some additional protection from cockpit fires.

29. Check canopy emergency release handle and coolant flap emergency release handle for safetying.

This is 1940's speak for "make sure the emergency handles are in the safety position so they won't release by mistake." They're automatically handled for you in Combat Flight Simulator. But here's the scoop. The coolant flap is a motorized door that controls the airflow to the two radiators on the belly of the P-51D under the wing. The emergency flap control mechanically opened this door in the case of a failure of the motorized system. The biggest quirk with this system is that once the door is opened with the emergency lever, you can't close it until you're back on the ground. You don't want it to open in flight unless it's an emergency.

30. Radio and communications switches OFF.

To turn off radio messages, press the B key. This key command essentially works like your radio but it will only disable the onscreen radio message text and the audio from your wingmen. In a real airplane, the reason for turning off all electrical equipment before starting the engine was to reduce the power load required and to prevent electrical damage to the fragile radios.

> **Note:** *Regardless of your radio setting status or radio condition, you'll always hear all ground control radio messages.*

31. Check landing gear warning lights

These are located on the lower far left of the instrument panel. In Combat Flight Simulator, this little panel also acts as the landing gear control—so you can operate it by clicking it with your mouse. You can use the G key command to toggle the landing gear as well.

There are two lights on this panel. Regardless of the aircraft you're flying, Combat Flight Simulator models them with a green light indicating a safe landing condition (gear down and locked) and a red light indicating an unsafe

The lights on the landing gear warning lights panel tell you whether it's safe to land on your landing gear.

landing condition. In the real world, you'd just be looking for a green light at this point.

32. Check generator-disconnect switch ON.

Combat Flight Simulator doesn't require you to mess with this. The generator produces power for the P-51D's electrical systems when the engine is running 1200 RPM and higher. The generator-disconnect switch connects the generator to the airplane's electrical system. Think of this as the ignition switch on your car (not the starter engage position and not the ACC position, but the position the key needs to be in for the car to run).

33. All circuit breakers pushed in.

Circuit breakers aren't modeled in Combat Flight Simulator. In a real aircraft, circuit breakers are the resetable, pop-out type. These breakers literally pop out when they reach load capacity. This not only makes them easier to identify from the multitudes in a typical airplane, but also allows them to be reset by just pushing them back in.

Starting Engine

By now you're probably starting to understand why Combat Flight Simulator has an Auto engine start feature. To use the Auto engine start feature, press the E key. If you choose to go this route, skip to the next section: Pre-Takeoff and Ground Check. For those of you continuing on, let's move along to the engine starting procedures.

1. Ignition switch and battery-disconnect switch OFF.

The ignition switch is the magneto switch discussed in the last section. The battery-disconnect switch (which isn't modeled) disconnects the battery from the aircraft's electrical systems completely. Confusing? Well, be relieved that Combat Flight Simulator only models the mag switch.

2. Mixture control IDLE CUTOFF.

It should still be there from the last checklist, but you can press Ctrl + Shift + F1 to double-check it.

3. Have ground crew pull propeller through several revolutions.

Okay, this probably sounds silly. First, the ground crew isn't trying to start the engine by hand. What they're doing is drawing some of the air/fuel mixture into the cylinders. This is a way to prime the engine to get it ready to start. Although the engine would eventually start if you didn't prime it first, this saves the starter motor and battery a lot of wear and tear.

4. External power supply connected (Battery-disconnect switch ON if external power supply is not available.)

5. Check throttle open approximately one inch.

6. Oil and coolant radiator air control switches at OPEN until flaps are fully opened, and then release switches to OFF.

Okay, number 4 isn't modeled (we're using internal power anyway). Number 5 (throttle) should be ready (where we set it earlier), and number 6 isn't modeled. But note that these doors are motorized (which is why you need to hold the switch in the OPEN position).

7. Check propeller is clear.

8. Hold starter switch ON.

9. Ignition switch to BOTH after six blades have passed.

10. Fuel booster pump switch to ON.

11. Prime engine three or four strokes when cold, one stroke when hot.

12. When engine starts, move mixture control to NORMAL. Do not jockey throttle. If engine does not start after turning several revolutions, continue priming.

13. Check oil pressure. If it is not 50 PSI within 30 seconds after engine starts, stop engine and investigate.

We've got several items that need attending to here, and due to the way that Combat Flight Simulator handles some of them, we have to alter the process a bit. Booster pumps are automatically handled by Combat Flight Simulator (the Merlin engine has a mechanical fuel pump and an electric manually-initiated

The starter switch is located just to the right of the mag switch on the P-51D.

booster fuel pump—the latter is not modeled), as is the priming pump. So we have to skip those. Finally, due to the lack of a virtual ground crew to hand turn the engine to atomize some fuel into the cylinders, we now have the following modified checklist.

7a. Increase fuel mixture lever to one or two clicks above idle cut off (press Ctrl + Shift + F3 twice). The Mixture Cutoff Setting is 100-percent efficient in Combat Flight Simulator, but in the real world there would be some fuel in the engine despite this setting.

8a. Normally you would yell out "clear!" as a warning that you were going to engage the starter. (Of course you can do this, but be aware that others may be in the room.)

9a. Next, press the M key followed by four presses of the = (Equal Sign) key while holding the key down on the fourth press until the engine starts. The fourth key press engages the starter just to make life easier for you. You can manually press the starter switch by clicking it with your mouse (it's the red rectangular thing located just to the right of the mag switch). Regardless of the method you use, you need to keep the starter engaged (switch or key pressed) until the engine starts (just as in real life).

10a. Once the engine comes to life, increase the fuel mixture to full rich (press Ctrl + Shift + F4).

However, in Combat Flight Simulator, you may have noticed that there's no such mode labeled on either of the American throttle quadrants. So if you want to simulate reality in your flights, enable auto mixture by checking the box of the same name in Settings. To access this, click Settings from the main screen or from the menu bar, next click Options, and then select Settings.

Note: *Although the P-51D and P-47D have mixture control levers on their throttle quadrants, they had automatic mixture control modes. You set it in RUN mode (known as NORMAL in the early P-51D) and leave it there, and your mixtures would be automatically adjusted for you. If for some reason the Automatic Mixture Setting control malfunctions, the pilot has the ability to override this feature and run the fuel mixture in EMERGENCY F. RICH (Emergency Full Rich) mode.*

For our flight, you may recall, at the beginning of this chapter, we disabled auto mixture. That's because

we want to detail the manual use of fuel mixture control—so you can understand the British fighters' operation when flying an aircraft with true manual fuel mixture control.

Ground Check

Just as an aircraft preflight is a safety inspection, the ground check procedures are more of the same thing with a few *reminders* added. The main difference between the two, besides the fact that you're sitting inside the airplane now, is that the ground check is performed with the engine running.

Ground check procedures are usually performed before taxiing out on to the runway. But since we're on the runway, we'll perform them here. Unlike the aircraft in Flight Simulator 98, the aircraft in Combat Flight Simulator are 100-percent reliable unless you damage them (through overstressing or getting them shot to pieces!) So one would think that there isn't much point to performing the ground check—you *know* everything is going to work. Nevertheless, we'll look at a few items you should check that aren't directly affected by reliability.

1. Fuel system check.

Rotate fuel tank selector handle and check fuel pressure for proper operating range of each tank. Fuel booster pump switch must be on EMERG. If drop tanks are installed, check fuel flow from each. Position fuel tank selector handle at MAIN TANK L. H. for takeoff.

Again, fuel booster pumps are handled automatically by Combat Flight Simulator. Cycle through the fuel tanks by clicking the fuel tank selector. After each switch, check the fuel pressure gauge to see whether you're getting the proper fuel pressure (which is 16-18 PSI with the maximum being 20 PSI on the real P-51D). When you've competed your check, switch to the MAIN L.H. tank for takeoff.

2. Radiator air outlet flaps.

Move coolant flap and oil radiator air control switches to OPEN and CLOSE positions and have outside observer verify their operation. Hold switches at OPEN until radiator air outlet flaps are fully open, and then release switches to OFF.

These radiator doors are handled automatically by Combat Flight Simulator. But like all mechanical devices, heat is an enemy and can destroy a perfectly good engine.

3. Check oil, coolant, and fuel gauges for proper indications. Place supercharger control switch at AUTO.

Check the Engine "T" 3-way gauge and the fuel quantity gauge for proper readings. Supercharger control is handled automatically by Combat Flight Simulator.

4. Ignition system check.

At 700 RPM, turn ignition switch OFF momentarily. If the engine does not cease firing completely, shut it down and warn all personnel to keep clear of the propeller.

As we mentioned earlier, the ignition switch is the magneto switch. Press the M key followed by the - (Hyphen) key three times. On the third press quickly press the = (Equal Sign) key once to keep the engine running. To finish, switch the mags back to both by pressing the = (Equal Sign) key two more times.

When you moved the mag switch to the OFF position, you should have heard the engine momentarily stop firing. We're making sure that there aren't any shorts in the magneto wiring that would prevent us from completely shutting the engine down safely. With a short in the mag systems, the engine could start if someone or something turned the propeller (hence the warning to personnel).

5. Propeller check.

Note: *If you did have a short in the magneto system (currently an impossibility in Combat Flight Simulator), you'd shut the engine down by placing the mixture lever to idle cutoff.*

With propeller control in full INCREASE, set throttle to obtain 2300 RPM. Move propeller back to DECREASE position to note maximum drop of 300 RPM. Return control to INCREASE.

This step is intended to place a load on the engine and prop pitch control system. Prop pitch movement is handled by a high-pressure hydraulic system fed off the engine oil system. Cycling prop

pitch accomplishes two things. First it warms up the prop pitch control system by cycling oil through it. Secondly, by stressing the prop pitch system, you can force a weakness, such as a system leak, to show itself. Although the checklist lists this step as one cycle, it's not a bad idea to perform two cycles to ensure the oil in the prop governor is warm.

To cycle the prop, press Ctrl + F1 on the keyboard or pull the prop control (the middle knob) all the way back with your mouse. Leave it for a second or two and take a quick look at the tach to make sure that the RPM had indeed dropped and remained above 2000 RPM. Also take a quick look at the oil pressure gauge. You want to make sure there are no sudden losses in oil pressure. Finally, check the next list item (number 6) while you're at it. Once these are checked, return the prop control back to the full forward position by pressing Ctrl + F4 or with your mouse.

6. Simmond's regulator check.

Watch manifold pressure during propeller check. Manifold pressure should remain constant within one in. Hg.

The Simmond's regulator is essentially a manifold pressure relief valve. You're looking to see that it's not stuck in the open or shut position.

7. Supercharger check.

At 2300 RPM, place supercharger control switch at HIGH—there should be at least a 50 RPM drop. Return supercharger control switch to AUTO.

Supercharger control is handled automatically by Combat Flight Simulator, so there's nothing to do here. In any case RPM drops when the supercharger control is placed in HIGH speed because you're forcing more air into the engine than it can use. This causes a load on the supercharger and its drive train, which is directly connected to the engine.

8. Deleading spark plugs.

Should prolonged ground operation, such as checking engine condition or performing numerous preflight checks, be necessary, run the engine at 61 in. Hg. manifold pressure and 3000 RPM for one continuous minute prior to takeoff.

Prolonged ground operation at a low RPM tends to foul spark plugs. A high-performance engine is designed to operate at a certain temperature range and load. When it isn't subjected to the proper conditions (such as those encountered when idling), the fuel and lubrication that enters the engine's cylinders doesn't burn as thoroughly as it's been tuned to. This causes a coating to form on the spark plugs that interferes with its ability to produce a hot spark—which in turn deteriorates the engine's performance.

Running the engine at a high power setting allows the spark plug to burn ("delead" in the 1940s) this coating off the spark plugs. Fortunately for us, the engines in Combat Flight Simulator don't have these kinds of problems, so you can idle all day long and never miss a spark.

Pre-Takeoff Check

The pre-takeoff checks are basically your last chances to make sure everything is A-OK before committing yourself to takeoff. As we mentioned earlier, takeoffs and landings are the most critical parts of a normal flight due to the proximity of the ground.

1. Primary Controls: Check surface controls for free movement.

This is the same item as Interior Check checklist number 5.

2. Instruments and Switches:
   - Altimeter set.
   - Directional gyro set.
   - Gyro Horizon set.
   - All instrument readings in desired ranges.
   - All switches and controls at desired positions.

After reading the last chapter, you should now be well versed on what the flight instruments are, where they're located, and how to read them. The ground check is the time when they're checked and calibrated. Unlike Flight Simulator 98, there's no need to calibrate your instruments—but you can do a visual inspection.

The first visual check is of all your instruments. Start on one side of the instrument panel and work your way to the other rather than skipping around. This will help you to avoid missing one. You are looking for proper

operation. The gyros on the AI, T/S, and DG should be spinning. (If one isn't, its display will be cockeyed or spinning around and the ASI and VSI should both read zero.)

   3. Fuel System:
- Check fuel tank selector handle on MAIN TANK L. H.
- Fuel booster pump switch at EMERGENCY (handled automatically). Primer switch OFF (handled automatically).

   4. Flaps:
- Flaps set for takeoff (UP for normal takeoff).
- Check the flap position indicator. Press F5 to raise your flaps fully.

   5. Trim:
- Trim tabs set for takeoff:

Fuselage Tank 0 - 25 Gal.	Fuselage Tank Full (65 gal.)
Rudder 6 deg. R	6 deg. R
Elevator 0 deg	2 to 4 deg nose-heavy
Aileron 0 deg	0 deg

   Trim tabs are adjusted as follows:

Trim Tab Adjustment Key Combinations	
Rudder trim left	Ctrl + 0
Rudder trim right	Ctrl + Enter
Elevator trim up	Num 1
Elevator trim down	Num 7
Aileron trim left	Ctrl + Num 4
Aileron trim right	Ctrl + Num 6

Unfortunately, there isn't any way to check your trim positions in Combat Flight Simulator's default aircraft. However, when you first enter the airplane the defaults are pretty close to neutral, so you can "guesstimate" the optimal Takeoff Trim Settings from there.

   6. Check all circuit breakers in (not modeled).

   7. Check that cockpit enclosure is locked and that canopy emergency release handle is safetied.

Pre-Takeoff Engine Check

We're almost there! The next checks are the final ones.

1. Check propeller at full INCREASE.

We want to generate full power on takeoff, and, you may recall, that requires the prop to be set at minimum pitch/full RPM. Press Ctr + F4 to put the propeller control at full INCREASE/maximum RPM.

2. Power check.

Advance throttle to obtain 2300 RPM. At this RPM, the manifold pressure should read 1/2 in. Hg less than field barometric pressure within +/-1/2 in. Hg.
Way back in Interior Checklist item number 23, we looked at the manifold pressure gauge reading. To save you from looking back, the reading we saw was 29.61 in. Hg. Advance the throttle to 2300 RPM by pressing F4 a few times. Manifold pressure should read 1/2 in. Hg less than field barometric pressure within +/-1/2 in. Hg.

3. Ignition system check.

At 2300 RPM, with propeller at full INCREASE, move ignition switch from BOTH to L, back to BOTH, then to R, and back to BOTH. A maximum drop of 100 RPM is allowable for the right magneto and 120 RPM for the left magneto. If RPM drop is more than allowable, spark plugs will have to be deleaded.
The magneto check requires several steps. First advance the throttle to 2300 RPM by pressing F4 a couple of times. (For accuracy's sake, don't use the mouse for this.) Check your progress by watching the tachometer.
Next we need to systematically turn on and off the magnetos. The magneto switch is similar to an ignition switch found in a car. The P-51D's magneto switch has four settings (OFF, R, L, and B), but as previously noted, the start switch is located next to it on the right.
The OFF position on the mag switch is self-explanatory, and you can think of right, left, and both as three different run positions. Right and left refer to the two magnetos found on the engine. They are redundant systems for safety. If one magneto goes out, the other will keep the engine running. You'll

normally fly with both magnetos enabled—if one goes out, the other will still be connected.

During the ground check, you check the condition of each individual magneto by systematically turning one mag off at a time. To do this, press M on the keyboard and then press the - (Hyphen) key to turn the mag switch counter clockwise or the = (Equal Sign) key to turn the mag switch in a clockwise direction. First move the mag switch to the L (Left) position, then move it back to B (Both), followed by R (Right), and finally back to B again.

Each time you switch from B to one of the other mags and back, you should be watching the tach for RPM changes. You're looking for RPM drops from the Both position to a single mag of less than 100 RPM for the right magneto and less than 120 RPM for the left magneto. Any higher RPM drops than the specifications call for indicate a worn magneto or, most likely, fouled spark plugs. Needless to say, you probably shouldn't fly if you find a problem here—unless you're looking to check out how well your airplane works as a glider.

4. Idle speed check.

Idle engine at 650 to 700 RPM with throttle against idle stop. Return the throttle back to idle by pressing F3 several times. Then check the tach for the proper RPM.

5. Acceleration and deceleration check.

With mixture control at NORMAL, advance throttle from idle to 2300 RPM. Engine should accelerate and decelerate smoothly with no tendency to backfire. Since the Combat Flight Simulator ground crew keeps your bird in perfect running condition, there should be no problems here.

6. Set throttle for 1500 RPM for best cooling during prolonged ground operation.

7. Carburetor ram-air control lever at RAM AIR (handled automatically).

8. Check mixture control at NORMAL.

NORMAL is full forward on the mixture control. Press Ctrl + Shift + F4 to double-check it.

9. Check supercharger control switch at AUTO
(handled automatically).

10. Oil and coolant radiator air control switches at AUTOMATIC
(handled automatically).

11. If necessary to wait long before takeoff, recheck magnetos to see if
any spark plug leading is present.

Takeoff

Now for the fun! Things happen quickly here, so you may want to read through
this section at least once before taking action.

1. Be sure takeoff area is clear, and check final approach for aircraft.

You're the only one flying in Free Flight mode, so don't worry about traffic
now. (But during your missions, you'll likely be flying with a wingman or
wingmen—chances are they'll be right in front of you when you enter
the mission.)

Your view directly in front isn't very good because the instrument panel
(and nose of the aircraft in a real taildragger) is blocking the way. (There are
three ways to correct this—we'll cover them later in our discussion on taxiing.
We know you're just itching to get up in the air.)

2. Release brakes and line up for takeoff.

To release the parking brake, press the . (Period) key.

3. Advance throttle smoothly and steadily to Takeoff Power.
Note: It is recommended that 61 in. Hg and 3000 RPM be used for
all takeoffs and that this power setting be reached as quickly as
possible after the takeoff run is started. Do not jam the throttle
forward, as torque will cause loss of control of the airplane.

Press F4 to increase throttle. If you've got the auto rudder option disabled,
you'll be using rudder to control the airplane on the ground. Moving the
ailerons won't help you to change direction. If you're using a set of rudder
pedals, add a little right rudder to compensate for the left-turning tendency and
hold it there. There's no exaggeration here—a little means a little. Make small

corrections to stay in the center of the runway. Unless there's a strong crosswind (and there won't be with this Flight), you won't need to do much to keep rolling straight down the runway.

> **Note:** *The real P-51D had NORMAL, AUTO RICH, and AUTO LEAN Fuel Mixture Settings. In Combat Flight Simulator, use the Full Rich Setting (fuel mixture control lever full forward) for NORMAL and AUTO RICH Checklist Settings.*

4. If rough engine occurs during takeoff run, immediately throttle back 4 or 5 in. Hg. manifold pressure to complete takeoff, if conditions permit. Throttling back tends to decrease the intensity of detonation or pre-ignition and minimizes the chances of engine failure. If this condition occurs on takeoff, the spark plugs must be changed before the next flight.

Your trusty virtual ground crew keeps your engine in tip-top shape, and they fuel you up with the best (virtual) aviation fuel there is, so you won't have to worry about this.

5. Do not attempt to lift the tail too soon, as this increases torque action. Pushing the stick forward unlocks the tailwheel, thereby making steering difficult. The best takeoff procedure is to hold the tail down until sufficient speed for rudder control is attained and then to raise the tail slowly.

The real P-51D has a locking tailwheel. It's "locked" when you hold the control stick in the neutral position or any position aft of neutral (slightly aft of neutral is recommended for takeoff). But the term locking is a bit misleading. In this case, when the tailwheel is locked, it really only limits its travel to 6 degrees right or left, and doesn't prevent it from moving totally—as you might expect. In any case, limiting the amount that the tailwheel can swivel helps the pilot avoid over-controlling the airplane during takeoff roll.

6. As soon as you're definitely airborne, retract the landing gear by pulling the landing-gear handle inboard and up. Check position of gear by warning lights.

The phrase "definitely air-borne" has been replaced by "when positive rate of climb has been achieved" in most modern checklists. Getting your wheels off the ground doesn't necessarily mean you're going to remain flying. By

Follow Your Feet

At best, steering with your feet feels very awkward—especially after years of conditioning from driving automobiles. I can recall the odd feeling of not knowing what to do with my hands while taxiing around the airport during my primary flight training days. But don't get discouraged. It's possible and it's done every day.

New pilots tend to use too much rudder and over-correct. These over-corrections lead to what's known in the test pilot biz as PIOs (Pilot Induced Oscillations). The secret to success is to add a little bit of corrective rudder and hold it there until you see its effect. From there you can set a new course of action.

Granted, this is easier said than done, but here are few more tips:

- *Try and relate your rudder inputs to a place on the airplane. The most common spot is the nose. If you want to move the nose to the right, press the right pedal. If you want to move the nose to the left, press the left pedal.*
- *Remember that it's better to apply less rudder than you need than to apply too much and have to correct it with opposite rudder input.*
- *If you're having an inordinate amount of trouble with this, your rudder controller sensitivity may be set too high, or your Null Zone needs to be increased.*

If none of the above helps and you're still having problems, practice high-speed taxiing down the runway. Keep your speed below 90 MPH IAS and don't use any flaps (so you don't take off). Also don't get discouraged. A taildragger is more difficult to control than an airplane with tricycle gear setup. Many a pilot has had to use this high-speed taxi training method to learn to handle a taildragger, so don't be shy. Get out there and practice.

checking your VSI and establishing that a positive rate of climb has been obtained, you can safely retract your landing gear with at least some confidence that you're not going to stuff it into the ground right then. To retract your landing gear, press the G key or click the landing gear position indicator.

7. Check coolant and oil temperatures and oil pressure.

Just check to see that all of your gauges are in the "green" (normal) ranges. If not, you want to find out why as soon as possible. The farther you fly away from the airfield, the harder it will be to get back there to land if something is wrong.

Finally, don't neglect to watch your heading on the DG and bank angle on the AI. Keep the wings level and continue the climb. If you've adjusted your bank at any time, check back with the T/S and step on the ball.

Minimum-Run Takeoff

Minimum-Run Takeoff is what we today call a short field takeoff. Basically it's the takeoff procedure used to get off the ground in the minimum distance and time. As you might imagine, this comes in especially handy when the enemy is attacking your airfield! That's why you might consider using this procedure for all of your takeoffs—practice makes perfect.

1. To accomplish a minimum-run takeoff, lower flaps 15-20 degrees.

Flaps increase your lift and subsequently lower your stall speed. This is all good stuff to have when you're taking off and landing (not to mention when you're so close to the ground, too). Combat Flight Simulator's P-51D flaps have five position settings—0 degrees, 10 degrees, 20 degrees, 30 degrees, and 47 degrees. The recommended Flap Setting depends on your situation (in this case 15-20 degrees). A real P-51D has hydraulically operated flaps that operate like the radiator door and can be set in any position. But because Combat Flight Simulator's P-51D doesn't work like that, use either the 10- or 20-Degree Setting instead.

Note the word "recommended" when we mentioned flap settings. Flaps are not *required* for takeoff, but they will reduce the takeoff roll required when you use them. For instance, using the 20-Degree Flap Setting will reduce your takeoff roll by about 20 percent.

To lower your flaps one setting increment at a time, press the F6 key. To raise them one setting increment at a time, press the F7 key. You can also adjust your flap setting by using your mouse and clicking the flap control lever.

2. Keep airplane in a three-point attitude and allow it to fly itself off ground in this position. Take off at minimum airspeed—95 to 100 MPH IAS.

Keeping the airplane in a three-point attitude means keeping the tailwheel on the ground. A lot of new pilots try and force the tail of the airplane off the ground early by applying down elevator, believing they will get in the air faster. Despite their good intentions, the additional induced drag imposed on the airplane by lifting the tail early actually increases takeoff distance.

3. As soon as you're airborne, allow airspeed to build up and climb out at 100 MPH.

Maintain constant climb, holding airspeed 100 MPH IAS until runway is cleared. Remember that pitch controls airspeed. Therefore, use your airplane's pitch to achieve the target 100 MPH IAS climb speed. (Pitch down to increase airspeed and pitch up to decrease airspeed.) You're just worried about getting into the air at this point. Don't worry about your climb rate or any other performance numbers right now.

4. After clearing the runway, lower nose slowly to allow airspeed to build up to climb speed of 170 MPH IAS.

170 MPH IAS is the best rate of climb speed (known as Vy) for the P-51D. In other words, if you climb at this airspeed, you'll reach the highest altitude in the least amount of time.

5. Retract landing gear as soon as definitely airborne.

Retract your landing gear by pressing the G key or clicking the landing gear position indicator.

6. Raise flaps above 200 feet altitude.

To raise the flaps one setting increment at a time, press the F7 key or use your mouse and click the flap control lever. While you can fully retract or deploy your flaps with a single key press (pressing F5 and F8 respectively), the general recommendation is to raise and deploy flaps gradually (in increments). Although the P-51D doesn't suffer from any major attitude changes when flaps are retracted or deployed, not all aircraft behave that way. For example, some aircraft may become nose heavy (pitch down) when you lower the flaps and become tail heavy (pitch up) when you retract the flaps.

Climb

The climb, or what's sometimes more descriptively called the cruise climb, is different from takeoff climb in how it's configured and what it's intended to achieve. The takeoff climb (when we first lifted off the ground and climbed at 100 MPH IAS) is designed to get you off the ground to the highest

altitude in the shortest period of time for safety reasons. (For example, if you lost your engine during takeoff, the greater the current altitude, the longer you can glide—which increases your landing options.)

On the other hand, a cruise climb trades off altitude gain for more ground distance traveled over a period of time. As we'll discuss later, depending on your mission, there will come a point where you won't want to climb any higher and you'll be more interested in airspeed for retaining energy, saving fuel, or making good time to your destination. That portion of the trip is known as the cruise. The cruise climb is a compromise between the takeoff climb and the cruise—which neatly explains the term's origin.

1. Allow airspeed to build to 170 MPH for normal climb.

Again, 170 MPH IAS is the best rate of climb (Vy) for the P-51D. Remember to use pitch to control your airspeed. If airspeed gets a little fast, ease the nose up slightly. If speed starts to drop, lower the nose slightly. It only takes a small pitch change to create big changes in airspeed and rate of climb.

Also remember to use the rudder to maintain coordinated flight. After lowering the nose, you won't require as much right rudder anymore. It's when the airplane is traveling at low speed with a high power setting (like the takeoff climb), that the right rudder is required to compensate for the airplane's left-turning tendency.

2. After reaching an altitude of 500 feet, throttle back to 46 inches of manifold at 2700 RPM.

Next, back down the power. Although Combat Flight Simulator's engine can run at full power all day long, it uses a lot of fuel. One of the goals of cruising is to find a balance of performance and fuel economy. The cruise climb more or less has the same goal.

Reduce the throttle to 46 in. of manifold pressure by pressing the F3 key. Then pull back the prop control by pressing Ctrl + F2 until the tach reads 2700 RPM.

3. Retrim the ship for climbing attitude desired.

Use the trim keys to trim the airplane to maintain the climb. Just remember that unless you've stabilized your airplane before trimming it, you'll just have

to do it again as your airspeed changes. Use the rudder trim keys (Ctrl + 0 and Ctrl + Enter) to reduce the amount of right rudder pedal requirements.

   4. If your airplane has a three-position booster pump switch, set it at NORMAL when an altitude of 500 feet has been attained. (The boost pump is automatically handled by Combat Flight Simulator.)

Cruise

There comes a time in a flight when you become interested in making good time rather than climbing any higher. Although not listed as a step in your checklist, at this point you need to level off at your cruising altitude. (When the wings of the AI rest on the top of the AI's horizon line, you'll be at a level pitch attitude.) Don't worry about letting the airplane accelerate. Whatever airspeed the airplane gives you is what you want.

With the increase in airspeed, you'll need to retrim the airplane. Just make sure you do this after the airplane has finished accelerating (reached equilibrium) or you'll have to do it again. That's not a big deal, but flying the elevator trim is like chasing the VSI. If your trim adjustment changes your airspeed, the new trim setting will no longer be correct. Generally, you'll need to wait about a half minute to reach equilibrium once you've leveled off.

Cruise Performance

There are three cruise options available to you: reduced flight time, fuel economy, or a balance of the two.

As you might imagine, reducing flight time requires you to fly faster, and flying faster requires more fuel. Conversely, flying while economizing to increase your range, won't allow you to burn the fuel necessary produce the power required to fly fast.

Performance and fuel economy rely heavily on atmospheric conditions (air is the working fluid for an engine—the more you can get in, the more power you can produce). Cruise power, which needs to be determined by a chart, is configured with throttle and prop control. Your cruise goal will determine the chart you use.

We've provided a sample Maximum Endurance (maximum range) and performance chart for the P-51D.

Maximum Endurance Cruise

Economy is a function of fuel mixture based on the throttle and prop settings. The Maximum Endurance cruise chart will provide you with specific prop and throttle setting and what they'll achieve at airspeed (in this point in history usually in CAS—Calibrated Airspeed— in MPH) at a specific altitude to achieve the maximum range. (Just what the general ordered for reaching Berlin and making it home.)

Tip: *One handy rule of thumb that can help you level off at the right altitude with minimal corrections is known as "The 10% Rule". This means you begin to level the airplane at an altitude 10% of your vertical speed below your intended altitude. For example, our cruise climb configuration should net you a climb rate of 2200 FPM vertical velocity. Therefore, to level off at a cruise altitude of 5500 feet, you should begin to level off at 5280 feet (220 feet below the final altitude).*

For a flight in the P-51D with a maximum weapon and fuel load cruising at 15,000 feet using the default weather, one throttle setting and one prop setting is 35 in. and 2050 RPM. This will net us 140 MPH CAS at 60 GPH (Gallons Per Hour) fuel burn.

Maximum Endurance Chart - Standard Day   P-51D

Configuration: Six 5" Rockets - plus Two 75 Gal. Tanks, Two 110 Gal. Tanks, Two 1000 lb. Bombs, or One 1000 lb. Bomb plus one 110 Gal. Tank
Gross Weight: 13,000 to 11,000 lbs.

GPH	Mixture	Approximate RPM	MP (In Hg.)	CAS (MPH)	Pressure Altitude (Feet)
48	NORMAL	1750	36	140	Sea Level
52	NORMAL	1750	35	40	5000
56	NORMAL	1800	36	140	10,000
60	NORMAL	2050	35	140	15,000

Legend: GPH - Fuel Consumption (Gallons Per Hour); CAS - Calibrated Airspeed; F.T. - Full Throttle

Normal Cruise

You may have noticed on the Maximum Endurance cruise chart that your airspeed is a rather unremarkable 140 MPH CAS. That's excruciatingly slow for a sleek fighter—but for optimal range, that's the price you pay.

Fortunately, long-distance bomber escort missions (more on these later) aren't the only duties you'll be asked to perform in Combat Flight Simulator. For those missions that don't require range to be absolutely stretched to the limits, you'll be able to use normal cruise settings and fly at faster airspeeds.

Mixture Leaning

We've got our performance set up, so next we look at economy. At cruising altitude we can lean the fuel mixture. The P-51D has an automatic fuel mixture system that would do this for you, but for the sake of understanding how this works and how it would operate on the user-flyable British aircraft in Combat Flight Simulator, we've unchecked Enable auto mixtures in Settings.

One way that fuel mixtures are normally leaned is by using some engine temperature reference. Your engine will heat up as it reaches peak efficiency but will cool off as you reach lean or rich conditions. If you're a Flight Simulator 98 veteran, you may recall that the EGT (Exhaust Gas Temperature) gauge is used to guide engine leaning. The way it's done is to systematically lean the fuel mixture until the EGT peaks, and then back it off in the rich mixture direction slightly (the exact amount depends on the engine manufacturer's specifications).

None of the user-flyable aircraft in Combat Flight Simulator has this handy instrument, so you need to rely on other means to measure peak. On the P-47D, you can use the CHT gauge, and on the P-51D, you can use the coolant gauge.

Another method is to listen to the engine while leaning the mixture. Slowly press Ctrl + Shift + F2 while listening to the engine. You'll hear the engine increase RPM slightly. If you further lean the mixture the engine will begin to sound rough and may even quit. At that point, press Ctrl + Shift + F3 to enrich the mixture for smooth operation. Enriching the fuel mixture about two to four clicks above misfiring should put you approximately in the right area. The visual temperature gauge method is more accurate, but if you're in a bind this second method will work reasonably well.

During flight, your fuel gauges should be a regular part of one of your sub-scans. Once you're configured for cruise, switch tanks to the fuselage tank. The fuel in this tank has the largest affect on the P-51's maneuverability, so it pays to burn this fuel first.

Combat Configuration

You probably have enough information now to conclude that the optimal combat configuration for a fighter would be full throttle, full prop, and full rich mixture. That's not too far from the truth.

Obviously in a combat situation, you want maximum power at your disposal. But as you'll see later, full throttle isn't always the best power setting for all combat situations. So for a combat configuration, we'll call it throttle as needed.

As for the prop setting, Full Forward/Max RPM is the setting of choice. Again, you want maximum power, and this setting will give it to you.

Finally, although you may be flying and fighting at high altitudes, you still want to run with your mixture set at Full Rich if you're not using automatic mode. Why? You're not interested in fuel economy, you never know if the battle might end up at a lower altitude, and it gives you one less thing to worry about. You're going to be busy enough in combat—you don't want to be worrying about your engine running too lean.

Descent

The descent, or what is referred to as cruise descent (as opposed to approach descents used in precision IFR operations), is made at cruising speed from cruising altitude to a lower cruising altitude or until transition to a landing approach descent.

Descent in a warbird like the P-51D can be made at any airspeed above the recommended margin of about 25 percent above stall speed with the landing gear and flaps up. (This is known as Vs—which is 101 MPH IAS@9000 lbs. in level flight. This would make your minimum descent speed about 125 MPH IAS.) You know that if you lowered the nose of the airplane your airspeed would increase. Our definition of cruise descent: a descent made at cruising speed. This means we need to reduce power.

Stall Speeds IAS MPH (Power Off)   P-51D

Gross Weight Lbs.	Gear Up Flaps Up			Gear Down Flaps 45° Down		
	Level	30° Bank	45° Bank	Level	30° Bank	45° Bank
Wing Racks Only						
10,000	106	115	128	101	110	123
9000	101	109	121	94	103	116
8000	94	102	114	87	98	108
Bombs, Drop Tanks, or Rockets (stall speeds with Rockets estimated)						
12,000	119	128	143	113	123	136
11,000	113	22	137	107	117	131
10,000	108	116	130	102	111	124
9000	102	110	123	95	105	117

When you reduce power, the nose of the airplane will pitch downward by itself if you let it (remember throttle controls descent). Pick a pitch attitude on the AI and keep the airplane there until the airplane reaches equilibrium again. You shouldn't have to mess with the elevator trim because we were trim for cruise speed—and you should now be descending at cruise speed as well. Finally, because we've changed power and pitch, you may need to add some left rudder; keep the ball in the T/S centered. Don't forget to check that. The last thing you need when you're getting closer to the ground is get into a spin.

With all things being equal, normally your mixture setting will automatically lean itself even if you're not running in automatic mixture mode when you descend due to the denser air below. This can be dangerous if you didn't reduce the power setting. Generally a leaner mixture at a higher power setting will become a slightly richer mixture at a lower power setting because the fuel flow requirements are reduced. Nevertheless, once you're established in the cruise descent you should enrich your fuel mixture.

Make sure you're watching the ASI, VSI and ALT during your descent. You don't want to descend beyond your target altitude. The 10% rule for leveling off applies to descents as well. The air-traffic pattern at Interlaken Airfield is 3423 feet MSL (Mean Sea Level). Traffic patterns are generally flown at 1000' AGL (Above Ground Level). So if we're descending at 500 fpm, to descend to Interlaken's pattern altitude you'll begin leveling off at 3473 feet.

Approach

The approach we're discussing here can be thought of as the level approach (as opposed to the Approach Descent—normal flight configuration (Number 5) listed at the beginning of this chapter) because you'll be flying level. Approach speeds vary from plane to plane and according to wind conditions, but in all cases they're executed at a slower speed than cruise.

Ideally, an approach speed should be at Vy. If you must abort your landing, you won't have to retrim during the flurry if you have to climb again to circle for another landing attempt. On the other hand, you also want your approach speed to be manageable so it will be easy to slow down. We know that Vy is 170 MPH IAS and the recommended engine out speed with no flaps or gear is 175 MPH IAS, so we'll shoot for something in this range.

Just as a preflight check was required when we took off, landing requires a prelanding check. This checklist not only serves as a reminder to remember important tasks like lowering your landing gear, but also is used to configure your airplane for approach.

Pre-Landing Checklist

1. Fuel tank selector handle on fullest internal tank.

2. Check that fuel booster pump switch is on EMERGENCY (automatically handled).

3. Check carburetor ram and hot-air control levers as needed (automatically handled).

4. Mixture control at NORMAL.

Part of the prelanding checklist is to help you prepare for landing. The other part is to prepare you in case you abort your landing and recircle for another attempt. Setting your mixture is one of these steps. The reason you want your mixture to be at Full Rich is just in case you need to punch the throttle through the firewall for a go around. It won't sputter and die from being overly lean just when you need it the most.

Press Ctrl + Shift + F4 to increase fuel mixture to Full Rich. (Remember,

Note: *Stall speeds increase as bank increases due to the loss of lift, as covered in Chapter Four.*

in Combat Flight Simulator, NORMAL1 and RICH Settings are considered the same as Full Rich. The RICH Setting merely overrides the AUTO Setting.)

5. Propeller set at 2700 RPM.

This is another go-around precaution. Depending on what your cruise and descent configuration was before reaching this point, you may have to either increase or decrease your prop's pitch to obtain 2700 RPM. To increase pitch (which will decrease RPM) press Ctrl + F2. Conversely to decrease pitch and increase RPM, press Ctrl + F3.

Although it isn't included here as a step, you'll likely need to adjust your throttle setting in order to maintain or increase your airspeed so it will equal 170-175 MPH IAS. A throttle setting of 25 in. Hg. combined with the 2700 RPM setting will achieve that target speed in level flight.

6. Oil and coolant radiator air control switches AUTOMATIC (handled automatically by Combat Flight Simulator).

7. Clean out engine at 3000 RPM and 61 in. Hg for one minute (unnecessary in Combat Flight Simulator).

8. Landing gear handle DN below 170 MPH IAS.

Press the G key to lower the landing gear.

9. Check gear position by use of warning lights, horn, and hydraulic pressure.

Neither the warning horn nor hydraulic pressure gauges are modeled in Combat Flight Simulator, but check the landing gear indicator panel for a green light.

10. Shoulder harness.

Lock harness and check by leaning forward against it.

11. Flaps down 15 (to give steeper approach if desired).

If you think you're going to overshoot the runway by being too high, you can lower your flaps to increase your angle of descent. This will get you on the ground faster without gaining airspeed. Lowering either the flaps or landing

gear, or both, greatly increases the gliding angle and the rate of descent. As we noted, 15 degrees of flaps is not obtainable in our P-51D, so use the 10- or 20-Degree Setting instead. To lower flaps in increments, press F7.

> **Tip:** *GUMP—no relation to Forrest Gump, but you'd probably be called that around the base if you landed your airplane with the gear retracted. GUMP is an acronym for the landing checklist:*
> *G = Gas*
> *U = Undercarriage (landing gear)*
> *M = Mixture*
> *P = Prop*

12. Recheck gear and flaps.

These items were covered in the prelanding checklist. But when you're landing, there's a lot to do. Rather than read through a checklist, remembering GUMP can cover the most important list items. This can be especially helpful if you're nursing home a wounded bird.

Landing

Because of the wide landing gear (and locked tailwheel on the real version), the landing roll characteristics are excellent on this airplane. Minimize the use of brakes during ground roll, and at the completion of landing roll, you should clear the runway as soon as possible.

1. Flaps full down at an altitude of at least 400 feet (below 165 MPH IAS).

Rather than drop your flaps one notch at a time (and due to the P-51D's mild flap deployment reaction), pressing F8 to fully deploy your flaps with one command can save you some time.

Drop your flaps early enough so that you'll have the time and altitude to stabilize the airplane. But as you gain experience, you'll probably want to avoid deploying them too far out because flying at such a low airspeed for too long becomes quite boring after the excitement of a successfully completed mission. But for now, it's better to err on the side of a long, slow-landing approach than to be too fast, too low, and unstabilized.

2. 120 MPH IAS at edge of field.

For a normal landing, plan your approach so you're over the edge of the airfield at 120 MPH IAS. Pull back the throttle and let the nose drop, but stay

Note: *The flaps on a real P-51D would take from 11 to 15 seconds to travel from full up to full down.*

on top of everything. Watch your VSI: you don't want to descend faster than 500-800 FPM as you near the airfield. If you're descending too fast, add a couple of inches of throttle for a couple of seconds, and then pull it back again.

You may need to add or reduce throttle based on your distance from the runway. If you don't think you'll make the runway, add throttle. If you think you're going to land in the middle of the runway, reduce throttle. You'll be tempted to lower or raise the nose, but use the throttle instead.

3. Throttle closed when landing assured.

4. Flare out.

Just before you cross the end of the runway, reduce power to idle and gently raise the nose until it's just slightly above the horizon. Use continuous back pressure on the stick to obtain a tail-low attitude for actual touchdown. You don't want to climb, but what really helps a lot of new pilots with their landings is playing a little game called "try to keep the airplane from landing." It sounds pretty silly (especially when you want to land) but here's how it works: instead of letting the airplane just drop in, if you try to keep it off the ground by increasing pitch, the airplane will stall just as it touches ground. As long as you don't attempt this when you're too high in the air or allow the airplane to climb, it will work perfectly.

5. Touch down 90 MPH IAS.

Because of the wide landing gear and locked tailwheel, the landing roll characteristics are excellent on this airplane. Minimize the use of brakes during ground roll. At completion of landing roll, clear runway as soon as possible.

Don't get discouraged if you don't get it all right away—keep practicing. Remember, as General Yeager says, there ain't no such thing as a natural pilot. With any landings (airplane or helicopter) the approach is key. Make a bad approach, and your landing will be more difficult (if not impossible) to perform.

At this point, you can press the X key to end the flight, but if you want to really do it all, let's look at taxiing.

Taxiing

Congratulations! Now that you're back on terra firma, taxiing will seem like a piece of cake.

1. Open canopy.

Sorry, I don't know anyone with a canopy over their computer chair—but that doesn't mean someone out there doesn't have one! Just let out a deep sigh of relief and that should suffice—you've made it home!

2. Open oil flap and coolant flap (automatically controlled).

3. Raise flaps.

Press F5 to completely raise the flaps. There are a couple of reasons for raising flaps while taxiing is done. The first is the potential for them to be damaged while taxiing around. The second is that theoretically a major gust of wind (as unlikely as that may be) might lift the airplane or cause a loss of control. The final reason concerns putting the machine back in ready condition for the next guy flying it. Performing these tasks now will reduce the likelihood that you'll forget later. The next pilot that flies this airplane—even if it's you—might be in a rush, so you can save someone some trouble.

4. Trim tabs NEUTRAL.

5. Prop control—full INCREASE.

6. Booster pump switch OFF (automatically controlled).

Here are some final tips to help with getting around on the ground.

- Watch your speed. It's much better to be too slow than to be too fast. You can add a bit of power to get rolling, but once you move back the throttle back down. A power setting of 1000 RPM works pretty well.
- Trying to see ahead of you is really tough in taildraggers. You can cheat by tilting the forward view down (press Shift + Enter or remove the obstruction—the instrument panel—completely with a press of the W key.) If you're into doing it the real way, use your rudder to zigzag (known as S-turns) around the taxiways while using the 2:00 and 10:00 views. Don't worry about the C.O. (Commanding Officer) thinking you've got problems—this is common practice for taildraggers.

- Every user-flyable aircraft has two brakes, one for each wheel. Pressing the . (Period) key applies both brakes evenly. To operate each brake individually (useful for turning while taxiing) press F11 to apply left brake, and press F12 for the right brake.
- Don't forget to reduce power when you want to stop. You'll stop a lot faster than if you only applied the brakes. Besides, you wouldn't want to ding the wings of that beautiful warbird!

Chapter Six

Air Combat Basics

In this chapter, we'll take a look at the five stages of an air-combat engagement. Instead of throwing flight maneuvers at you, I think you'll find it easier to comprehend what's happening when maneuvers are presented in context. The combination of knowing a maneuver and where it can be used within a battle will empower you with the knowledge needed to transform you from the hunted to the hunter.

To keep things simple, we'll discuss one-vs.-one tactics here. We'll discuss multiple fighter tactics in the Advanced Combat Training chapter and bomber attacks in the Intermediate Combat Training chapter.

Because air combat is a fluid event—one stage flows into the next—some tactics that we'll discuss will spread beyond the particular stage in which it's first presented. What's important to gain from this chapter is an overall understanding of what goes on. Don't get carried away with trying to memorize each of these stages. When you're engaged in a furball, you don't have time to think in those terms.

Detection Stage

If you can see the enemy before he sees you, it not only often affords you the advantage of surprise, but also gives you some control over the battle—taking the fight where and when you want it to be. The detection stage contains three basic objectives—what we'll call the three W's: who, what, and where.

Combat Flight Simulator gives you four ways to detect the enemy—through the Tactical Display, on the map, through the viewing systems, and through the game engine (from radio calls).

Note: *You can extend your radar viewing range (which is 5000 meters from the center to the sides) by flying a zigzag pattern. This is because the radar screen is square in shape. This naturally makes the distance (which relates to radar range) to the corners of the screen slightly longer than the distance directly to the sides. By flying a diagonal path relative to the radar target, you'll be able to detect it earlier than if you flew directly towards it.*

Using the Tactical Display

To toggle the Tactical Display on or off press the F9 key. The Tactical Display is essentially all-knowing radar that also acts as a flight director. We'll discuss how this feature works when we discuss navigation in a later chapter. For now, let's concentrate on the combat benefits of the Tactical Display.

The Tactical Display makes a fighter pilot's life easier because it answers most of the W's for you. You're able to see the affiliation, position, and, to a limited extent, even the flight condition of any aircraft within range. You can also usually approximate the heading of other aircraft by their relative rate of separation or closure compared to your flight path.

What's not conveyed to you is altitude information and type of fighter aircraft. It's difficult not knowing exactly which aircraft the bandit is flying—until you do, it's difficult to choose the appropriate tactics. Other than the partial obstruction of your view (there's really very little imposition), there is no disadvantage in keeping your Tactical Display activated. Use it to watch for approaching enemies, and to keep track of friendly aircraft. Your airplane is the yellow cross at the center of the radar display. Other aircraft will appear as colored dots:

Tactical Display works like short-range radar and allows you to see the affiliation and position of any aircraft before you're in real trouble or within visual range.

- Green = Friendly
- Red = Enemy
- Yellow = Selected Target
- Black = Destroyed Enemy Aircraft

Here are some additional pointers for more effective use of radar for detection-stage combat:

- The Tactical Display offers a 360-degree view.
- The yellow cross at the center represents your airplane.
- The top of the Tactical Display coincides with the front of your airplane. (It turns when you do.)

Using the Map

Press Shift +] to open the map window. (Press the] key to close it, or if you have multiple windows open, first click the window you want to close before pressing the] key.) You can adjust the zoom factor of the map by pressing the = (Equal Sign) and - (Hyphen) keys.

At certain zoom factors the map works like the Tactical Display because it provides affiliation and position information, but, if you have aircraft labels enabled, the map also provides the added benefits of aircraft type and range information. Although the map may seem like the ultimate detection feature, it has limitations.

The map takes up valuable screen space and, unlike the Tactical Display (which is semi-transparent), will block whatever it covers. The map's zoom restrictions for viewing detection information makes its detection duty range smaller than that of the Tactical Display. Also, the ground textures visible on the map tend to clutter up the view, making it difficult to use. In the heat of battle, you want quick information. Anything you can do to diminish your cockpit workload will help— a cluttered display works against that goal.

Basic map tips:

Tip: *You can extend your radar viewing range by flying a zigzag pattern. This is because the radar screen is square in shape. This makes the distance (which relates to radar range) to the corners of the screen slightly longer than the distance directly to the sides. By flying a diagonal path relative to the radar target, you're to detect it earlier than if you flew directly towards it.*

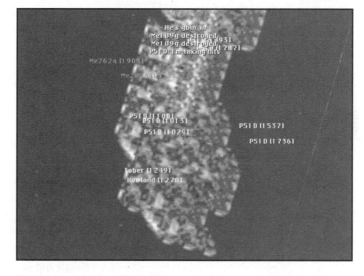

At close zoom levels, the map provides the same information that the Tactical Display does, plus aircraft type and range information if you have labels enabled.

- Like the Tactical Display, the map provides a 360-degree view.
- The red colored cross in the center of the map represents your airplane.
- The top of the map coincides with the front of your airplane. (It turns when you do.)
- To enlarge the map window, bring up the pop-up menu with a right mouse click, and then select Maximize Window.

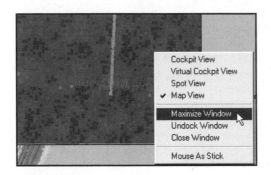

To enlarge the map window, right-click on the window and select Maximize Window.

Labels identify other planes and make them easier to see.

Tip: *The aircraft belonging to the label is located just below the center of the text.*

Note: *Label color designations are the same as Tactical Displays except that yellow (for selected target) and black (destroyed enemy) are not used.*

Labels

Labels display the distance of the object from you, the object type (in this case, aircraft), and faction affiliation information. Labels will appear at 12,000 meters and the color of the Label will indicate the target's affiliation. Just as with the Tactical Display, Green = Friendly, and Red = Enemy.

Naturally labels won't appear if the aircraft in question is not in your current view. This means that tags will show up even if hidden behind your airplane's artwork if outside the borders of your current view. Move your airplane or view so that labels appear. Use the Forward Slip (see the sidebar of the same name later in this chapter) or invert.

Visual Detection

If you decide not to use the Tactical Display and choose to keep labels disabled, you're forced to discover the three W's yourself. But even with the Tactical Display enabled, altitude and aircraft model is only determined by visual sighting.

The most basic and effective way to avoid becoming a statistic on the enemy kill list is to vigilantly scan all areas of the sky. This isn't difficult if you develop a *detection scan pattern*. A good detection scan can also help you avoid missing or skipping some areas of the sky. This skill will also increase your situational awareness abilities.

Detection Scan

The concept of the *detection scan pattern* is similar to an instrument scan pattern used for Instrument Flight Rules (IFR) flight. As with all scan patterns, there's no ideal detection scan pattern for all pilots or all situations. Most pilots need to develop their own patterns to maximize efficiency based on personal habits. Let's look at one example of a detection scan main pattern, but keep in mind that you'll probably have to develop your own.

Start by scanning the forward view and then move your eyes to the Tactical Display. (If it's disabled, you could scan the map.) Then scan the rear view and back to the forward view. Next, scan right and then back to the front. Now scan left, back to the front, and then finally up and back to the front. Now start over.

Intertwined between the main pattern cycles are scan sub-patterns. These sub-patterns include banking the airplane to see under your wings and nose. A quick flip to Padlock mode can alert you if anything got by your other scans.

> **Tip:** *Always include the sun in your scan. It's a popular and effective attack position. Any airplanes flying within the center of the sun or within the haze surrounding it will become appropriately shrouded from view. Labels may become difficult to see.*

The key of a scan pattern is to keep your eyes moving so that you can continuously cover all areas around you. A common mistake is fixating on the forward view or the radar screen—or omitting or skipping some areas. At this point, you're looking for dots in the sky or on the ground which depict aircraft (or their shadows) at long range. As you get closer, their labels (if enabled) appear onscreen.

The Final W's

The next W's you'll want to discover are what the bogey is doing and where it's going. Sometimes you can even figure out the next objective (who) based on what the bogey is doing and where the bogey is going. Because Combat Flight Simulator can generate random-traffic positions, you can never be sure whether or not any bogey not in your immediate flight group is a bandit

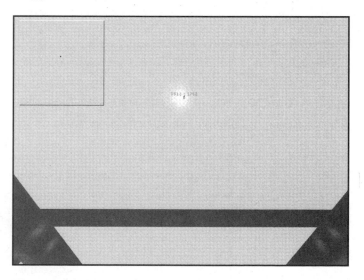

The sun can be used for tactical purposes.

The Forward Slip

One maneuver that's effective for detection purposes at high altitudes is a forward slip. It allows you to bank your wings without changing your heading. While a forward slip is normally used for losing altitude, a less aggressive slip (using less control input) doesn't cause an appreciable loss in altitude. Pilots at high altitude normally accept either changes in heading or losses in altitude associated with steep banks. Some pilots temporarily fly inverted and use the up view to see what was previously below them. Normally this is fine, but aircraft with slow roll rates can suffer great E (energy) losses with such a maneuver. These airplanes will benefit the most from the forward slip. Basically, the forward slip is a bank using ailerons with enough opposite rudder added to keep the airplane from turning. You'll usually need to apply a bit of up elevator to keep the aircraft from descending as well. It may take a little getting used to, but with some practice, the forward slip will become second nature.

While the forward slip is handy for visual detection duty, note that it's usually used for losing altitude without gaining airspeed. This is especially useful for those fast landings required by a bandit in pursuit of your smoldering airplane.

without closing on it first. Always assume the worst until you make contact. While you will receive radio reports of bandits in the area, the reports are of little use if there are several out there. Also remember that the most reliable reports are the ones you discover yourself.

Based on the bandit's appearance, location, heading, and altitude, you can sometimes guess what they're up to. This can help you determine whether to close in to take a closer look. Here are a few common situations.

If a bogey is:

- Smoking and at low altitude, it's damaged and trying to get away.
- At low altitude near an enemy runway and lined up with it, it's probably taking off or landing (if there are no enemy aircraft in its path).
- At low altitude near an enemy runway with enemy aircraft near it, it's using its Ack for protection (more on this a little later).
- At low altitude near a friendly runway, it's picking off pilots taking off and landing from that airfield, or attacking it.
- At medium altitude and outside the main furball, it's likely trying to gain altitude.
- At high altitude, it's ready to attack (and is selecting a target).
- Surrounded by friendly aircraft, it's under attack.

Finally, your current condition determines the value of the *who* objective. If you're damaged or out of ammo, this can make a big difference as to whether

The forward slip can help you see what's below without losing much altitude.

you choose to stay on course or run. If you're neither damaged nor especially low on anything, it doesn't matter who the bandit is—you're in pursuit!

Stealth

If the axiom "You can't shoot 'em if you can't see 'em" is true, then the opposite is also true: "They can't shoot you if they can't see you." This is the basis of anti-detection (known as *stealth* today). We're dealing with the same issues again: radar and visual—only now we're on the other side. Being able to see the labels of your enemy without them seeing yours would be nice, but unless you have Tactical Display working and they don't (an impossibility in Combat Flight Simulator unless you're playing in Multiplayer mode), you'll be spotted as soon as you spot them.

Defense against Visual Detection
If Labels are disabled in multiplayer mode, NOE (Nap Of the Earth), or terrain, following flight can help you evade visual detection —but it won't foil the

Tactical Display. If you fly behind mountains and other physical obstacles when they're located between yourself and the suspected location of the enemy, it'll make it very difficult for the enemy to spot you—because visual detection is (obviously) line-of-sight.

Distance is also your friend. As soon as you've become close enough to recognize a bandit as a Label—you're too close. You've blown your cover. Another tip is to fly very high (over 12,000 meters above the enemy). You'll just be a dot in the sky and if you keep your separation from any dots below you, you'll remain dots to them (not appearing as a Label that'll give your allegiance away).

Closing Stage

In the world of air combat, the Closing stage doesn't imply end of battle. In fact, it's where the battle begins. With regards to this stage, the term Closing means getting closer. Sandwiched between the Detection and Attack stages, the transition from Closing to Attack is determined by weapons' range. As you'd imagine, the Closing stage is crucial—if you make a bad decision at the beginning of the battle, it can devastate your chances to win.

Regardless of wheher you've identified the second or third of the three W's (Where, What, and Who) in the Detection Stage, you must make an assessment of your present situation and mission goals. Even though situation and mission goals are separate criteria, both must be considered in order to make a sound Closing decision.

Situation Relations

Closing takes place outside weapons range. If you're already offensive or defensive, you've jumped to the Attack or Maneuver stages, so we need to back up. When placed in a Closing situation, you must decide two things: if and how. If, of course, means deciding whether to proceed with closing, and how means how you're going to close (dictated by the type of attack you're going to make). Let's examine the big *if* first.

Your decision for proceeding to the Closing stage is based on your current condition. If you're low (on ammo, fuel, energy, or airplane parts), you may want to make a break for home, in which case you would jump directly to the Disengage stage.

Your first consideration when flying propeller-powered fighters is the E-to-danger ratio. "E" is energy, and danger is proximity, quantity, quality, and the relative E state of the enemy. The E-to-danger ratio will dictate what you can do and how you'll be able to go about doing it. The more elements in your favor, the more likely you'll emerge victorious.

If it's just you and your lone wingman against an entire enemy air force, attacking would likely be a greater challenge than you want. The same may be true if the enemy has an enormous E advantage over you. While you might be ridiculed for running from a battle when flying against human players, it really all comes down to what's important to you and what you want to get out of your Combat Flight Simulator experience. Some pilots fly to preserve their virtual skin, and others fly just because they enjoy the thrill of battle, not caring if they get shot down. We'll continue on the assumption that you're looking to stay alive and increase your kill total.

Multiple Bandits

Although we're still talking in terms of one-vs.-one combat, we should insert a few words about multiple bandits. Given equal planes and equal E states, any side with superior numbers has, of course, an inherent advantage. This isn't to say one couldn't overcome the odds with tactics and skill—two ace pilots can defeat three average pilots *most* of the time. But when the odds reach 5:2, the five average pilots have a much better chance of prevailing, regardless of the skill level of the other two pilots.

Remember that even when you enter a fight with a numerical advantage, things can change quickly. Keep an eye on your Tactical Display (if you have it enabled) and map. It's more likely than not that other planes (including enemy planes) will be busting up your shindig shortly.

Mission Goals

Your mission objectives will also dictate whether or not you'll even want to proceed to the Closing stage. For example, if your primary objective is to escort bombers, you may choose to ignore low flying enemy targets in favor of taking care of your mission—protecting your bombers.

Because we're discussing fighter tactics now, we'll only superficially discuss traditional fighter missions such as CAP (Combat Air Patrol), Sweep, or Escort here. We'll cover the details of those and other tactics in Intermediate Combat Training chapter.

Tip: *Watching for enemy fighters is even more critical when fighting close to or in enemy territory. The enemy has less distance to cover to enter the fight than your countrymen have to cover you.*

And Now...How

Your current position in relation to your enemy will dictate your Closing strategy. An acronym that says it all is PASSS: Position, Altitude, Speed, Surprise, and Sun. The way many pilots remember PASSS is by thinking of air-combat engagement as starting with a first PASSS. Individually each element yields its own advantage, so the more of these elements you can gain over your opponent, the greater your total advantage.

- For *Position* against fighters, you want to gain a position in the order of desirability as discussed earlier: H2T, T2T, H2H, and T2H.
- *Altitude* dictates the terms of the battle with prop-based fighters. You'll understand why by the end of this chapter.
- *Speed* and *Surprise* go hand-in-hand. Unless you can surprise your enemy, the bandit will attempt to maneuver so that you'll gain as few advantages as possible. Additionally, speed offers another advantage as well—a fast moving target is harder to hit.
- The *Sun* can help you gain the element of surprise. It's difficult to use this strategy, so don't put too much effort into trying to achieve it.

Before We Close...

Here are a couple of final tips that will serve you well:

- Before closing on the enemy, make note of the bearing of important landmarks. In particular, note where friendly territory is located in relation to where your fight will take place and the direction of your mission objective(s). This means knowing the heading of your charges in an escort mission or direction of your mission target. From here on, things get pretty busy so you'll find it's better to get your bearings straight now while you're not being fired upon. It will save you from having to waste time and energy during battle just to figure out where to find help or safety.

- *Fight your own fight.* This means you must have the courage to avoid battles that aren't on your terms. Don't be suckered into a fray that you can't win unless other lives depend on you (again like in an escort or strike mission). While it may not seem courageous to run

away from a fight, there are no medals or rank advancement for being shot down. There's no dishonor in surviving a successful mission even if it means avoiding some or all of the battles put in your path.

Attack Stage

The Attack stage follows the Closing stage. What separates the two is your proximity to the bandit. When you've reached weapons range and have ammo, you've entered the Attack stage. Depending on which side of the gun you're on, this is where the bullets fly—or where you start sweating bullets. There are three important parts to the Attack stage:

- Tactical considerations
- Methods
- Technique

Before we look at these stage subdivisions, let's consider the aspects they have in common.

Being Aggressive

In all traditional fighter missions, if you can fight, you fight—there's no question about it. This means being aggressive, and the old cliche "The best defense is a good offense" applies here. You can force your opponent to take a defensive posture, and a defensive bandit can't shoot at you.

Real fighter pilots made every effort not to think about getting killed or shot down because it hindered performance and abilities. The best real fighter pilots were aggressive, and the more aggressive they were, the higher their kill ratio.

Being aggressive and taking the fight to the enemy has other advantages. It will give you maximum separation from the asset you're protecting and put you closest to the target you're trying to take out. But keep in mind that being aggressive doesn't mean being suicidal. Although you'll encounter suicidal players (usually human ones) in your sorties, that can sometimes work in your favor. Every second that a bandit overstays his welcome without killing you, it decreases his chances of survival—which increases your chances of killing him. After all, it's not a matter of whether or if any pilot gets shot down, it's a matter of when.

Marksmanship

In the most basic terms, fighter aircraft are flying gun platforms. Learning to make gun kills is really about learning to fly. Among other things, your job as a fighter pilot is to fly your aircraft to a favorable position so you can fire your weapons at your target.

Now, there are favorable positions and there are even *more* favorable positions. Exactly what makes for the latter depends on three things: what you're shooting (your weapon), what you're shooting from (your aircraft and how it's being flown), and what you're shooting at (your target). These criteria make up the backbone of good marksmanship. Here are some ideas that will help you increase your hit ratio (bullets that hit compared to bullets fired).

Weapons

The basic air-to-air fighter weapons offered in Combat Flight Simulator are cannons and machine guns. Some aircraft have both and some have only machine guns. The number and abilities of each vary from one type of plane to another. The best advice is to *know your airplane*. We'll outline specifics in the next chapter, but generally on a fighter, guns are mounted in one or two of three possible positions—on the nose, on the fuselage, or on the wings.

Nose-mounted guns or cannons (such as what's found on a P-38 or Bf 109) pose the least amount of computational problems, and wing-mounted guns cause the most. This is because a nose-mounted gun fires straight in front of your aircraft, and wing-mounted guns are usually set so that their line of fire converges somewhere out in front of your aircraft.

Of course, the location of this convergence point is very important because your greatest fire and killing power is where these bullet streams meet. So knowing exactly where in space your six .50 caliber bullet streams meet is important—targets hit at this distance will inflict the most damage with the least ammo. This is why the label "distance-to-target information" is so valuable.

Lethality

Unless you're flying with unlimited ammunition enabled, conservation should be a key concern. In addition to learning to restrain yourself from spraying bullets all over the place, be aware that different aircraft have different ammo loads—and we're not talking about ammo round counts either.

Some aircraft fire cannon shells in addition to their standard machine gun shells, which can dramatically increase your killing potential, (or decrease it after your cannon shells run out). But the killing potential of each weapon is measured by the distance to target because each projectile has a finite range. (Ranges vary from gun to gun and cannon to cannon—multiply the muzzle velocity by a factor of two to calculate them.) At relatively close range, one might conclude that a cannon-equipped fighter would be the ultimate weapon.

Unfortunately, cannon (and machine guns for that matter) have their limitations.

Cannon don't fire very fast (in rounds per minute). On the other hand, machine guns fire quickly but have a shorter lethality range, also inflicting less damage when they hit.

We'll discuss weapon lethality in more detail in the next chapter, but in the meantime, these hints will help maximize your weapon lethality:

- Press the 1 key to fire the primary weapon and press the 2 key to fire the secondary weapon. Pressing the Space bar will fire both the primary and secondary weapons together. If your aircraft is equipped with both cannons and machine guns, machine guns are considered the primary weapon and cannons are considered the secondary weapon.
- If your aircraft is equipped with cannon and machine guns, all weapons fire at once when you pull the trigger of your joystick.
- Don't fire your weapon(s) when you're out of range unless you have a tactical reason to do so (scare the bandit). You may run out of ammo before you really need it and then find yourself in REAL trouble.
- Rely on cannon for long-range attacks and machine guns for close-in fighting.
- If your aircraft is equipped with both cannon and machine guns, consider using machine gun fire to "line up" your target and following up with cannon fire when you're getting hits. This can maximize your ammo lethality because you'll carry many more machine gun shells than cannon shells.

Wing-mounted guns are usually set so their line of fire converges out in front of your aircraft.

Straight Shooter

We already know that because your guns and cannon are in fixed positions you must maneuver your aircraft to aim them, but we haven't talked about what to use as references and how to use them. There are two types of gunsights modeled in Combat Flight Simulator: the fixed optical gunsight and the Lead Computing Sight (LCS). Let's see how they're used.

Using the Static Gunsight

The name fixed optical gunsight comes from its being static (it doesn't move in relation to the aircraft), and because it's an optical reflection rather than a physical object like the old iron ring-and-bead gunsights found on WWI airplanes. A real reflective sight is a light pattern shaped like the gunsight that's beamed onto the slanted piece of glass atop the instrument panel.

When shooting with a static gunsight, you have to interpolate where your bullets will end up based on your current position, speed, effects of gravity, and distance from your target. Unless your opponents want a place in your kill statistics, they won't be flying straight and level when you shoot at them. This means you need to "pull lead" (shoot ahead of your target) and compensate for gravity drop. While even the greenest fighter pilots know this, what isn't always known is how much lead must be pulled to get hits.

There are basically two manual methods you can use in Combat Flight Simulator. The first is best understood using a *garden hose* metaphor. The concept behind this method requires you to envision your tracer stream as a stream of water from a garden hose. You simply need to maneuver your airplane so that the stream hits your target. But be aware that you can waste a lot of ammo if you're not careful.

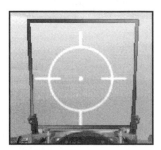

The static optical gunsight found on every fighter in Combat Flight simulator requires you to interpolate where your bullets will end up based on your current position, speed, and distance from target.

The second method relies on pilot instinct. Of course instinct is always enhanced with a little knowledge. First, your bullet steam will appear to follow a slight arc and drop off towards the end of their path. Note the word *appear*. Bullets generally fly in a straight path and then drop off as velocity decreases. When you move the nose of your airplane, the bullets appear to arc in the sky because the nose/gun moved slightly during the interval between each individual projectile fired. The direction of arc is also in the exact opposite direction of the movement of the nose of your aircraft. In other words, your bullet stream will appear to arc to the left when the nose of your airplane is pointed to the right.

The static gunsights in Combat Flight Simulator, like the old ring-and-bead gunsights, depict a circle with a center point. And if you use your imagination a bit, the innermost points of the horizontal and vertical slash marks in the 12 o'clock, 3 o'clock, 6 o'clock and 9 o'clock positions depict a

smaller circle. The sizes of the depicted circles are not randomly selected. They represent range information. If the wings of a fighter (bombers have larger wingspans) touch the outside circle, the target will be approximately 250 meters

> **Tip:** *Regardless of your airplane's orientation, a bullet stream will arc slightly toward earth. Keep this in mind and compensate for it.*

away. If the wings of the target touch the inner circle it is approximately 500 meters away. You're not obligated to use only one of these methods. Use your instincts to start your shot, and then move to the garden hose method to fine-tune your aim. Nothing helps you more with marksmanship skills than practice. That's what unlimited ammo, Quick Combat, and the training missions are for—so make use of them.

Using the Lead Computing Sight

The LCS (also known as the gyro gunsight), relies on the gyroscopic principle of rigidity in space to predict where your bullets will land even while your aircraft is turning. Combat Flight Simulator's only lead-computing gunsight is found on the P-51D and is toggled by the \ (backslash) key.

"...later models of the P-51...came out with the K-14 lead computing gunsight, which, if you operated it right, took all of the guesswork out of

deflection shooting," wrote Brig. General Chuck Yeager, USAF, 13 kills.

As General Yeager points out, without an LCS a pilot needs to rely on skill and experience to determine how much lead is necessary to achieve hits. But as useful as it is and as simple as its use may first sound, the use of the LCS has a few pitfalls.

First, a LCS can mislead you (pardon the pun)! In reality, the LCS predicts where your bullets will fall based on the range setting.

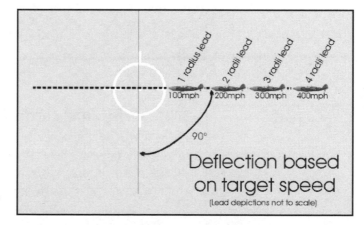

The amount of lead required to hit a moving target increases as the speed of the target increases. It's a 1:1 ratio (if target speed increases 100 percent, lead must increase 100 percent) at 90-degrees AOT (angle off tail).

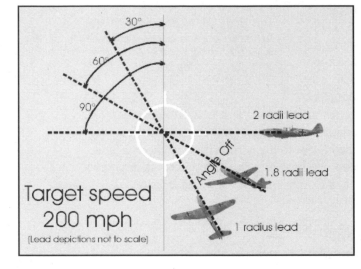

30°

60°

90°

2 radii lead

Angle Off

1.8 radii lead

**Target speed
200 mph**
(Lead depictions not to scale)

1 radius lead

The amount of lead also increases with AOT increases.

Tip: *You'll know approximately when a fighter is at 250 meters distance when one wing appears to be equal in size as the diameter of the LCS pipper.*

So if your target isn't found within your range setting, chances are pretty good that you'll miss. The LCS in Combat Flight Simulator is set for 250 meters. This means that lining the LCS pipper up on the target will only net maximum hits if the target is approximately 250 meters away. (Note that this number is the same as the convergence range of the P-51's guns.)

The LCS pipper can be distracting. Many new pilots tend to fixate on the gunsight floating around rather than watching the bandit and bullet path—which is definitely not good. On the other hand, the LCS can help new pilots gain a better understanding of the relationship between the motion of projectiles and the motion of the platform. So trying to use the LCS can pay big dividends even if you end up not using it.

The lead computing gunsight is only found on the P-51D while using the fixed front view.

Durability and Damage Modeling

Firing at the right distance and lead angle isn't always enough to kill your targets. This is because Combat Flight Simulator models damage areas on each airplane. This causes certain areas of an aircraft to correspond with higher or lower hit/damage values (this is how protective armor is modeled into the system as well).

There are a maximum of 44 hit boxes (as they're called in the simulation business) or hit regions on each aircraft in Combat Flight Simulator. Depending on a particular aircraft's complexity, this number changes. For instance, four-engine

bombers have the most numerous hit boxes while single-engined fighters have fewer.

Partial Listing of Typical Hit Boxes for Fighters and Bombers

P-51D	P-51D, continued	B-17G, continued
Nose Structure	Starboard Flap	Nose Structure
Coolant Reservoir	Starboard Aileron Control Cable	Coolant Reservoir
Oil Reservoir	Starboard Gear	Port Oil Reservoir
Engine One	Starboard Wing Tip Structure	Starboard Oil Reservoir
Hydraulics Reservoir	Starboard Aileron	Engine One
Radio	Tail (fwd) Structure	Engine Two
Fuel Tank	Tail (rear) Structure	Engine Three
Fuselage Structure	Port Elevator	Engine Four
Rudder Control Cable	Starboard Elevator	Hydraulics Reservoir
Bomb Release	Rudder	Radio
Bomb	Cockpit	Starboard Fuel Tank
Elevator Control Cable	Port Machine Guns	Port Fuel Tank
Port Wing Structure	Port Rockets	Fuselage Structure
Port Flap	Starboard Machine Guns	Rudder Control Cable
Port Aileron Control Cable	Starboard Rockets	Bomb Release
Port Gear	**B-17G**	Bomb Bay
Port Wing Tip Structure	Port and Starboard Cheek Guns	Elevator Control Cable
Port Aileron	Port and Satrboard Waist Guns	Port Wing Structure
Starboard Wing Structure	Upper, Lower and Tail Guns	Port Flap

Damage to some aircraft parts can be critical for flight—other parts less vital. Hits to the wing, for example, may not be as critical as a hit to the engine although wing damage may well affect associated systems such as flaps, ailerons, or landing gear. That kind of damage may cause control problems and an eventual crash, but if you want to take out an enemy aircraft quickly, target critical systems, such as the engine—or pilot. (Sawing a wing off with your machine-gun fire would classify a wing a "critical system" as well.)

Assessing Damage

If you fly with the Combat Status Messages text display disabled (press the F key to toggle), you can still determine how much damage you've inflicted on a target by carefully watching what happens when your projectiles reach their

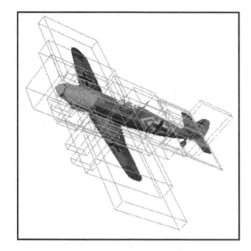

These are the hit boxes for the Bf 109E from very early in the development cycle. Although the hit box sizes were dramatically reduced to reflect the actual size and shape of the aircraft, these larger boxes better illustrate the complexity of Combat Flight Simulator's damage modeling.

target. When you damage another aircraft, you may see sparks, pieces of the aircraft falling off, smoke, or an explosion.

Light-colored smoke indicates damage to the coolant or fuel systems, black smoke indicates burning oil or damage to the engine. In addition to the color of the smoke, the rate that the smoke is expelled indicates the level of damage. Sputtering smoke means the aircraft is slightly damaged, intermittent smoke means the aircraft is moderately damaged, and a steady stream means serious damage.

Attack Tactics

Boiled down to its essence, there are really two basic attack positions—H2H (Head to Head) and H2T (Head to Tail). The nose is where your guns and other weapons fire from and your target will face you with either its head (nose) or tail (any other part of the aircraft). For our discussion purposes, the distinction between head and tail is based on offensive capability. Anything other than the nose can be considered the tail (because it can't shoot at you).

The most desirable position is H2T because you're on the offense and your target is in a defensive position. (Remember, we're talking about fighters—bombers have tail gunners!) By contrast, H2H is dangerous. while you're in an offensive posture, so is your opponent. Let's look at each attack individually.

Head-On Merges

Taking out an opponent on a first head-on pass is efficient and exhilarating because it's quick and usually spectacular. But most of the time it's a big gamble. So in an H2H confrontation, you must make a decision to go for it or try to avoid it. If you try to avoid the head-on, you become defensive. While voluntarily putting yourself in a T2H situation seems like suicide, it's sometimes the only way to stay alive.

When faced with superior firepower, such as a Fw 190 or a pilot with superior marksmanship skills, going toe-to-toe will usually result in your going down in a ball of flame. If you choose the alternative—avoiding the H2H confrontation, you're jumping to the Maneuver stage. Let's look at two methods for increasing your chances of coming out on top in H2H attacks.

Bob-n-Weave

As you've probably surmised, the H2H attack is like trying to choose the lesser of two evils. For the best chance at shooting your opponent down, you need to fly a steady course relative to your target's position. While this increases your chances of putting holes in your opponent's shiny airplane, it unfortunately also increases the ability of your intended target to reciprocate the gesture. Conversely, flying a course that gives your opponent a difficult shot at you (a high angle of deflection shot) also makes your shot more difficult. Okay so what's a budding fighter pilot to do?

By far the best and safest solution is a compromise. Fly a weaving course enroute to your H2H pass. Fly your pattern so that your bullet stream will cross over your target. When your target's lined up, squeeze off a few rounds. The pattern you fly is up to you, but as an example, try flying so that your gunsight/bullet path draws a figure 8 around your target. This can give you double the targeting opportunities in addition to adding altitude and heading changes intended to complicate your opponent's shots. A side benefit is that this technique will also reduce the likelihood of head-on collisions. While properly executed weave-and-fire attacks won't net as many spectacular kills as when you gambled on toe-to-toe fights, your H2H survival ratio should improve.

Shoot 'em in the Back

Although it may not seem chivalrous, the best attack position against fighters is a H2T shot. Why? First, the enemy can't shoot at you. Second, you don't need to lead your target as much to shoot at it. And third, you can see what your enemy is doing—making his evasion attempts easier to counter.

While attacking unsuspecting fighters from the rear is the most desirable position, you'll rarely get the opportunity for such attacks without some effort on your part or blunder from your enemy. The majority of gun opportunities you'll find will be deflection shots. In either case, because the guns of your intended target are facing away from you, you're usually not in immediate danger. So you'll be able to plant your gunsight on your target and keep it there. Even if this sounds easy, there are pitfalls to avoid with rear and flanking attacks.

Under the Cowling

Because Combat Flight Simulator is poised as an open standard, you have access to information unavailable to pilots during WWII (or pilots of other air-combat simulations for that matter). The best ways to determine which hit boxes/aircraft systems are most vulnerable is by viewing the .dp files of each aircraft with a text editor such as Notepad.

These .dp files (one per aircraft resides in its respective aircraft folder under the Combat Flight Simulator folder) contain the information of the aircraft's damage profile. (An Excel-based editor will become available shortly after the release of Combat Flight Simulator). Here's a brief rundown to help you decipher what each damage parameter means.

The first section header [BOXES] lists the damage box names and their locations based on X, Y, and Z coordinates in meters from the aircraft's center of gravity. The next section named [SYSTEMS] lists the system name as a variable (determined by the names in the [STRINGS] section further down in the file), and how many hit points are required to destroy that particular system.

For example in the b17g.dp file, system.0 (which is the Nose Structure from the listing in the [STRINGS] section) can take 800 damage points before it's registered as destroyed. Now if you jump down to the [EFFECTS.0] section (the corresponding effects section for system.0) it lists what percentage of damage will cause what effect. In this case 100 percent damage will result in a BREAK.

There are three possible levels of damage: LEAK, BREAK, and BOMB. LEAK will result in a leak, BREAK is a total loss, and BOMB is an explosion. The nature of the component/system will determine which effects are assigned to it—an aileron, for example, would never leak or explode, but it could break.

The two numerals after the damage effect listing are the visual smoke effects associated with that level of damage. The first number indicates the color of the smoke (1= light, 2 = dark, and 3 = reddish brown—the color of hydraulic fluid), and the second number specifies the rate (1 = sputter, 2 = intermittent, and 3 = steady).

To get back to our B-17 example, [EFFECTS.1] the coolant reservoir will leak at 25 percent and put out light color smoke at the sputter rate. (Light color smoke indicates a coolant leak, dark smoke indicates an oil leak, and reddish smoke indicates a hydraulic leak.) At 50 percent, the smoke color will remain the same, but the rate will change to intermittent. At 75 percent damage, the color of the smoke remains the same, but the smoke rate will change to steady. Finally, at 100 percent the coolant reservoir will break and the aircraft's engine will critically overheat all the while trailing a steady stream of light smoke. While this information can come in handy for determining how much damage you've inflicted on a bandit when you have the Combat Status Messages text display disabled (press the F key to toggle), lets not forget why we're discussing this. For Attack stage potential targeting, you should be looking at the hit boxes/sections of the aircraft that can explode (BOMB effect) with the least number of hit points. Those are the most vulnerable.

E = Energy

Energy or "E" management is arguably the most important concept and skill a fighter pilot needs to learn and fully understand. E management skills (conservation and expenditure) are what separate the aces from the targets.

There may be too much of a good thing with altitude and speed, because they can eliminate your advantage. In this light, don't sacrifice too much of one for the other. Moderation best describes what you're after. It's generally better to have a little of each than to be really high and very slow, or very low and really fast. There are, of course, exceptions to this rule of thumb, but moderation is safe—it doesn't present inherent disadvantages.

Tip: *The basic fighter energy conversion equation is: altitude can be traded for speed, and speed can be exchanged for altitude. Still, always be aware of your aircraft's performance envelope.*

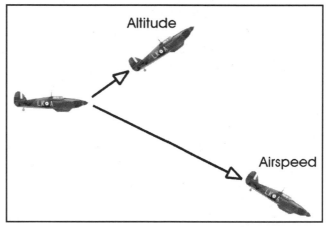

Potential energy (altitude) can be converted into kinetic energy (airspeed) by diving, and kinetic energy can be converted into potential energy by climbing.

E is categorized as either kinetic energy or potential energy. Kinetic energy is airspeed, and potential energy altitude. Potential energy can be converted into kinetic energy by diving, and kinetic energy can be converted into potential energy by climbing. Although both may seem of equal importance because one can convert itself into the other, in the world of air combat, potential energy has the edge most of the time. This is because even if you have a massive amount of kinetic energy (airspeed), that energy will only allow you to achieve a lesser level (altitude) of potential energy. For example, diving from 30K feet down to 15K feet will net you a very fast airspeed—but it will only allow you to climb back up to, say, 25K feet before you go below your starting airspeed. Consequently, you've lost 5K feet of potential energy.

E can be airspeed, altitude, or both. At maximum throttle the only way you can increase your airspeed is to dive, but in order to dive, you must have some altitude. In spite of the fact that you can trade one form of E for the other, the maximum total you can achieve is relative to the E you possess at that time. The bottom line: altitude will get you airspeed, and airspeed will get you altitude. But if your total is less than a nearby enemy's, you're at a severe disadvantage. Here are a couple of things you can do to avoid or lessen the effects of that kind of situation.

- When grabbing E (climbing), at the very least retain enough airspeed to make good use of the vertical plane (do a loop). If you lack the airspeed and try some vertical maneuver, you'll become too slow near the top and the bandit will kill you as you hang in the air in front of it.
- If you get caught unprepared (with less airspeed than required to go vertical) you'll only be left with the option of turning toward earth or on the horizontal plane. Neither is ideal because each severely limits your options and makes your flight path more predictable for the enemy.
- If you have virtually no airspeed (as in barely enough to remain in the air), turn your nose low to use gravity to assist in the turn. You can accelerate very quickly with the assistance of gravity, but never forget that after any potential E trade, you almost always end up with a net loss.

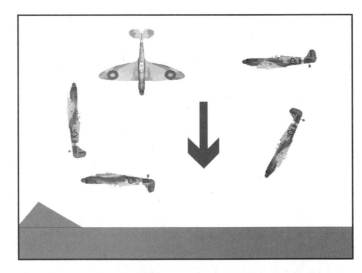

Your relationship with gravity remains constant regardless of your aircraft's orientation, but its effects can help or hinder your aircraft's performance.

Gravity... It's the Law

Turning toward the ground will increase your airspeed because of the assistance of gravity. Conversely, gravity will work against you in a climb. If you understand how to work with gravity, you can take advantage of it—or at the very least minimize its unwanted effects.

A good maneuver that illustrates the benefits and consequences of gravity quite well is a straight loop. When you break up a loop

maneuver into smaller components and analyze them, you'll recognize portions of other maneuvers performed frequently in air combat. Both the Split-S and the Immelman are examples. They're both comprised of half loops with a half roll added before and after the loop sections, respectively.

Unless you go out of your way to fly a perfectly symmetrical loop (like a perfect circle), a loop will look like a hastily written, script lowercase E. The loop entry starts smoothly, goes vertical, sharply curves at the top, and then the exit gently curves, finally ending at an altitude lower than where it started.

Let's look at what happens by breaking the loop down into sections. At the start of the loop, you generally make a smooth pull-up because you'll either black out or exceed your aircraft's performance limitations. At this point, gravity and centrifugal force work against you. While

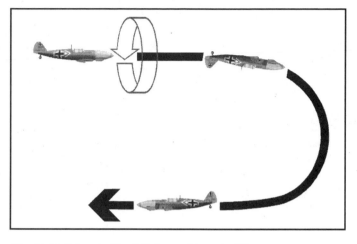

The Split-S is a half roll followed by a half loop.

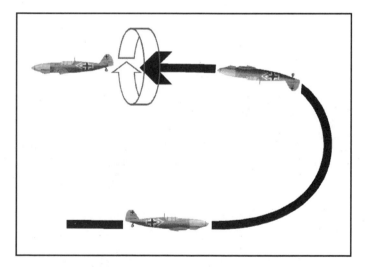

The Immelman is a half loop followed by a half roll after the loop.

you're trying to climb, gravity is pulling you down and bleeding off your airspeed. Near the top of the loop, your aircraft slows down even more. The combination of gravity pulling you back toward earth, lower centrifugal force, and your slower airspeed produces a tighter turning radius. Because gravity is

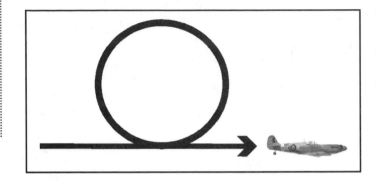

Symmetrical Loops do not happen by accident. They require skill and effort to perform.

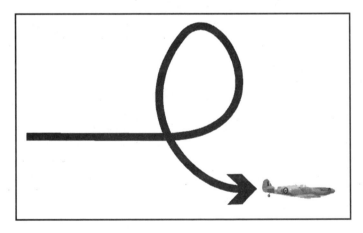

In practice, most Loops more commonly resemble a hastily written lowercase (script) e.

pulling in the direction you want to go, it causes the top of the loop to narrow.

As you travel toward the bottom of the loop, the exact opposite occurs. Your airspeed picks up, increasing centrifugal force, which subsequently increases your turning radius. Gravity is also back to fighting so you have to deal with blackouts again. These conditions cause the loop exit curve to straighten. Most of the time you'll also find that you're at a lower altitude than when you started. That's because in order to exit the loop back at your starting altitude, you'd have to decrease your airspeed on the way down and end up at a slower airspeed at the finish. Whether you end up at your starting altitude at a slower airspeed, or at a lower altitude with a comparable airspeed, the results are the same—a net loss of E.

(Virtual) Physical Performance

Blackouts are a result of G-forces impeding blood flow to the brain. They occur when you pull up at high speeds or turn at very high rates. Redouts, which occur in steep dives, result from G-forces creating too much pressure in the brain. In either case, the effect is progressive and can result in complete unconsciousness if the action causing it continues for too long.

These virtual physiological effects in Combat Flight Simulator are nothing more than minor inconveniences when you have them enabled. The only effect is degradation in what you're able to see (your instrument panel will remain visible and functional). The net effect is similar to turning down the brightness control on your monitor—inconvenient perhaps, but you still have control over your aircraft. In any case, your vision will clear when you ease up on your speed and/or angle of attack.

> **Tip:** *Reduce the effects of gravity on your virtual self by controlling your airspeed diligently. Keep at corner speed (covered in Chapter 7) and just stay slow enough to achieve max turn rate without blacking out.*

Coping with the virtual physiological effects may seem like minor inconveniences, but they can be pretty dangerous. Even though your controls will work while you're blacked out, moving your joystick wildly while your screen is blanked could get you killed. It may not mean running into the ground, but every accelerated stall or spin (or both) you enter reduces your turn rate and bleeds E—giving your opponent a chance to gain on you.

The ways blackouts and redouts have been modeled are:

- Blackout if you pull more than eight G's.
- Redout if you experience more than negative three G's.
- Either effect can occur suddenly or gradually, depending on the suddenness of the Gs, or prolonged G exposure. The effects are also cumulative, so the longer you're in them, the longer it takes to recover.

There are basically three ways to regain "consciousness" after a G-related lapse in vision—reduce control input, slow down, or do a combination of the two. While reducing control input is straight-forward enough, resist the temptation to violently reverse control input—you might reverse your condition. For example, if you've blacked out, applying full down elevator may relieve the blackout—but it may move you straight into a redout condition—which is just as bad, if not worse.

Reducing your airspeed can also help you regain consciousness—we'll discuss this more in the next chapter. For now, the quick answer is that airspeed increases lift, and lift is responsible for G loading forces—so if you reduce airspeed, you'll reduce lift and subsequently G forces on your virtual body. This is fine in theory, but reducing airspeed doesn't happen as quickly as controls change, and then if you've got a bandit on your six, unless you've got an absolute E advantage, think twice before giving up that hard-earned E.

Boomin' and Zoomin'

One of the oldest, and arguably best, air-combat tactics is known as the Boom and Zoom (BnZ). The ideal BnZ goes something like this:

1. From a position of superior altitude, dive on your (preferably unwitting) target to gain airspeed.

2. Blast the target as you close.

3. Speed out of harm's way.

4. Enter a climb to regain E.

5. Turn around and do it all over again until the enemy is dead or you run out of E or ammo.

Although this seems simple enough, there are a few things you need to consider in order to become an accomplished BnZer.

Where the target is in relation to you and how it's oriented will determine the danger potential and how you want to carry out the dive. As always, you also need to consider your aircraft's limitations. This will determine your dive angle and attack options. If your aircraft can fly at high speeds, you may not want to dive at a steep angle—or you may not be able to pull out before becoming a grease spot on the ground. One way to avoid this is to reduce your throttle.

Note: *While deploying your flaps or dropping your gear can help you keep your airspeed down, for attacks on fighters this isn't recommended due to the length of time it takes to retract them.*

There are four types of BnZ attack runs: the level run, high slashing run, vertical run, and the low slashing run. The traditional BnZ lines you up for a head-on level pass at your opponent or a high slashing (about 45 degrees or so) attack. Unfortunately each has its problems. We already know the level, high-speed head-on attack can be dangerous

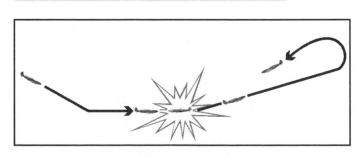

The BnZ consists of a diving attack followed by a high-speed climb out of harm's way, and then reversing course until the bandit is dead or you run out of E or ammo.

because you can be shot at and your bullet flight path is usually almost identical to your flight path during level flight. But for what it's worth, the benefit is that you're not expending E when flying level. Although you can use the weave and fire technique and attack from a slight angle, a level attack is pretty dangerous.

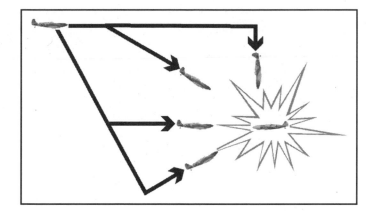

The four basic BnZ attack runs are level, high slashing, low slashing, and vertical.

High slashing attack runs cause gun lead calculation (aiming) problems for yourself. As the enemy flies under your nose, you'll tend to increase your dive and try to spray bullets on the target as he passes under you. This will increase your airspeed and cause additional loss of potential E as well. While less than ideal, this situation has advantages. First, it makes your opponent's shot at you harder, so you're on even ground in this respect. However, if the bandit tries to climb to meet you, even though he's gaining potential E, he's slowing down—which makes him easier to shoot.

Your target may try to evade you as you make your attack run. This may require you to turn, but be aware that at high speeds your aircraft won't turn very well. If you try to turn with the target, chances are good that you'll overshoot and put yourself in your enemy's gunsights. Also, turning requires an expenditure of E. Every little bit of E you waste without a kill moves the battle in favor of your opponent. So unless you think you can absolutely slow down enough to turn inside the turning arc (path) of the bandit to make the kill, don't turn more than 30-40 degrees on your BnZ attacks.

Vertical BnZ'ing

The vertical BnZ attack comes in handy because you're able to attack aircraft from an angle other than head-on. The vertical BnZ's greatest asset is the high starting altitude it requires—because your target usually can't shoot at you without trading a tremendous loss of speed. If your opponent raises his nose to shoot at you he'll bleed E and make him an easier target for your next pass. This is especially true if the bandit's acceleration is poor. Moreover, his

> **Tip:** *Watch your airspeed closely. You'll lose E like crazy with vertical attacks if you're not careful. Remember that any time you move the nose of your airplane, you lose E, and the further you dive, the more total E you'll lose. That's why you'll want to keep your dives as short as possible.*

maneuvering options are limited, and all of them are within your visual sight during your attack. Regardless of where the bandit tries to run, you'll see him. And, if he does run, regardless of direction, you will net a H2T shot.

The low slashing attack consists of a dive below your target and a climbing attack run at your target. The only good time to use this kind of attack is when you're facing a target without a belly gunner or one who is more or less committed to flying level (as in a bombing run). Fighter/Bombers (but not all) most commonly fit these criteria. The biggest disadvantage is that you'll lose the most E with this type of attack run because you dive lower than your target.

Zoom for Room

Now let's assume that you pinged the enemy, but didn't get the kill. Your best course of action is to sprint out of harm's way. If your E level is high enough, you can usually escape any danger posed by your (hopefully) lower E opponent. Ideally you'll want to level out your wings and climb while you extend to regain some of your original E advantage. If your airspeed is quite high, you'll have no problem climbing and you'll be able to put enough distance between yourself and the enemy. Unfortunately, the reality is that your airspeed is probably not as high as you'd like it to be—so you'll need to sacrifice (decrease) your rate of climb in an effort to exchange altitude for greater separation distance.

At this point your main goal is to extend to the minimum range required to turn around and begin your next attack run—without having the approaching bandit shooting at you before you're ready to shoot back. This distance varies based on your airspeed and the bandit's E state, turning skill, and resolve to chase you. But a good extension distance is generally around 2000-2500 meters. After a few attacks, your E level will bleed low enough so that climbing and extending will be impossible. This would probably be a good time to bug out—head for home and reinforcements. These options may not sound courageous, but reversing when you're offensive is no good if you can't get a shot off. You're expending E for no reason—never a smart idea.

Reversals

In terms of BnZ, reversals are turns. Which reversal you should use is based on your E state.

A classic textbook BnZ reversal is the Half-Cuban 8. If your airspeed is fairly high, a Half-Cuban 8 is a good choice because it allows you to gain maximum potential E before resuming your attack run. This helps offset some of the E lost in your prior attack run. It's basically a 3/4 loop with a half roll on the down side.

If you're fighting a good pilot (or if your marksmanship skills aren't great), and your E reserve starts to dwindle in subsequent attack runs, the Chandelle becomes the reversal of choice. It requires less airspeed (you're not pushing the nose over the top of a loop). The Chandelle is almost like a Half-Cuban 8, except that it isn't performed perpendicular to the ground, but rather at an oblique angle

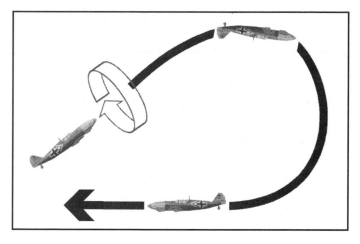

The Half-Cuban 8 is a good vertical turn to use if your airspeed is fairly high.

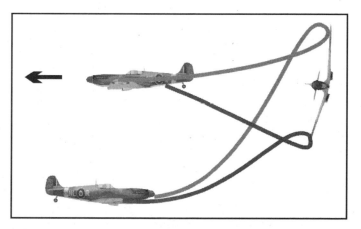

The Chandelle requires the same amount of airspeed as the Reverse Half-Cuban 8, but it won't cost as much altitude.

to the left or right. In addition, the half roll isn't a roll at all. You merely level your wings on the way out. The biggest drawback with this maneuver is that you won't gain as much E as with a Half-Cuban 8.

The Wing Over is a variation of the Chandelle. This maneuver relies on the rudder to tighten the turn at the top of a climb at an oblique angle instead of

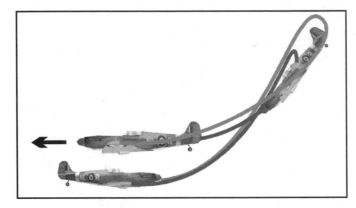

The Wing Over is a variation of the Chandelle but isn't a good choice unless your target is well below you.

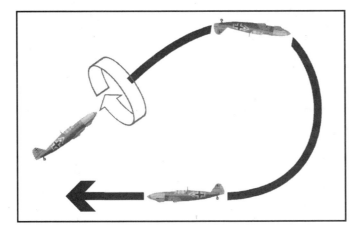

The Reverse Half-Cuban 8 is another good vertical turn to use when your airspeed isn't as high as you'd need to go over the top. But gravity will hurt your turn rate.

using aileron to roll or elevator to tighten the turn. Although it may look similar to a Hammerhead, the Wing Over is less vertical. While you'll gain some E with this maneuver, the biggest drawback is the lowered airspeed at the top. That's why it's generally only useful when your target is well below you.

If your airspeed drops further, you can zoom and use the Half-Reverse-Cuban 8. This maneuver looks much like a Split-S preceded by a slight climb. Although you can gain some E during the climb, your turn rate suffers because you have gravity working against you at the bottom of the loop.

If you've failed to see the writing on the wall, hung around and tapped out your E reserve and must now reverse, you're starting to sweat big time. Your choices now become the Slice Back or Split-S. Neither is very enticing because, despite retaining air speed, you've gained no potential E for your reversal. Consider these final tips when executing BnZ attacks:

- Impatience is the most common causeof BnZ failure. Many new pilots either get caught off guard with bandits closing in on them before they've stored enough E, or are too anxious to get into battle and just attack before they're really ready. Don't be in a hurry to get shot down!

- The second most common mistake is hanging around in the battle too long. If you don't kill your target within a few passes— get out.
- Don't bleed E unnecessarily. Be smooth and deliberate with your control movements.
- Don't turn to engage— turn only to kill. Don't get suckered into the turning fight unless you know you have at least an equal or better match in aircraft, E, and skill.

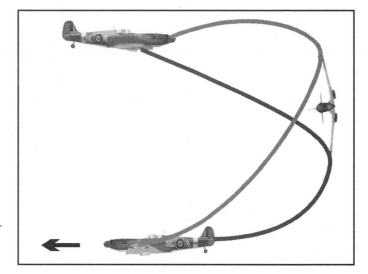

The Slice Back becomes particularly useful when you're low on E, but if you've reached this point during BnZ attacks, you're probably in trouble.

- If you reverse too soon, you'll need to fire while inverted (upside down). Avoid the temptation of following the bandit under you in this situation. A vertical fight is a turning fight done in the vertical plane, so the rules regarding turning fights (more on these later) apply.
- Use your flaps when going over the top of a vertical maneuver if you're low on airspeed. It will increase your lift, and subsequently lower your stall speed—which will reduce your chances of inadvertently entering an inverted spin.
- The secret advantage of the vertical attack is that any airplane will roll faster than even the best turning airplane can turn.
- Apply rudder in the same direction of your roll to improve your roll rate (but not too much or you risk entering a spin). Just remember to move it back to neutral when you've finished your roll.
- Even though your gun range is limited, fire earlier in head-on attacks. The combined velocities of your two converging aircraft will quickly decrease that maximum distance in short order, and you may just land a

hit. An extraneous ping (even when little or no damage is actually done) can be very demoralizing to the enemy and can yield you an advantage if you can cause the bandit to turn.

Avoiding the Overshoot

As we've seen, attacking from the rear with adequate speed isn't a problem if you have enough speed to extend to safety. It's when you don't have enough airspeed to extend that gets you in trouble. You whiz by your target and suddenly find yourself with the bandit on YOUR six and can't get away! This scenario is known as an *overshoot*. You can try to dive away to put some distance between you and the enemy, but the bandit will most likely be able to squeeze off a few rounds before you get away. If you find yourself in a position where you're flying past your target, it's better to punch the throttle and keep on going rather than to try to force a bad position.

If you try to turn at high speed, your turn radius is large and that usually allows the bandit to pull lead and shoot at you. (High speed will increase your turn radius—we'll discuss exactly why in the next chapter.) How well your aircraft performs will dictate how critical this situation is. If your aircraft is a poor turner compared to your opponent's, slowing down to try to avoid the overshoot puts you in a bad position as well. You may get more rounds off, but if you don't make the kill right away, you will have bled off some of your E and be stuck facing a turning fight with you at a disadvantage.

On the other hand, if your aircraft is the superior dogfighter, you can bleed off your speed and enter the turning fight with the advantage. Under those circumstances, excess smash (another term for E) isn't as big a problem. The High Speed Yo-Yo is one way to reduce excess speed (and subsequently the rate of closure between your two aircraft). It uses our simple E conversion formula—trade off speed for altitude.

Basically the Yo-Yo is a simple turning battle maneuver that utilizes the vertical plane for energy management. You turn at an oblique angle to use gravity for tighter turning. The High Speed Yo-Yo is a turning climb followed by a turning descent. (Using the rudder on the top of a Yo-Yo can help your roll performance because

Note: *Staying nose-high for too long can lead to a stall, and banked stalls often result in spins. Either will result in E losses and very poor turn performance.*

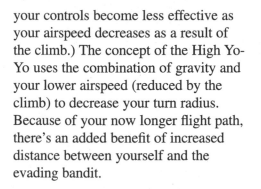

your controls become less effective as your airspeed decreases as a result of the climb.) The concept of the High Yo-Yo uses the combination of gravity and your lower airspeed (reduced by the climb) to decrease your turn radius. Because of your now longer flight path, there's an added benefit of increased distance between yourself and the evading bandit.

Final Attack Advice:

- Never break off an attack once you initiate it. Once within weapons range, if you decide to turn and run, you're setting yourself up as an easy target.
- Attack first. This means firing before (but just slightly before) you're within effective weapons range. The idea of firing now is to force the bandit to evade your fire. Although the chances of getting a kill are nearly nil, getting that bandit's gun off your general direction is almost as valuable. If you succeed, you place yourself in the highly desirable H2T position.

Tip: *If you feel that pulling some G's won't bleed off enough speed, reduce throttle, use your spoilers (none are currently modeled in Combat Flight Simulator), deploy flaps and/or gear. All of these create drag and will slow you down but their effect at high airspeeds is reduced (mimicking partial deployment). Use whatever it takes to slow you down. This will result in a net loss of E, but it's worth it if it gets you the kill.*

Also don't forget about the proximity of other bandits. The tradeoff may not be worth it if you're caught out of E and other bandits are around ready to pounce. It's better to temporarily save your skin and make more kills later in the battle than to sacrifice yourself for just one measly kill.

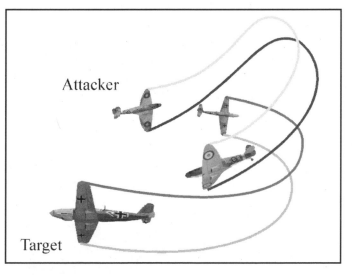

The High Speed Yo-Yo is one way to trade airspeed for altitude in order to achieve a tighter turning radius.

- Only attack when you have the clear advantage, and only fire when you're sure you'll get a hit. This was the advice of Manfred von Richthofen—also known as The Red Baron. Although this may seem cowardly, you can't argue with his kill record (80 kills). Although it sounds like a very boring way to fly, it's really the best way to increase your kill tally and stay alive long enough to brag about it.
- Master deflection shooting. In descending order of danger, there is T2H (your tail toward the pursuing enemy's head), H2H, T2T, and H2T. Obviously, the H2T situation is easier and safer to shoot when the bandit can't get any shots off. Since the bandit will also want to shoot you out of the sky, this scenario is rare and requires some work to achieve. You'll generally find yourself faced with mostly T2T situations and H2H shots, and the odds are you'll live longer if you don't seek H2H shootouts—meaning you'll make mostly high angle of deflection shots.

Maneuver Stage

The Maneuver stage of air combat generally takes place after the Attack stage, but it doesn't always work out that way. At its most basic level, maneuvering is precisely what air combat is all about—maneuvering your gun platform into a position to make a kill. That's it. Everything else just helps you reach that goal. While it's definitely preferable (for a long life) to get kills in the Attack stage and avoid the Maneuver stage altogether, skilled opponents usually won't allow that. (Let's be honest, the harder the kill, the more satisfying it is, right?)

Let there be no mistake about the goal of air combat—kill your target. You need to be on the offensive to do this. Maneuvering is designed either to maintain your offensive or to convert a neutral or defensive position into an offensive one. Basic Fighter Maneuvers (BFMs) by themselves are neither offensive nor defensive. If you recall, your relative position in relation to the bandit is what characterizes your posture.

Combat Scan

"Lose sight, lose the fight" is another one of those air-combat axioms that combat sim players like to recite. While there is some truth to that saying, it's possible to lose visual contact with bandits, and still come out victorious. The key to success is to develop good situational awareness skills by using the

viewing systems until they are second nature. You can almost reestablish
visual contact at will.

The combat scan is an extension of the detection scan, which now includes
the relative positions and orientations of other aircraft in your vicinity. Unlike
the detection scan, the combat scan is based around a bandit view, instead of
front view. You're sometimes unable to see the ground in the front view, so
you'll have to resort to one of the other views with a horizon. Based on what
you see, you'll then have to correlate your orientation according to that
information. You're looking for whether or not you'll hit the ground or run out
of E, if you continue on your course—or if you can perform the maneuver you
desire. (E status information is gathered through your instrument scan.)

A basic combat scan alternates between the bandit view (which can be any
fixed, Virtual Cockpit, or Padlock view); the forward view or other view that
shows the horizon; the airspeed indicator; and the altimeter. The bandit view
gives you information on maneuvering strategy, the horizon view warns of
impending flying trends, and both airspeed and altimeter indicate whether
you're flying at the best performance parameters.

This may sound complicated; an effective, basic combat scan pattern would
first scan the bandit view, then scan the front view (or other horizon view), and
finally go back to the bandit view. Next scan over to airspeed and altimeter
before starting over again at the bandit view. Next mix in sub-scans that include
the ammo counter (on the HUD), Tactical Display or map, and some standard
instrument scan stops, such as the heading indicator, flap status, manifold
pressure gauge, and radio/system/damage messages.

Although some pilots are able to knife fight using the padlock view
exclusively, another effective viewing strategy is to use only the padlock view
to locate bandits, and then switch to the viewing system you're most
comfortable with. For most pilots this is the fixed view system.

Just as with any kind of scan, always keep your eyes moving. A common
mistake is fixating on one display, bandit, or view. Another mistake is omitting
or skipping some display or aircraft. You have to constantly read, compare, and
analyze what you see, or you will lose the fight—guaranteed.

Defending Against the BnZ

The Attack stage does not need to precede the Maneuver stage. As we've noted,
you should never break off an attack after you've initiated it. Avoiding the
head-on attack is a strategy that may seem to go against that recommendation,

but it really doesn't. Why? Avoiding the head-on attack is only temporary. Your goals for avoiding such an attack are twofold: It gives your opponent a very difficult shot at you, and it allows you to maneuver to an offensive position.

As we know, the most difficult shot in air combat is the high angle of deflection shot. If you are forced to give a shot to your enemy, this is the only shot you'll want to give them. You can accomplish this by showing the side of your airplane to your opponent at the highest rate of relative speed. To do this, fly at full throttle on a flight path that will put the bandit on your 10:00 or 2:00 position. An additional shallow dive or shallow climb will further complicate things for your opponent. The key to getting a quick kill or staying alive after the merge is to time your next turn correctly and turn in the right direction. We'll cover how to do this, but first let's look at the factors you must consider before you can make these decisions.

Know Yourself and Know Your Enemy

Know your abilities as well as the capabilities of your aircraft. It doesn't hurt to know the capabilities of your opponents' aircraft either. The specifications and characteristics of all of the user-flyable aircraft modeled in Combat Flight Simulator are listed in the next chapter. Armed with this information, you can decide on a basic attack strategy. In any case, your goals are to outturn the bandit and make it bleed E.

Fighter doctrine can be boiled down to two basic aircraft flight-performance characteristic types—a dogfighter or an energy fighter. Generally, if your airplane is more maneuverable than your opponent's, it is advantageous to lure them into a turning fight.

On the other hand, if your aircraft isn't as maneuverable as your opponent's, you want to avoid the turning fight because then you're at a disadvantage if you get into one. If your maneuverability is equal or better than your opponent's, you'll want to turn as soon as possible so that you can shoot him before he can shoot at you. This maneuver is known as the Early Turn. If your maneuverability is inferior to your opponent's, but your speed is greater, you'll want to make your turns as far away as possible from him so that you can turn before getting shot at. This of course is the basis of the BnZ attacks.

The Early Turn

In addition to which direction to turn, one of the most important aspects of maneuvering is *when* to turn. When you start your turn can affect the position of the outcome. If you turn too early, you'll give the enemy a rear-quarter shot at yourself. If you turn too late and the enemy is also turning, he'll arrive at an offensive position sooner than you will. But if you time your turn just right, you can equal or outturn a better turning aircraft. The Early Turn maneuver embodies this goal.

Stating that everything in air combat must be relative to something else sums up why the Early Turn works. Although air combat takes place in three-dimensional space, one can't discount the relative effect of time. Of course, what matters most to us for beating a BnZ attacker is your turn performance relative to the attacker—and time.

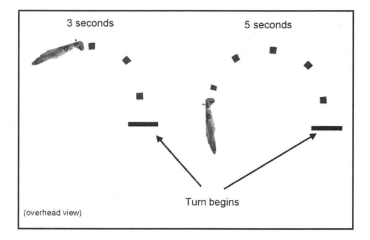

The early turn is based on the principle that the nose of your airplane will move more if you spend more time turning.

The theory behind the early turn is if your airplane can turn X degrees per second, the more seconds you turn, the greater number of degrees your airplane's nose will move. If you can turn for enough additional time over the enemy, you can theoretically outturn an opponent in a better turning aircraft with superior E.

In the simplest terms, turning faster doesn't necessarily require a faster turn rate (e.g., more degrees of direction change per second). Make no mistake about it, a faster turn rate *is* extremely useful in air combat, but arriving at your desired heading/guns solution faster is really what matters most.

Therefore, the most important factor to the ultimate success or failure of this theory is *when* (time) each turn begins. If two airplanes begin turning at the same moment, regardless of how many seconds the inferior turner turns (assuming both pilots are equally skilled), the superior turner will always turn more. But everything changes when the inferior turner begins turning an ample amount of time before than the superior turner.

The way to use the Early Turn against a BnZ attacker is to begin your turn just as the enemy comes into weapons range. This can yield several advantages:

- It only allows the BnZ attacker a high angle of defection shot at you.
- You may lure your opponent into following you through a turn—which will cause him to bleed off a lot of his E.
- You may sucker the bandit into a turning fight.
- You'll arrive at an offensive position faster than your opponent will.
- You can procure a tail shot if he tries to zoom by. This is commonly referred to as a *stern-conversion.*

Because air combat takes place in a three-dimensional environment, the directions you can turn include up or down in addition to left or right. As always, your current E state, aircraft abilities, and enemy position will dictate your best options. Although you can climb or descend while turning, you're basically dealing with left or right combat turns (maximum rate, minimum radius turns). Which way you should turn depends on the relative position of the bandit, the angle of the bandit's attack run, and your airspeed in relation to your present minimum-turn radius.

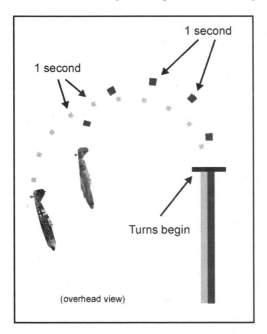

1 second

1 second

Turns begin

(overhead view)

Discounting potential angular advantages, if you can turn for enough additional time over the enemy, theoretically you can equal or even outturn an opponent in a better turning aircraft and or with superior E.

If you were to look at this problem from strictly an airspeed perspective and if your airspeed is fairly high, you'll want to use one of the more vertical turns, such as the half-Cuban 8, half reverse Cuban 8, or Chandelle. This is because you can turn around faster if gravity is helping you. If your E is low, a slice back or Split-S will work nicely, because gravity will help you build speed on your attacker as he tries to extend.

The offset between your position and the bandit's attack run will decide which direction you should turn. When facing a BnZ attack run and countering with an early turn, turning away from the attacker yields an advantage. Although this goes against one of the basic rules of thumb, this is an exception for the following reasons:

- Although turning in either direction causes gun solution problems for the attacker, an early turn toward the bandit gives him a snapshot chance to shoot as you pass across his nose.
- Turning away may sucker the bandit into turning with you in an attempt to get a shot off. This will bleed some of the bandit's E.
- If the bandit turns with you even a little, it decreases the radius you need to turn to get on his six as he tries to extend.

Regardless of any BnZ defensive tactics you may use, always:

- Lead-Turn the bandit and shoot it as it attempts its Zoom. If you can get a few hits with each pass, you can eventually kill the bandit—that is, if you can keep from getting shot down yourself.
- Make the attacker bleed airspeed with every pass. Make the bandit dive lower than you, or turn as much as you can on every pass.
- Know that a well-timed lead turn will make it hard for the BnZ attacker to get away. This usually causes inexperienced pilots to try to climb vertically or dive away. Either will bleed the attacker's total E level further.
- If you can maintain your E level as high as possible, the bandit will slowly lose any E advantage it may have had over you. Of course, if your opponent really knows his stuff, he'll be hard to beat. Most inexperienced BnZers don't know when to quit. So when the bandit gets too slow, you'll be able to kill it because you'll now have the E advantage, and if you've absorbed what we've been talking about, you'll also be in an aircraft that turns better.

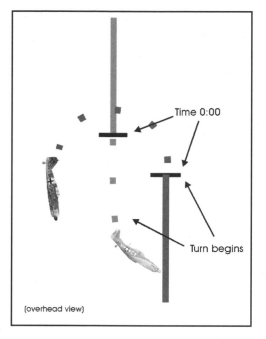

Time 0:00

Turn begins

(overhead view)

The Early Turn can help you arrive at an offensive position before your opponent.

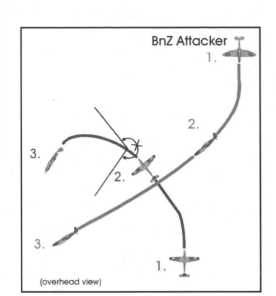

BnZ Attacker

(overhead view)

Turn away from a BnZ attacker to avoid the head-on to lure the bandit to turn with you and decrease your radius to get on his six.

Turn and Burn, Baby!

"Turn and burn" is a phrase used for dogfighting. Although there are no hard-and-fast rules that apply for every situation, if you don't know the relative performance of your opponent, or if you have trouble identifying the exact model of the opposing aircraft and you're not flying one of the slowest airplanes around, consider attempting an Energy fight before trying the Angle fight. This is because once you've bled off any energy in a turn, it's very difficult to recoup that E again while bandits are trying to kill you.

If you're ever going to attempt an Energy fight, it's best to do it when you have the most energy yourself. This means you must execute the Energy fight before making any turns because turning or climbing will cost

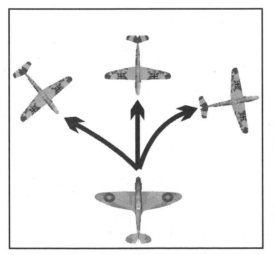

It's preferable to keep bandits ahead of your 3:00 through 9:00 line.

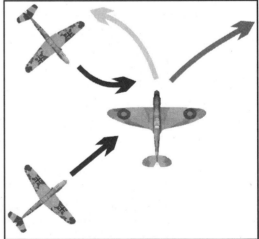

If you're in a purely defensive position, always turn toward the bandit or you'll just give the bandit a low angle of deflection shot at yourself.

you E. If you decide the time is right for the Angle fight (rather than find yourself in one—you always want to fight *your* fight), and then you want to undertake *Turn and Burn* (TnB) fighting.

Regardless of posture the most preferable relative enemy aircraft position is ahead of your 3:00 through 9:00 line because you can change or maintain any posture into a more favorable purely offensive or offensive and defensive one with the least amount of effort. When faced with this situation, always turn towards the bandit. Although this usually results in some sort of head-on pass, it accomplishes two things: It points the nose of your aircraft in the general direction of the enemy, which increases your ability to shoot at it (making you offensive), and it denies the bandit a T2H shot at you.

If you're purely defensive, regardless of the bandit's relative spatial position, always turn toward the bandit unless you're jinking, avoiding another head-on, or doing an Early Turn. If you turn away, you just give the bandit a lower angle of deflection shot.

The best way to keep yourself out of that defensive position is to pick your attack and make the kill. But that's easier said than done. Here are a few techniques you can use to increase your abilities to make the kill in a turning battle.

"Drivin' to the Corner"

If you're behind the 3-9 line of a bandit and relatively far back from the aircraft, if you turn as hard as possible when the bandit turns, you'll end up in front of it—not good! Instead, continue straight to the approximate position where the bandit started his turn. This is known as "driving to the corner." (Note that if you start your turn a little earlier than the corner, it can decrease the separation between you and the bandit.)

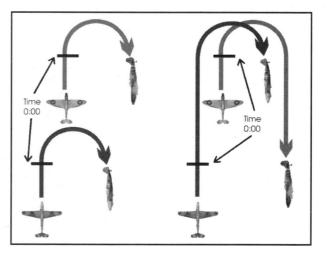

"Driving to the corner" can help you remain behind your intended target.

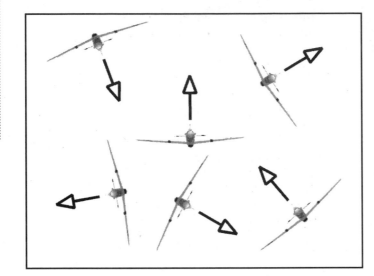

Your lift vector always acts perpendicular to your wings regardless of your plane's orientation.

Lift Vector Dogfighting

Regardless of your airplane's orientation, your lift vector acts perpendicularly (at right angles) to your wings. The fact that an airplane generates more positive lift than negative lift (nose up as opposed to nose over) is the basis for high performance turning in a dogfight. If you find yourself in a turning fight, and without regards to E maintenance for now (we'll come back to this in a minute), the way lift vector dogfighting works is like this:

1. Roll in the direction of the bandit and pull back on the stick.

2. Switch to your Up view (Shift + Num 5) as you continue your roll. Stop rolling when the bandit is centered in your Up view. Adjust your roll to keep the bandit centered in your Up view. This is known as *putting your lift vector on it.*

3. During all of this, keep pulling back on the stick. This will cause the bandit to move toward the upper section of your up view, which is exactly what you want to happen.

4. Switch back to the forward view and keep pulling. If you can get a shot off while inverted, take it.

When turning like this without vigilantly watching your E level, you'll expend all of your E. Your airplane will wallow in the air like you're flying an aluminum lawn chair. The only way to prevent such a catastrophe is to learn good E management techniques.

The Other Yo-Yo

In any turning battle, your goal is to out-turn your opponent to gain an angular advantage. To turn tighter, you need to pull maximum Gs at the lowest airspeed possible—quite difficult. This is known as *cornering speed*. As you pull G's, you bleed airspeed, and if you lose too much of it, your wings won't be able to generate enough lift to return the required G. Because the elevator (or rudder, depending on your orientation) controls airspeed (throttle controls altitude), use the Low Yo-Yo, an energy management technique for maintaining corner speed. If you can accomplish this and your opponent can't (in roughly equal aircraft), you'll eventually gain the advantage—even if you're defensive to begin with (and not blown to pieces by a bandit right away).

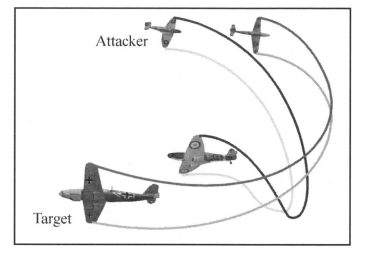

The Low-Speed Yo-Yo begins with a descending turn followed by a climbing turn.

At first glance, the Low Yo-Yo may seem identical to the High Yo-Yo; but it's actually the exact opposite in both execution and result. Instead of beginning with an initial climbing turn, the Low-Speed Yo-Yo is an initial descending turn followed by a climbing turn. In a more practical sense, the chief difference between the two is when they are used.

The classic example for use of the Low Yo-Yo is when you have the throttle pushed to the firewall and you're below cornering speed (probably turning with low or no energy reserve). The initial turning dive increases your airspeed and rate of closure with your target. Since the initial dive converts altitude to airspeed, you're in a more favorable position on the turn performance curve. The increased airspeed also decreases the distance between you and your target.

In essence, the Low Yo-Yo moves your airplane's nose above and below the horizon to increase and decrease airspeed while turning. Take into account the following tips for when performing the Low Yo-Yo:

- At the top of a Yo-Yo, you may require some rudder input because your controls may become less effective due to reduced airspeed resulting from the climb.
- If you keep your nose high too long you'll stall—and banked stalls often result in spins. Either will cause an E loss with no gain and very poor turn performance.
- A series of small Yo-Yos are more effective than a single large one.
- Avoid extreme dives or climbs and you'll be able to maintain your airspeed. But if you get a kill and it won't put you in immediate danger, go for the kill!

Loop Fighting

You'll find that many of the turning battles with experienced pilots in Multiplayer mode will take place on the vertical rather than horizontal plane. This type of fighting commonly degrades into what is known as *loop fighting*. Going vertical is popular because it presents a more efficient way to turn. The deciding factor for which is best depends on pilot proficiency, specific aircraft performance, E state, and your current strategic positioning with regard to your opponent.

Nevertheless, going vertical to turn does offer an inherent advantage over a high-rate level turn—a level turn will bleed your E without recouping any of it. After a level turn, you end up with a loss of kinetic E because level turning to the left or right nets the same losses—but when moving in the vertical plane, going up or down yields very different results due to the effects of gravity. These differences affect both your E status and your turn rate. If you can use the vertical and cause your enemies to bleed E faster than yourself, you'll out-turn them—a necessary prerequisite to killing them in a turning fight.

There are several tactics to be used against a loop fighter:

- Break out of the looping pattern and extend and begin a BnZ attack against the looping bandit. The key is to time your extension so that your opponents either can't see you leaving or are at a point where they don't have the E to do anything about it. All things being equal, you'll find this is usually on their climb up.
- Use a climbing turn in a one-vs.-one situation. As the bandit loops over you and starts back down, roll over and kill it.
- Practice good speed control and you may *out-loop* the bandit.

Stay as slow as possible on the way down, but maintain exactly enough E to make it back over the top again with flaps. With luck, you'll be able to out-turn the bandit or cause it to stall or spin. When it does, kill it.

- Follow the bandit, but at a slower rate, when he moves in the vertical plane. The idea is to expend your E at a lower rate than your opponent. This will give you the opportunity to nail the bandit up at the top of his loop if it gets too slow or to meet it with a higher airspeed on his way down if he goes that way. By not immediately following the bandit up and over, you can see what it's going to do, and you'll have the E to do something about it.

Retaining E

Regardless of the direction of a maneuver, as you're probably aware by now, it's quite easy to throw away E, so be careful. A well-executed level turn can easily outperform a very sloppy vertical maneuver any day. Rather than describing the proper way to fly your airplane (topics such as stick movement are pretty abstract for our purposes), here are some pointers on what *not* to do.

> **Tip:** *Even though excess control inputs can affect both ailerons and elevators, aileron movements create a lot less drag than elevator movements. Excessive elevator input leads to stalls and accelerated stalls—avoid both at all costs because they'll steal your E.*

Yanking the stick around and being imprecise with your movements contributes to wasting E. If you're constantly adjusting your stick movements with corrections and overcorrections, you're wasting E. Of course, some stick corrections are inevitable—just remember that the more you correct, the more it can drain your E reserves.

It helps to think a little ahead of where you want the stick to be (again, visualize!) and move the stick slowly—but not too slowly—to where it should be. This will cut down on the overcorrections and you'll be able to judge better just how much movement is necessary before you actually get where you need to be. This reduces the tendency to overshoot your goal.

Disengage Stage

Although the Disengage stage is presented as the last air combat stage, you should understand that its placement doesn't necessarily signify the end of an air-combat confrontation. To *disengage* means to put as much space between you and your opponent until you're out of weapons range. While you can choose to disengage to end air combat at that time, you can also choose to disengage for other combat-related reasons. Without considering mission objectives, there are only four ways to resolve an air battle:

1. Shoot your opponent down (you're left flying).
2. Go down in flames (your opponent is left flying).
3. You both go down (both of you crash).
4. Neither gets shot down, and you both continue on your course of wreaking havoc and destruction.

In terms of desirability and difficulty, shooting down your opponent is the most desirable. While killing your opponent is usually difficult, it isn't always the most difficult way to end the battle. Conversely, getting yourself shot down is definitely the easiest, but it's also the least desirable. A draw will gain you a kill if you ping your opponent before he crashes into the ground—but if you net a draw through a collision, you'll also get a Total Failure mission rating. Getting away when it's mutually agreeable is also easy. It's when your opponent(s) aren't cooperating (and why would they?), that you'll find disengaging to be the most difficult—and the most dangerous.

The criteria you use to base your decision whether to disengage is anything from tending to your mission objectives (such as escorting bombers to their targets), to being damaged or out of ammo. But if you're flying a damaged aircraft, it will severely decrease your chances of disengaging or surviving (not to mention making additional kills).

Damage and Flying a Bent Bird

Because damage plays such a big role in your decisions to disengage, let's talk about damage calculations, repercussions, and solutions. Anytime you take a hit, the amount of damage inflicted is based on:

- Where you've been hit—wing, fuselage, tail, elevator, horizontal stabilizer, etc.
- How many times you've been hit—more is worse (naturally)
- What you've been hit with—cannon or machine-gun fire

These variables are reflected by a cumulative damage percentage per hit box. If you don't blow up first, when your damage reaches the point where you can no longer fly or land in one piece you're considered killed in action. A visual indication to your conditions is represented by aircraft smoke and flames—and the darker the smoke the more serious the damage.

If flying a damaged airplane isn't enough to worry about, the sight of a smoldering aircraft has an effect similar to pulling a large banner from the tail of your aircraft with "Kill Me First" on it.

To make matters worse, depending on where you've been hit, damage can affect your flight performance. Conditions such as sluggish controls, lost control functions from severed control cables, locked flaps, inoperative landing gear, fuel leaks, oil leaks, coolant leaks, and hydraulic failures are all modeled. While not all damage will cause a drop in performance, the more damage your plane takes, the easier you'll be to kill. So if you're damaged, it's best to make a run for home.

Control Loss

If you've lost a control surface you'll either have a total loss of range of movement (pitch, roll, or yaw) or a partial loss (such as when you've lost one aileron or one elevator). If you have a total control loss, you've got no choice but to bail out (press the O key three times) unless you've lost pitch control. In that case there's a *slight* chance that you might be able to control pitch with the throttle or elevator trim or both.

On the other hand, if you've got a partial control failure, you may be able to nurse your wounded bird home. Partial aileron failures generally manifest themselves as being able to roll in one direction with control, but not the other. Partial elevator failures usually result in an airplane that will not change pitch without rolling to one side or the other, and as you'd suspect, partial rudder loss will make an airplane that will yaw in one direction better than the other.

Common sense dictates. If your airplane will only roll left, don't try to roll right. Fly as level as possible and only make extremely shallow left turns. Also, if you have rudder control, you may be able to use right rudder to reduce the right roll control loss.

In the case of partial elevator loss, you can try to control pitch with throttle and/or trim, but whatever you do, forget about any kind of vertical maneuvers unless you're really in trouble. Just be prepared for the twisting (roll)—you might be able to off set it with aileron (if they're still working).

Leaks

You basically have two main systems to worry about—the engine and the hydraulic system. Of course without an engine, you won't be flying for long. As you're probably aware, an engine requires three things to keep running: fuel, lubrication, and keeping cool.

If your fuel system develops a leak, you'll still be able to fly as long as you have fuel (and nothing else is damaged). In this case, you may be able to continue your battle and/or make it home.

But if you develop an oil leak, when your oil is depleted the engine will eventually seize from lack of lubrication. Similarly, coolant leaks will cause a rise in engine temperature, eventually causing a seized engine. All you can do in those situations is to reduce throttle, keep your eye on the engine temperature gauges, and hope you make it to a safe landing spot.

Hydraulic leaks result in hydraulic systems failures. The landing gear and flaps on some aircraft are hydraulically operated. If you have a leak, you may be able to still operate them. The loss of flaps isn't a big deal for landing (just land with a little more airspeed than normal, and you'll be fine), but landing without landing gear could be hazardous.

To manually pump your landing gear down, press Ctrl + G repeatedly. If the gear still won't lower, your choices are to bail out or attempt a belly landing.

Miscellaneous Damage

The following items may be damaged, but there isn't much you can do about them.

Radio Damage: Losing your radio isn't a big deal. Although you'll lose contact (both audio and text) with ground control and your wingmen, you'll still receive the Combat Status Messages text if the display is enabled (press the F key to toggle).

Airframe Damage: If your aircraft vibrates at normal maneuvering airspeeds, or your airspeed is lower than normal for your power and pitch settings, you've likely sustained airframe damage. All you can do is avoid high-stress maneuvers and fly slower until you can get your aircraft back down on the ground.

Fire: If your airplane catches on fire, you need to get on the ground as soon as possible—with or without your airplane (bail).

Here are few suggestions that may come in handy while you prepare for landing—on or off field:

- Slow down and configure your airplane for landing (flaps and gear) as soon as reasonable.
- Use your flaps to slow down and reduce your stall speed.
- Stabilize your descent speed by using your throttle.
- Fly your landing approach at the published Best Glide airspeed listed in Pilot's Manual.
- Control your airspeed with elevator/pitch.
- After touchdown, hit the wheel brakes by pressing the . (period) key.
- If you're going to overshoot the runway, pitch up your nose, raise your gear, slowly apply full throttle, and go around.

Gettin' Outta Dodge

By far, the best way to deal with damage is never to be damaged in the first place. So let's back up a bit and talk a little about some tactics to help you avoid getting shot to pieces:

Speed Away: The most basic way to disengage your attackers is to fly away from them. If your airplane is much faster or you possess a great deal more E than your enemy, this is easily accomplished as discussed in the BnZ sections.

Spiral Turn: This is a steep climbing turn in either direction. Separation is gauged by distance, so in a general sense, it doesn't matter which direction the separation is calculated—1000 meters separation is 1000 meters separation whether it's horizontal or vertical. If your airplane is a better climber and you have even the slightest E advantage over your opponent, you should be able to outclimb them using the spiral turn.

Red Eye Express: This isn't a maneuver you'd try in a real airplane, and its effectiveness is sketchy—especially in a negative G sensitive aircraft. The basic idea is to pull up into a climb and then jam the stick forward. You'll red out, but if your pursuer noses over to follow you, he'll red out, too.
As you recover, roll to another angle and pull out. If you dive for the ground and pull out at the last minute, it can only help you. If your opponent doesn't *push over* and does a Split-S instead, he will lose sight of you as you fly under his nose.

Call for help in Multiplayer mode: Get on the radio and call for the cavalry. Most pilots love jumping into fights when they can outnumber the enemy or attack an enemy low on E.

Fly toward friendlies: If no friendlies are near or if they lack sufficient E to help you, just fly toward friendly airspace. If there's friendly AAA available, make sure you fly low enough so your AAA can get good shots at your pursuer.

Use the Clouds: Although flying into the clouds will not evade computer-based opponents, it can be a powerful tool for escape in Multiplayer mode (provided the enemy isn't flying with the Tactical Display or the Enemy Indicator enabled). Once you enter the clouds, the key is to turn 90 degrees in any direction. If you follow this procedure every time you enter the clouds, chances are good you'll evade the enemy. Once you've accomplished that, you can make for home.

Spin to Win: Intentionally going into a spin may sound foolish, but sometimes it works for evading some pilots. They think you've been shot down and/or they're unwilling to lose all of that E following you down.

Downward Spiral: Fly around in circles while decreasing your altitude a little at a time. Before you know it (or rather, your opponents know it), they'll be too low and will end up as a smoking hole in the ground.

Dive, Dive, Dive!: Bring the battle down to ground level if you ever find yourself totally out of ammo, airspeed, and ideas. Only use this tactic in final acts of desperation. Many times, the enemy won't follow you down. If so, you can get away. If your pursuers do follow you down, you can *hope* that they aren't very good pilots. Less skillful pilots will auger into the ground because they're concentrating on shooting instead of altitude or airspeed.

Low Split-S: Do a Split-S very close to the ground. Pull your throttle all the way back and drop your flaps on the way down. This will allow you to decrease your airspeed so that you can squeeze the bottom of the loop and (hopefully) not hit the ground. If your pursuers are too preoccupied with following you, by the time they catch on, they'll be flying too fast and do that gear-up-landing-with-too-much-vertical-velocity thing.

Bail: You can always get out of a bad situation by *bailing out* (by pressing the O key three times). But bear in mind that bailing will net you an incomplete mission. If you've been pinged by the enemy in multiplayer mode, it'll count as a death for you and a kill for the attacker.

Anti-Aircraft Artillery, British

Gun	Shell Weight	Range (Ceiling)	Muzzle Velocity
40 mm Mk 1	1.98 lb (0.9 kg)	5000 ft (1525 m)	2700 ft/sec (823 m/sec)
3-inch (76.2 mm)	16.5 lb (7.5 kg)	15,700 ft (4785 m)	2000 ft/sec (610 m/sec)
3.7-inch Mk 1 (94 mm)	27.94 lb (12.7 kg)	32,000 ft (9755 m)	2600 ft/sec (792 m/sec)
4.5-inch Mk 2 (114.3 mm)	53.9 lb (24.5 kg)	35,000 ft (10,515 m)	2410 ft/sec (732 m/sec)
5.25-in Mk 2 (133.3 mm)	80 lb (36.3 kg)	43,000 ft (13,105 m)	2800 ft/sec (853 m/sec)

The primary AAA in the Battle of Britain campaign is the 3-inch (a.k.a. the "17-pounder").

Anti-Aircraft Artillery, German

Gun	Shell Weight	Range (Ceiling)	Muzzle Velocity
37 mm Flak 18	1.32 lb (0.6 kg)	15,750 ft (4,800 m)	2700 ft/sec (820 m/sec)
88 mm Flak 18-37 (BoB)	21 lb (9.4 kg)	26,240 ft (8000 m)	2700 ft/sec (820 m/sec)
88 mm Flak 41 (BoE)	21 lb (9.4 kg)	35,000 ft (10,675 m)	3280 ft/sec (1000 m/sec)
105 mm Flak 39	32.5 lb (14.8 kg)	31,000 ft (9450 m)	2900 ft/sec (881 m/sec)
128 mm Flak 40	57 (26 kg)	35,000 (10,675 m)	2900 ft/sec (880 m/sec)

* Note that the primary German gun, the "88," is more powerful in the Battle Over Europe campaign than during the Battle of Britain. In the Battle Over Europe campaign, 88 mm guns are used in greater numbers than 105 mm and 128.

Anti-Aircraft Artillery, American

Gun	Shell Weight	Range (Ceiling)	Muzzle Velocity
40 mm M1	2 lb (0.9 kg)	11,000 ft (3355 m)	2870 ft/sec (875 m/sec)
3-inch M3 (76.2mm)	12.75 lb (5.8 kg)	28,000 ft (8504 m)	2800 ft/sec (853 m/sec)
90 mm M2	23 lb (10.6 kg)	33,800 ft (10,300 m)	2700 ft/sec (823 m/sec)
105 mm M3	32.5 lb (14.8 kg)	37,000 ft (11,275 m)	2800 ft/sec (853 m/sec)
120 mm M1	50 lb (22.7 kg)	47,400 ft (14,445 m)	3100 ft/sec (945 m/sec)

In the Battle Over Europe campaign, the 90 mm is the primary American AAA.
*AA gun specs are from The Oxford Companion to World War II. Ed. I.C.B. Dear and M.R.D. Foot. Oxford and New York: Oxford University Press, 1995.

Doin' Fancy Pilot Stuff

If your airplane doesn't possess a distinctive speed advantage or you don't possess a large enough E advantage over your enemy, disengaging becomes much more difficult. Your disengaging choices now narrow down

The best chance you'll ever have to get away from a bandit is when its nose is pointed 180 degrees from where your nose is pointed.

to dogfighting. This is where your fancy pilot stuff either pays off or gets you killed.

The best chance you'll ever have to get away is when the nose of the bandit's airplane is 180 degrees off where your nose is pointed. But to get to this highly desirable position usually means that you've bled E while turning to get there in the first place—all of which greatly reduces your ability to safely speed away again.

Herein lies your dilemma—if you keep your E high (by making gentle turns), you'll most likely get your tail shot off. By contrast, pulling major G's to achieve the coveted 180 degrees T2T (tail-to-tail) position will usually make you too slow—allowing the bandit to catch up with you and line you up again for the kill. In other words, you need to do something that'll put you in that magic 180 degree T2T position (with lots of E to spare), and that'll leave your enemy's E reserves as low as possible. Your E advantage must be sufficient enough to increase your separation distance to at least 1700 meters (the maximum effective distance of projectiles).

Here are some tips that can help your disengage stage efforts that just might save you from early retirement:

Be unpredictable: When you're defensive, the only thing in your favor is that your pursuers must react to your maneuvers. You get to move first, and your pursuers' reaction time works against them. If you can keep them guessing, it'll increase your chances of getting away.

Use the vertical: Any escape maneuver you try should incorporate a vertical element (whether your vertical component is up or down depends on your E state), and your vertical maneuvers should contain a horizontal element as well. In other words, if you have sufficient E to pull up, don't just loop straight over. Roll out of your climb to the left or right. The same goes for dives. Adding a roll (of any degree up to 360) or consecutive rolls will make it harder for your opponents to predict your next direction. If they can't predict your next move, they won't be able to figure out the amount of deflection required to shoot at you with any success.

Ack

AAA (Anti Aircraft Artillery), or more as it's more affectionately known—Ack, can be an asset or a nightmare, depending on whose side it belongs to. Each important asset in Combat Flight Simulator (as in real life) has two to eight Ack emplacements situation near it for protection.

In the most general terms, Combat Flight Simulator's Ack emplacements have a range of 34,000 feet and they are extremely lethal if you get hit. It's killing zone resembles an umbrella in shape (now you know where the phrase "ack umbrella" comes from) and extends a full 360 degrees around the center— but

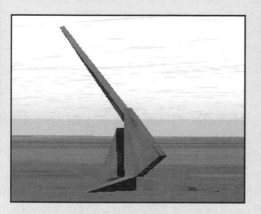

Each important asset has two to eight Ack emplacements.

it's base does not meet with the ground. The lower border actually varies with the distance from the point of origin at a slight upward angle. What this means is that you can safely fly below 1000 feet and not get shot at by Ack.

Finally, Ack can be destroyed. The hit points required to disable or destroy them are listed in the aaa_gun.dp file in the objects_dp folder located in the Combat Flight Simulator folder. The file is laid out similar to the aircraft damage modeling we described earlier.

Jink: Jinking is moving *out of plane* (out of level) with the enemy when he shoots at you. Basically, as your opponent gets lined up for a shot, roll your aircraft a random amount and pull back on the stick. This moves you out of plane with your opponent and forces the him to line up another shot all over again.

Naturally, in order to do this, you need to be looking out the rear view— so you can wait as late as possible to jink. If you have quick reflexes, they'll help you determine which direction to jink in order to evade the bullets being fired at you. But if you guess wrong, you'll get pinged. Keep jinking as many times as necessary—until you can get away, the bandit runs out of ammo (only in multiplayer mode—computer driven aircraft cannot run out of ammo), or you get shot down. (Hopefully for one of the former rather than the latter, of course.)

The Scissors: There are many descriptions of the Scissors, but for our Disengage stage purposes, the Scissors is a maneuver that consists of a series of turns made back and forth in an attempt to cause your pursuer to overshoot. Most pilots who scissor use it as a last resort and just weave back and forth without really watching the opportunity to take advantage of the move. Success with the Scissors relies on timing and learning to recognize when the maneuver is working.

To begin the Scissors, make a turn in either direction. Using the Up view to spot your opponent, reverse your turn just as he appears in the Up view. Each time you reverse, the bandit should move slightly farther forward in your up view, and you'll see more of the top of his cockpit instead of the front of his plane (and guns!). The farther forward he moves, the closer to overshooting he'll be. Then it's just a matter of timing your reverse turn so it puts him in front of you—or gives you that magic 180-degree chance to get away.

Even if you're equipped with the best training, strategies, and information, in reality, disengaging the enemy may not be possible without some "assistance" from your opponent. The bandit usually either has to screw up or has to let you go—or you'll need some intervention from friendlies. The fancy flying you use to dazzle everyone is intended to get your opponent to screw up. Despite what you see in the movies, there isn't any magic maneuver that will get you out of all situations every time.

The best solution is to never let yourself get into such a situation in the first place. That's the brutal reality of air combat. As you've probably summarized from this chapter, being well-versed with the performance of your airplane as well as that of your opponent, is highly valuable and can help you gain an edge over the enemy and make all of this a lot easier for you.

Chapter Seven

Aircraft and Flight Performance

The more you know your airplane and the airplanes you're flying against, the better off you are. Knowing the capabilities of your enemy's airplane is really as important as knowing about your own airplane when it comes to air combat. The combination of combat tactics, piloting skills, and knowledge of aircraft performance can transform any pilot into a most formidable fighting opponent combination. This chapter is all about getting the most from your aircraft.

In order to achieve these lofty ideals, we'll not only discuss the aircraft performance specifications for the various aircraft, but we'll also go into why things happen in certain situations. Knowing how and why certain things happen gives you the knowledge to exploit those situations—or once again, avoid them if possible.

Performance Basics

You may have heard the phrase "pushing the envelope" from time to time. The origin of that phrase comes from the early days of aviation and flight-testing. If we were to plot the flight performance limits of an airplane on a graph, we'd end up with a diagram that looks like a slanted square or rectangle. This box is commonly referred to as the *flight envelope*. In the simplest terms, the lines that mark the outer edges of the envelope illustrate the exact points where an aircraft transitions from flying to not flying.

If you can fly your airplane at its performance limits (pushing the envelope), you're able to turn tighter, fly higher, and fly faster than your (hopefully less-skilled) opponent. Obviously this is an advantage if your opponent is flying an equal or less capable airplane than you, but a common misconception is that this skill is of less value if you're flying a lower performance aircraft. In actuality, if you're flying a lower performing airplane than your opponent, being able to fly your airplane at the outer edge of the flight envelope is sometimes the only way to even out an uneven

> **Tip:** *Although being armed with your own specs will help you fly "out on the edge," it's generally more advantageous to learn the specifics about your enemies' limitations in comparison to your own. This helps you decide on a basic plan of attack by exploiting your strengths against your opponents' weaknesses.*

playing field. The old axiom, "It's the man—not the machine," says it all.

Riding the Edge

We'll cover the specs for all of the user-flyable fighters in Microsoft Combat Flight Simulator shortly. Experienced pilots only need to look up and memorize the airspeeds and they're fine. But if you wish to fine-tune your piloting skills to fly out on the edge, we need to break down the process into three steps:

1. Learning the limits.

2. Learning to recover if you go beyond the limits.

3. Learning how to stay within the limits.

When learning to *ride the edge*, you have to know what the limits (and beyond) look like and feel like—even though you're equipped with the numerical limits of an airplane. Combat Flight Simulator makes this easy for you to recognize. Stall buffeting, spins, and loss of control are all modeled. The stall buffeting communicates maximum limit warnings, and spins and loss of control authority tell you that you've crossed the limit.

Crossing the Line

Learning how to recover from going slightly over the edge of the performance limits is critical for survival because once you're over the edge, you're transitioned into *not* flying. And as some pilots put it, "If your airplane ain't flyin', you're dyin,'" As it turns out, stalled flying surfaces cause the majority of flight performance problems.

We've already discussed stalls and stall recovery way back in Chapter Four: Ground School, so let's just continue with how stalls affect your aircraft's flight performance.

Although the critical angle of attack varies with different wing designs, recall that an airplane can stall at any airspeed or at any flight attitude, altitude, or power setting. That may sound pretty intimidating, but again the

good news is that stalls are pilot induced. In other words *you* have direct control over them. Taking it easy on the elevator can help prevent stalling by keeping you away from the critical angle of attack, but the problem with that technique is that it makes for sloppy and wide turns—which generally lead to bullet holes in your tail feathers. So, as you probably realize, turning tighter increases your maneuverability and survivability (and probably your kill total as well).

If you fail to recover from a stall or let the stall progress by ignoring the stall signals, you can enter a spin. Just to re-cap, this is because stalls also cause spins. Spins result when one wing is producing lift while the other is stalled. In order to spin, an airplane must first and always be stalled. This means that if you never stall your airplane, you'll never spin. The best solution to beating the spin is to never to get into one in the first place. You do that by never stalling your airplane, and you achieve this by being smooth and easy on the stick and never exceeding the critical angle of attack.

Two crucial points about spins that you should remember are:

- Not all spins are recoverable.
- You may recover from spins faster in some aircraft if you reduce throttle during the recovery. Reducing throttle as a regular procedure for spin correction will decrease your loss of altitude as well.

Flying the Line

Now that we've examined what the edge looks like and how to come back if you cross over it, let's talk about how to stay on the edge. The benefits of flying as close to the performance edge as possible without crossing over are easy to understand when you accept the fact that once you cross the edge, recovery usually consumes any gains that you might have made up until that point.

To fly out on the edge, a pilot must fly right up to the start of the buffeting and then let off. (The same procedure applies to blacking out.) Once you've become familiar with the limits, it's all a matter of trying to keep the plane's performance as close as possible to that point. Of course, this is much easier to say than do because it requires precision control and feel (this is where a Force Feedback joystick can yield an advantage), but if it were easy to do, everyone would be doing it. That's where the advantage over your opponent(s) lies.

Performance Factors

Aircraft performance in Combat Flight Simulator can be broken down into two separate factors. Specifically, we're referring to an airplane's power output, and to its turning capabilities. Let's take a look at each of these factors and how they affect aircraft performance.

Power Output

Of course, when we talk about power output we're talking about engine horsepower. With a more powerful engine pulling your airplane through the air, the higher your top speed, the faster you'll accelerate and climb, and the better you'll be able to retain your E in a turning fight. We've already discussed the finer points of energy management and power management skills. But there are two engine power concepts you need to be aware of, so let's study them next.

WEP

War Emergency Power (WEP) was a special addition made to engines of some of the airplanes in WWII. In Combat Flight Simulator there are two types of WEP modeled that we'll call Type 1 and Type 2. Type 1 uses some sort of expendable material such as the injection of nitrous oxide, an alcohol derivative such as methanol, or a water and alcohol/methanol mix to boost performance.

Type 2 boost uses a mechanical device—such as a supercharger or turbocharger. Both types of WEP have a limited duration—so once they're gone, they're gone for good.

Combat Flight Simulator Aircraft WEP Specifications

Aircraft	Duration	WEP
Bf 109G	300 seconds	Type 1 (methanol and water injection)
Fw-190A	300 seconds	Type 1 (methanol and water injection)
P-47D	300 seconds	Type 1 (water injection) and Type 2
P-51D	300 seconds	Type 2

To enable WEP in aircraft equipped with it, press F10. You can also view it when you're using War Emergency Power when your manifold pressure gauge goes past redline—although a message is displayed as you engage and disengage WEP (and you hear a higher engine rpm whine). Then once you've expended your WEP allotment, WEP will immediately shut off (even if it's engaged again).

High Altitude Performance

As you fly higher into the atmosphere, the air becomes thinner and the performance of normally aspirated aircraft engines decreases. This is because the obtainable maximum engine compression decreases as the air thins. While supercharged, turbocharged, and turbine aircraft can delay this thin air problem by enabling these engines to produce an increase in power (compared to their normally aspirated cousins), none totally eliminates the effect. This explains why most flight performance envelopes are slanted to the right near the top. By delaying the loss of engine power, you're able to make gains on the thinning air.

Your manifold pressure gauge will go past redline when you use War Emergency Power.

How each aircraft accomplishes this depends on the particular aircraft's engine design. The P-51D has a second stage supercharger that kicks in after 19,000 feet (Combat Flight Simulator handles this for you automatically), while the Fw-190A used nitrous injection WEP. Again, this is another reason why flight envelopes vary for different aircraft.

This message appears when you engage War Emergency Power.

A fundamental rule of thumb for energy management is "Speed is life." Thinner air also produces less drag, which in turn results in higher airspeeds. As your altitude increases, so does your airspeed. So if "Speed is life," this is an advantage. Unfortunately, like most good things, there is a limit (although it's not as obvious in jet turbines until you reach very high altitudes).

Note: *The real Bf 109's had double the WEP duration of any other fighter modeled in Combat Flight Simulator. Also, the real Fw-190A used nitrous oxide injection WEP, so it didn't provide the same amount of boost that WEP did on other fighters at low or medium altitudes. Over 20 K, the Fw-190A's WEP increases climb performance, and above 25 K it boosted overall engine performance.*

➤

> **Tip:** *Even if you fly with Automatic Mixture setting enabled you'll still reap the benefits of longer range at higher altitudes.*

With high performance prop-driven aircraft, this is easy to illustrate. Combat Flight Simulator's P-51D will do 357 TAS at 10 K feet, 380 TAS at 20 K feet, and 429 TAS at 30 K feet in level flight. However, at 35 K feet, maximum speed at the same exact power setting drops to 427 TAS. The benefits of dogfighting in a Mustang below 30 K feet become especially obvious if your opponents' aircraft doesn't perform as well at this altitude.

High Altitude Range

Combat Flight Simulator allows you adjust fuel mixtures. In real aircraft, thinner air allows you to lean out your fuel mixture. This allows you to conserve fuel, which in turn will increase your total range.

There are those who believe that high altitude fuel savings is a myth because in order to obtain the same TAS at the higher altitude, it requires more engine power. They argue that this will require more fuel, but if you take both measurements at full military power (100% throttle and no WEP or afterburner in jets), while there is a power decrease with altitude, there is no additional greater power setting being called for by the pilot.

Engine Torque Effects

Although engine torque effects aren't generally thought of as a performance enhancement, they are related to engine power output and can be used to extract an advantage. But perhaps we should back up a bit. Torque effect may be explained through Newton's Second Law of Motion, which roughly states that for every force there is an equal and opposite reaction.

This means that the engine on a high-powered prop fighter in Combat Flight Simulator turns its propeller in one direction—causing the airplane to want to roll in the opposite direction. This effect is most prominent during the application and reduction of power (throttle) such as a low power to high power throttle change while at a low airspeed (as during takeoff or steep climbs near minimum stall speed), and from high power to low power at high

> **Note:** *Recall that energy management tells us that altitude can be traded for airspeed, so altitude can also be considered life. As altitude increases, so does airspeed and subsequently range, but this only happens up to a point. This complicates things, but it probably explains why this concept isn't conveyed with a catchy phrase like "Speed is life."*

airspeeds. Naturally the latter results in a roll in the opposite direction than the power on torque effect roll.

> **Note:** *Left-turning tendencies such as engine torque are reduced at the lower Flight Model Realism Settings.*

If you understand this principle, you can (with the application and reduction of power) use torque effect to gain a slight advantage over your opponent because you're able to increase your roll rate under the right conditions. However, note that numerically even (unit wise) multi-engine aircraft (none of which are flyable in Combat Flight Simulator) such as the P-38 series reduce the effect of engine torque on their airframes.

Turn Performance

One of the most important things you'll ever do in a fighter is turn it. Generally, there are two ways that you can execute a turn in your airplane—as a precision turn or as a non-precision turn. A non-precision turn is one that's made with little or no regard to bank or rate. Non-precision turns range from the leisurely, wallowing turns used by sightseeing pilots, to the *bank and yank* desperation turns used to evade a bandit's bullets.

On the other hand, a precision turn is one that's made with very high regard to bank and rate. Although the precision is commonly thought of as the standard rate turn used in instrument flight, in the air combat world, the combat turn is also a precision turn. Let's take a look at what makes for a good turn.

Airspeed vs. Lift and Turn Radius: Lift is a critical component for turning, and lift generally increases with airspeed. But higher airspeeds increase turn radiuses—which decreases your turn rate. This is because centrifugal force begins to exceed the lift capabilities of the wing just as when you drive a car very fast into a turn; centrifugal force will exceed the grip of your tires. The radius of a turn in an airplane is larger than if

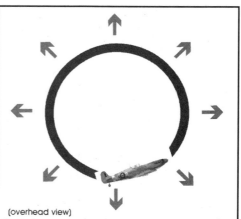

(overhead view)

When you're in a turn, centrifugal force always affects your aircraft from the same direction regardless of the direction of gravity's pull.

Left-turn, Clyde

There are three other phenomenon that can cause a propeller-driven airplane to want to turn under certain conditions. They are P-factor, Slipstream, and Gyroscopic Procession. When combined with the effects of engine torque they produce an even stronger tendency to turn left (in airplanes that have propellers that turn clockwise when viewed from the cockpit).

P-factor*: If you looked at a cross section of a propeller blade you'd notice that each blade is shaped like an airfoil. That's because each propeller blade is essentially a wing. In the simplest terms, when these little wings move through the air (when the propeller spins) they produce lift in the direction that we call thrust.*

When your airplane flies at a high angle of attack, the propeller blades on the downward cycle's (the starboard side of the airplane on a clockwise-rotating propeller when viewed from the cockpit) relation to the oncoming air have higher angles of attack than the blades on the upward cycle (port side). This produces more thrust than the upward-moving blades because they produce more lift, and subsequently causes the airplane to want yaw to the left. This effect is known as P-factor or asymmetric disk loading (a spinning propeller has the net effect similar to a solid disk).

Slipstream*: A clockwise-turning (viewed from the cockpit) propeller causes a spiraling mass of air (in relation to the prop shaft) to accelerate toward the tail of the airplane. This air mass (called a "slipstream" or "propwash") strikes the left side of the vertical fin and rudder and causes the airplane to yaw to the left.*

Gyroscopic precession*: A spinning prop has the same properties of a gyroscope. The gyroscope resists any effort to tilt its axis (or plane of rotation). Think of a gyro as a toy top. If you tried to push it over while it is spinning on the floor, it would instead move parallel to the plane of rotation (across the floor). This property is known as "rigidity in space."*

The property of procession is illustrated when a force is exerted against the side of the rotation gyro. The gyro would react as if the force was exerted at a point 90 degrees around the wheel (in the direction of rotation) from the actual place of application. This means that in an airplane with a clockwise-rotating prop airplane (when viewed from the cockpit), a sudden climb would cause the nose of the airplane to turn to the right. Conversely, any sudden dive would produce a turn to the left. Note that in both of these examples sudden control inputs produced gyroscopic procession effects.

you took the same turn at a slower speed because the effects of centrifugal force become greater than the centripetal (holding force) that's created by the cross component of lift when the airplane is banked.

> **Tip:** *We know that elevator trim changes are required with airspeed changes in level flight. But what many pilots fail to realize is that trim can help or hinder your turn performance, too. So if you notice your airplane isn't turning very well, or you're stalling all over the place in a turn, try adjusting the trim.*

Airspeed vs. Turn Rate: *Turn rate* is the time it takes to move the nose (aviation conventions reference the nose) of an aircraft a certain number of degrees. It's natural to reason that by going faster, you'd increase your rate of turn because your lift would increase from the additional airspeed. But when you consider the maximum lift curves we just discussed, going too fast also results in a turn-rate decrease because of the increases in centrifugal force.

Altitude vs. Lift: Without even considering the engine power losses due to increases in altitude we just discussed, altitude also affects lift. Basically, the higher you fly, the less dense the air becomes—and the less dense the air, the less air there is to create lift, and less lift decreases turn performance. Under such conditions, you need to fly faster to get the same number of air molecules under your wing to achieve the same turning rate achievable at a lower altitude. Unfortunately, as we've discussed, you may not have the power to increase your airspeed enough to make this possible.

Air Temperature vs. Lift: Again, without considering engine power losses due to altitude, air temperature is another factor that affects lift. Just as air density decreases with increased altitude, increases in temperature also decrease air density.

Corner Speed

We now know that turn rates decrease and turn radii increase with airspeed. As a combat pilot you want maximum turning performance. This means you're after maximum turn rate and the minimum turn radius. Because turn radii increase with speed, we can conclude that maximum turn rate is found at some minimum airspeed. This magic airspeed number is known as *cornering speed* or *cornering velocity*.

Tip: *Corner velocities may require diving turns to achieve or maintain them.*

By now you've probably gathered that cornering speed is not an absolute airspeed number that works in all situations even in the same exact aircraft. It's a "moving target" dependent on all of the lift variables we've discussed.

Cornering Velocities for User-Flyable Aircraft (IAS)

	P-47D		Fw-190A		P-51D		Spitfire I		Bf 109G		Bf 109E		Hurricane I		Spitfire IX	
	MPH	KPH	MPH	KPH	MPH	KPH	MPH	KPH	MPH	KPH	MPH	KPH	MPH	KPH	MPH	KPH
S.L.	260	418	229	369	216	348	213	343	213	343	207	333	201	323	171	275
1000	265	426	233	375	219	352	216	348	216	348	210	338	204	328	174	280
2000	268	431	236	380	222	357	219	352	219	352	213	343	207	333	176	283
3000	272	438	239	385	226	364	222	357	222	357	216	348	210	338	180	290
4000	278	447	242	389	229	369	227	365	227	365	219	352	213	343	181	291
5000	281	452	247	397	232	373	230	370	230	370	224	360	216	348	184	296
6000	285	459	250	402	235	378	233	375	233	375	227	365	219	352	187	301
7000	290	467	254	409	239	385	237	381	236	380	230	370	222	357	190	306
8000	293	472	259	417	244	393	239	385	239	385	233	375	226	364	193	311
9000	299	481	262	422	247	397	245	394	245	394	236	380	228	367	196	315
10,000	302	486	266	428	250	402	248	399	248	399	241	388	233	375	199	320
11,000	308	496	271	436	254	409	251	404	251	404	245	394	237	381	203	327
12,000	312	502	274	441	259	417	256	412	256	412	248	399	240	386	206	332
13,000	318	512	279	449	262	422	260	418	260	418	251	404	244	393	209	336
14,000	324	521	283	455	266	428	266	428	263	423	256	412	249	401	212	341
15,000	329	529	289	465	272	438	269	433	268	431	260	418	252	406	216	348
16,000	333	536	292	470	275	443	273	439	272	438	265	426	256	412	219	352
17,000	339	546	297	478	280	451	278	447	277	446	268	431	261	420	222	357
18,000	345	555	303	488	285	459	283	455	281	452	274	441	265	426	226	364
19,000	351	565	307	494	290	467	287	462	286	460	278	447	270	435	229	369
20,000	357	575	313	504	296	476	292	470	291	468	283	455	272	438	234	377

Cornering Velocities for User-Flyable Aircraft (IAS), continued

	P-47D		Fw-190A		P-51D		Spitfire I		Bf 109G		Bf 109E		Hurricane I		Spitfire IX	
	MPH	KPH	MPH	KPH	MPH	KPH	MPH	KPH	MPH	KPH	MPH	KPH	MPH	KPH	MPH	KPH
21,000	363	584	319	513	299	481	296	476	296	476	289	465	272	438	239	385
22,000	366	589	324	521	305	491	294	473	301	484	286	460	269	433	242	389
23,000	368	592	330	531	311	500	292	470	307	494	285	459	268	431	245	394
24,000	368	592	328	528	314	505	291	468	313	504	280	451	266	428	251	404
25,000	367	591	325	523	320	515	288	463	318	512	279	449	263	423	255	410
26,000	368	592	323	520	326	525	286	460	324	521	277	446	260	418	261	420
27,000	366	589	321	517	332	534	285	459	324	521	275	443	256	412	264	425
28,000	366	589	320	515	339	546	283	455	322	518	272	438	252	406	270	435
29,000	365	587	316	509	345	555	279	449	320	515	270	435	247	397	273	439
30,000	361	581	313	504	351	565	278	447	320	515	266	428	244	393	279	449
31,000	360	579	309	497	355	571	276	444	316	509	262	422	239	385	284	457
32,000	358	576	304	489	352	566	273	439	313	504	261	420	234	377	290	467
33,000	355	571	302	486	349	562	272	438	309	497	257	414	227	365	296	476

Instantaneous vs. Sustained

Turn rates are classified as either instantaneous or sustained. The difference between the two is the period of time they're able to maintain that rate. While you can achieve a high instantaneous G-load by pulling hard on the stick, you won't be able to maintain that high turn rate for very long because high G-loading will increase drag and slow the airplane—subsequently reducing the maximum G obtainable. Conversely, a lower G-load produces less drag.

If you keep on pulling the stick back for all it's worth, eventually you'll reach a point where thrust will be sufficient to overcome the drag being produced. This allows you to maintain the current G-load and airspeed. When you reach this point, you've reached the airplane's sustained turn rate.

Many pilots rely on an aircraft's sustained rate performance figure and generally ignore the instantaneous turning ability when comparing fighters. That's because an aircraft with a high sustained turning rate is easier to fly in combat. But ignoring instantaneous turn rates can be a costly mistake.

A superior instantaneous turn rate can not only be very useful for defensive maneuvering, but when used effectively, it can be very deadly in an offensive capacity as well. This advantage can potentially allow you to line up a shot faster. But the downside is if your sustained turn rate is inferior, if you fail to make the kill immediately, you're in for trouble. It's exactly this point which illustrates why a superior sustained turning rate aircraft is "easier to fly"—meaning it's more forgiving when your marksmanship is less than super-human.

Maximum Instantaneous and Sustained Turn Rates for User-Flyable Aircraft (degrees per second)

	P-47D		Fw-190A		P-51D		Spitfire I		Bf 109G		Bf 109E		Hurricane I		Spitfire IX	
	IST.	SUS.	IST.	SUS.	IST.	SUS.	IST.	SUS.	IST.	SUS.	IST.	SUS.	IST.	SUS.	IST.	SUS.
S.L.	28.8	15.6	37.0	19.3	34.8	20.3	39.7	24.2	39.9	23.2	41.0	23.2	39.6	24.0	36.9	28.0
1000	28.4	15.3	36.5	18.5	34.4	19.9	39.1	23.6	39.3	22.7	40.4	22.7	39.9	23.9	36.4	27.4
2000	28.1	15.2	36.0	18.1	33.9	19.5	38.5	23.1	38.7	22.2	39.9	22.2	38.4	23.4	35.8	27.2
3000	27.6	14.9	35.5	17.7	33.4	9.0	37.9	23.0	38.1	22.1	39.2	21.7	37.9	22.9	35.2	26.6
4000	27.2	14.6	34.9	16.9	32.9	18.6	37.4	22.5	37.5	21.6	38.6	21.3	37.3	22.4	34.8	26.0
5000	26.8	14.2	34.4	16.6	32.5	18.5	36.9	22.0	37.0	21.1	38.0	20.8	36.8	21.9	34.3	25.4
6000	26.4	13.9	33.9	15.8	31.9	18.1	36.4	21.5	36.5	20.6	37.5	20.3	36.3	21.4	33.8	25.2
7000	26.0	13.6	33.4	15.5	31.4	17.7	35.8	21.0	35.9	20.1	36.9	20.2	35.5	21.3	33.3	24.6
8000	25.6	3.3	32.8	14.8	30.9	17.3	35.2	20.5	35.3	19.7	36.4	19.8	35.2	20.8	32.8	24.0
9000	25.2	13.0	32.4	14.4	30.5	16.9	34.7	20.0	34.8	19.2	35.8	19.3	34.6	20.3	32.3	23.4
10,000	24.8	12.7	31.9	14.1	30.1	16.2	34.2	19.9	34.3	18.4	35.2	18.9	34.0	19.8	31.8	23.2
11,000	24.5	12.4	31.4	13.8	29.5	15.8	33.6	19.1	33.7	18.0	34.7	18.4	33.6	19.4	31.3	22.7
12,000	24.0	12.1	30.9	13.5	29.1	15.5	33.1	18.7	33.2	17.6	34.2	18.0	33.1	18.6	30.8	21.8
13,000	23.7	12.0	30.4	13.2	28.7	14.8	32.6	18.2	32.7	17.2	33.6	17.2	32.5	18.1	30.3	21.3
14,000	23.3	11.8	29.9	12.8	28.1	14.2	32.0	17.8	32.1	16.8	33.1	16.8	32.0	17.7	29.8	20.4
15,000	22.9	11.5	29.4	12.5	27.8	13.3	31.6	17.3	31.7	16.4	32.6	16.4	31.5	17.0	29.4	19.6
16,000	22.5	11.2	28.9	12.2	27.3	13.0	31.0	16.9	31.1	16.0	32.0	16.0	30.9	16.3	28.9	19.2
17,000	22.2	10.9	28.5	11.9	26.9	12.7	30.6	16.5	30.6	15.6	31.5	15.6	30.5	15.9	28.4	19.0
18,000	21.8	10.7	28.0	11.4	26.4	12.4	30.0	16.1	30.1	15.2	31.0	15.3	30.0	15.2	27.9	18.5
19,000	21.5	10.4	27.5	11.1	26.0	11.8	29.5	15.5	29.7	14.8	30.5	14.3	29.5	14.5	27.4	18.3
20,000	21.1	10.2	27.1	10.6	25.5	11.5	29.1	14.8	29.1	14.5	30.0	13.7	28.8	13.9	27.0	17.9
21,000	20.8	9.7	26.7	9.8	25.1	11.3	28.5	14.0	28.6	13.9	29.4	13.1	27.8	13.3	26.6	17.1
22,000	20.2	9.3	26.2	9.3	24.7	11.0	27.3	13.4	28.2	13.5	12.4	12.4	26.6	12.7	26.1	16.4
23,000	19.7	9.1	25.8	8.5	2.2	10.5	26.2	12.8	27.7	13.2	11.6	11.6	25.5	11.8	25.6	16.0
24,000	19.0	8.7	24.8	8.0	23.8	10.2	25.1	12.0	27.2	12.6	11.0	11.0	24.4	11.2	25.2	15.4

Maximum Instantaneous and Sustained Turn Rates for User-Flyable Aircraft (degrees per second), continued

	P-47D		Fw-190A		P-51D		Spitfire I		Bf 109G		Bf 109E		Hurricane I		Spitfire IX	
	IST.	SUS.	IST.	SUS.	IST.	SUS.	IST.	SUS.	IST.	SUS.	IST.	SUS.	IST.	SUS.	IST.	SUS.
25,000	18.3	8.2	23.7	7.2	23.4	9.5	24.1	11.4	26.7	12.0	10.4	10.4	10.7	10.7	24.8	14.7
26,000	17.7	7.8	22.7	6.7	23.0	9.0	23.1	10.9	26.2	11.5	9.9	9.9	9.8	9.8	24.3	14.1
27,000	17.0	7.5	21.8	6.2	22.6	8.5	22.1	10.2	25.5	11.0	9.1	9.1	9.3	9.3	24.4	13.5
28,000	16.3	7.1	20.9	5.7	22.2	8.1	21.2	9.6	24.4	10.2	8.5	8.5	8.5	8.5	23.5	12.9
29,000	15.7	6.7	19.9	5.2	21.8	7.4	20.1	8.9	23.4	9.7	7.7	7.7	7.6	7.6	23.1	12.4
30,000	15.0	6.3	19.0	4.3	21.4	7.0	19.3	8.4	22.4	9.3	7.2	7.2	7.1	7.1	22.6	11.8
31,000	14.4	5.9	18.0	3.7	20.9	6.3	18.4	7.9	21.4	8.6	6.6	6.6	6.2	6.2	22.3	11.0
32,000	13.7	5.5	17.1	3.2	19.9	5.6	17.5	7.2	20.3	8.1	5.8	5.8	5.7	5.7	21.9	10.5
33,000	13.1	5.1	16.2	1.8	19.0	5.1	16.7	6.8	19.3	7.4	5.2	5.2	4.7	4.7	21.4	10.0

The Flap on Flaps

In order for a wing to fly, you must generate lift. But to a limited extent a pilot can generate additional lift by increasing the AOA or adding flaps incrementally by pressing F7. (Press F6 to retract flaps incrementally or F5 to retract them fully.) Increased lift can (as we've just seen), increase turn performance. Although some airplanes have multiple flap settings that include Battle and Maneuver flap settings (the first flap setting in the P-51D), you can sometimes obtain turning benefits by using the greater flap settings (such as Takeoff or Landing or both flap settings) if the combat flap settings are not available on the airplane.

Unfortunately, the byproduct of lift is drag, and increased lift creates increased drag. So beware—the use of flaps will slow you down. While this can be useful for slowing down to execute tight turns and for landing, make sure your flaps are retracted:

- After taking off
- When you're flying straight and level
- When you're trying to escape from a bandit

Note: *You can deploy your flaps at any airspeed in Combat Flight Simulator and they won't be damaged.*

Performance Limitations

As with most things in life, you can only take so much of a good thing before it becomes tiresome. When it comes to airplane performance, there are limitations. But as always, if you understand them you can limit their effect or avoid them totally.

External Factors

Although they will not increase your aircraft's turn performance like flaps will, other external aircraft factors will decrease your flight performance. So you should be aware of them. How you have your aircraft configured will have a profound effect on your aircraft's flight performance. We're talking about external appendages and accessories that hang off your aircraft like external stores such as bombs and rockets, and general aircraft equipment such as flaps (which we just discussed) and landing gear. (Auxiliary fuel drop tanks are not modeled in Combat Flight Simulator, although their fuel is.) The main penalty for having any of the above attached or extended on your aircraft is increased drag. And as we've discussed, drag will decrease your airplane's airspeed (which affects lift/turn performance), and range (although drop tanks net a gain in range despite their increased drag). Drag is created by these items in two ways—form drag and weight.

Form drag is a type of parasite drag. Basically the object(s) increases the frontal area of the airplane so more air has to be pushed out of the way. Increased weight causes performance problems as well because increases in weight require more lift to perform the same flight maneuvers on a lighter airplane.

Regardless of how it is created, weight and drag affect your aircraft the same way—they drain your performance potential by placing you further up the performance curve than you want to be. While there isn't much you can do about additional aircraft weight not attached to a hard point on your aircraft (after all, you can't just throw stuff out your canopy in Combat Flight Simulator), here are some guidelines.

Basically, the only steps you can take to minimize these external drag factors is retract your landing gear as soon as possible, and drop your external stores if you need maximum performance in a crunch. Of course you need to balance that decision against whether or not you believe you can complete your

mission without those items, as well as your assessment of your chances of staying alive. It's these types of decisions that make heroes or corpses.

Effects of Airspeed on Control

You've probably noticed that your flight controls become less effective (mushy) when you're flying at a low airspeeds. This occurs because low airspeeds create a decrease of airflow over the control surfaces. This is an easy concept to understand. As your airflow decreases, more control deflection is required to divert the same volume of air.

Conversely, as your airspeed increases, the amount of control input required for maneuvering decreases. Just as with other concepts we've discussed so far this trend only continues to a point. As you approach the other end of the flight envelope your controls become "heavier" and (again) less effective. Depending upon the aircraft design, you may actually lose all control. This phenomenon is caused by an aerodynamic state known as *compressibility*.

Lift is generated by airflow moving faster over the upper portion of the wing than the bottom, as explained via the Bernoulli effect. When you start flying very fast in a non-supersonic aircraft (usually experienced in a high-speed dive), the airflow going over the top of the wings reaches the speed of sound (Mach One). This means the airflow over the top of the wing is traveling faster than the airplane itself.

This supersonic flow produces a strong shock wave that leads to the separation of the boundary layer (layers of air that flow near the surface of the wing) which causes the loss of control authority. The actual point that compressibility occurs varies due to wing airfoil designs. A high lift wing will enter compressibility before a low lift wing. For example, the high lift wing of a real P-38J (which was designed as a fighter-bomber and could haul a bomb load equal to a medium bomber) will enter compressibility at Mach .67 while a Spitfire encounters compressibility at .82 Mach.

Fighter Comparisons

Just like their real life counterparts, every aircraft in Combat Flight Simulator has its own individual mixture of strengths and weaknesses (known as *Disparity of Performance*). What's particularly interesting about aircraft development during the time period modeled in Combat Flight Simulator is no one aircraft has an absolutely decisive advantage over every other aircraft in all situations.

If you're going to become a good pilot, you're going to have to learn the assets and liabilities of nearly every plane in the sim and appreciate how these various planes behave in combat. The concept is to try to incorporate your plane's *virtues* against any enemy planes' *vices*. Before we discuss the specific concepts, let's briefly outline the plan. The plan is quite simple:

- Out-gun those with weak durability
- Out-climb the slower climbers
- Out-accelerate the slower aircraft
- Out-turn the zoomers
- Out-zoom the TnB'ers

As you know, some planes are much better suited to one style of fighting over another. The Fw-190A and P-47D are good BnZ type planes. They dive well, have lethal guns, and probably more importantly, they're not strong turners. BnZ fighters are fast, handle well at high speeds, and regain altitude well in the zoom. This can result from either low drag or a powerful engine.

Conversely, a Hurricane Mk I turns well, but it's practically worthless as a BnZ fighter because it isn't very fast and doesn't climb particularly well. A TnB fighter needs to turn quickly—a good climb rate can only help you as well. It's also very much to your advantage if your fighter has a relatively low stall speed and gives you plenty of feedback that it's going to stall. Some aircraft just snap into a stall with little or no warning. Those are very difficult to fly when pushing the envelope. By contrast, some planes such as the Spitfire IX can fly well either way.

Negative G Issues

We discussed the effects of positive and negative G's on your virtual persona in the last chapter. Just as positive and negative G's can affect your virtual persona's physical "systems," these same forces can affect your airplane's

systems too. We've already discussed how positive G's affect your turn performance and structural integrity, so let's move on to the affects of negative G's.

Tip: *Negative G cutout is toned down at the lower Flight Model Realism Settings.*

Essentially there are two ways to encounter negative G's in an airplane. One's by flying inverted, and the other is by pushing the nose over on your airplane by applying down elevator. (G polarity is determined by normal lift orientation.)

Note: *Early Spitfires and Hurricanes were not the only aircraft that suffered from negative G engine cutoff. Japanese Zeros also experienced the same problem.*

The most famous negative G performance disparity conflict took place during the Battle of Britain. Spitfire Mk I's and Hurricane Mk I's suffered from negative G carburetor float cutout. Whenever these aircraft were subjected to negative G's for more than a second or two the engines would sputter and stop running for as long as negative G was experienced. This limitation was caused by the float design of the upright carbureted Rolls-Royce Merlin V-12 engine. Whenever these carburetors experienced negative G, the carburetor floats would literally shut off fuel flow to the engine.

Conversely the German Bf 109's that fought against these handicapped Spitfires and Hurricanes used a Daimler-Benz DB-600 series fuel-injected inverted V-12 engine. The advantage of fuel injection enabled the German aircraft to "bunt" as the British called it (push negative G at the top of a vertical maneuver or climb) without losing power.

Although the tactical benefit of the bunt maneuver by the Germans is still debated today, the maneuver worked like this: When a German fighter was on the defensive with a Spitfire or Hurricane on its six, the German pilot could use the bunt to evade his attacker. If the British fighter attempted to follow with a similar maneuver, his engine would cut out and allow the German pilot to fly away. However, if the British pilot attempted to roll inverted and then followed the German fighter under (a Split-S), the extra time required to first roll the aircraft inverted would give the escaping pilot enough of an edge to get away cleanly.

The solution to this disadvantage/problem came with the development of the negative G carburetor, which was invented in December 1941 and first installed in the Merlin 50. Although people tend to classify the aircraft affected

How Negative G Engine Cutoff Was Solved

The first problem with inverting an upright carburetor is keeping the fuel in the float bowl so the venturi/jet pickup line stays in contact with the fuel. The second problem is with the float. When it's inverted, it shuts off all fuel flow.

To help you understand how this works, think of the carb float bowl as the water tank on the average toilet. The floats in either work the same way (although the pickup doesn't, you can get the idea just the same). The float maintains the fuel level in the float bowl just as the float in your toilet tank maintains the water level. When the water or fuel is below the float's shut-off point, it allows the water/fuel to enter, but when it reaches the shut off point, it shuts off the water/fuel coming into the bowl/tank.

Next picture the flapper on the bottom of the toilet tank. That can roughly equate to the throttle butterfly control of a carburetor (not exactly, but close enough to understand the negative G conditions). Picture inverting your toilet tank—what would happen? (Of course, imagining that the water in the tank would stay inside—what a mess!) What happens is the fuel/water will no longer sit on the top of the tank (which is now the bottom because we're inverted), so when you flush the toilet/open the throttle, you'll only suck air.

Second, depending on the ratio of water/fuel to the size of the float bowl/toilet tank, the float will now move to the shut-off position from the force of negative G and cause the influx of water/fuel to stop. That's because even if there's enough fuel to keep the float in the feed position while inverted, if you push enough negative G, that can force the float to move to the shut-off position.

The original negative G solution was a diaphragm-operated carburetor. This "restriction" type fuel system became known as "Miss Schilling's orifice" named after the woman engineer who invented it. The story goes that it was modeled after a birth control device, but how true that is is another matter of discussion altogether. Regardless, by the time the P-51 Mustang received the Merlin engine another solution known as the pressurized carburetor was available and fitted to all Markes of Merlin from then on.

Another negative G problem that affected a larger number of aircraft was oil starvation. When some aircraft were flown inverted or stayed in a spin for more than 10 seconds, the engine crankcase oil would either slosh to one side or to the top of the engine where the oil return pickup couldn't reach it—causing the oil starvation problem.

Of course oil is required to keep engines cool (back in the 1940's there weren't any late-night infomercials selling miracle engine treatments that allow you to run your engine without oil back in the 1940's) and to lubricate moving parts. Without oil, engine damage would occur often resulting in the engine seizing up (and a really angry crew chief when you get back!).

by negative G cutout by their model or model version, there were plenty of exceptions at the time (some Spit IX's are on record as having non-negative G carbs). But generally from the Spit version V onward, most Spits were equipped with the negative G carburetor.

Lethality

Being able to out-turn any aircraft in the virtual skies of Combat Flight Simulator is only part of the equation. If your airplane is only equipped with *pea shooters* or very few rounds, it's very difficult to capitalize on your flight performance advantage. For weaponry specifications listed by aircraft, see below.

Combat Flight Simulator Aircraft Armament

	Nose MGs	Wing MGs	Nose Cannon	Wing Cannon	Nose MGs Ammo	Wing MGs Ammo	Nose Cannon Ammo	Wing Cannon Ammo
Bf 109E	2x7.9 mm		1x20 mm		2x1000		1x60	
Bf 109G	2x13 mm		1x30 mm		2x300		1x60	
Fw-190A	2x13 mm			4x20 mm	2 x475			2x140, 2x250
Hurricane I		8x.303				8x 334		
P-51D		6x0.5				2x400, 4x270		
P-47D		8x0.5				8x425		
Spitfire I		8x.303				8x300		
Spitfire IX		4x.303		2x20 mm		4x350		2x120

Machine Guns

   Browning Mk 2 .303-in./7.7 mm (Spitfire I and Hurricane I)
   Projectile Weight: 0.344 oz.
   Muzzle Velocity: 2660 ft/sec
   Rate of Fire: 1150 rpm
   Ammo Types: Armor piercing, incendiary
   High lethality requires: >30 hits on fighters

   Rheinmetall-Borsig MG 17 7.92 mm (Bf 109E)
   Projectile Weight: 0.45 oz.
   Muzzle Velocity: 2450 ft/sec

Rate of Fire: 1100 rpm
Ammo Types: Armor piercing, incendiary
High lethality requires: >30 hits on fighters

Browning Mk 2.50-in./12.7 mm (P-47D and P-51D)
Projectile Weight: 1.6 oz.
Muzzle Velocity: 2750 ft/sec
Rate of fire: 800 rpm
Ammo types: Armor piercing, incendiary
High lethality requires: >20 hits on fighters

Rheinmetall-Borsig MG 131 13 mm (Bf 109G and Fw-190A)
Projectile Weight: 1.5 oz.
Muzzle Velocity: 2460 ft/sec
Rate of Fire: 900 rpm
Ammo Types: Armor piercing, incendiary
High lethality requires: >20 hits on fighters

Cannons

Oerlikon MG FF 20 mm (Bf 109E)
Projectile Weight: 4.82 oz.
Muzzle Velocity: 1800 ft/sec
Rate of fire: 520 rpm
Ammo types: Incendiary or high explosive
High lethality requires: >10 hits on fighters, >20 hits on heavy bomber

Mauser MG 151/20 20 mm (Bf 109G and Fw-190A)
Projectile Weight: 3.5 oz.
Muzzle Velocity: 2500 ft/sec
Rate of Fire: 750 rpm
Ammo types: Incendiary or high explosive
High lethality requires: >10 hits on fighters, >20 hits on heavy bomber

Hispano Mk II 20 mm (Spitfire IX)
Projectile Weight: 4.4 oz.
Muzzle Velocity: 2750 ft/sec
Rate of Fire: 750 rpm
Ammo Types: Armor piercing, incendiary
High lethality requires: >10 hits on fighters, >20 hits on heavy bomber

Rheinmetall-Borsig Mk 108 30 mm (Bf 109G)
Projectile Weight: 11 oz.
Muzzle Velocity: 1750 ft/sec
Rate of Fire: 660 rpm
Ammo Types: Incendiary or high explosive
High lethality requires: 1 hit on fighters, 5 hits on heavy bomber

Machine Guns vs. Cannon

There are seven factors that you need to consider when it comes to determining weapon lethality: firing rate, muzzle velocity, size of the round, chemical load, range, ammo load, and the other part of the puzzle—what you're shooting at. Of course the more lethal the armament your aircraft carries, the less rounds and time are required to destroy the enemy.

Machine guns have a high rate of fire (rounds per minute) and fast velocity. A higher muzzle velocity helps the round reach its target because the faster the round the faster it can hit its target before it can move out of the way. (Note that with similarly sized and shaped projectiles, higher muzzle velocities mean greater hitting power.) The third advantage is because the round is smaller and lighter, you can carry more of them.

On the other hand, cannons are slower in both rate of fire and muzzle velocity—but because of their larger projectile sizes, they have more potential destructive power. Additionally, many contain some sort of explosive charge. But due to the increased size and weight of cannon shells, you can't carry as many.

When you're studying the specifications of each aircraft in Combat Flight Simulator, make a point to note the amount of ammo each airplane is armed with. After all, having the most lethal guns in the world may not be all that valuable if you don't have any shells left to shoot! Obviously, if the bandit is on the short side of the ammo count (which is only important in multiplayer mode), it can work to your advantage as well.

Although it's generally understood that because cannons fire relatively slower and fighters can almost fly through their firing stream, it is equally understood that cannons are good against bombers. That's because bombers are bigger, slower, and less maneuverable than fighters. Conversely, machine guns are thought to net a higher rate of return against small, more agile fighters. But, in addition to machine guns' reach to target(s), you need to factor in the kind of damage they can inflict on various targets.

According to Brig. General Chuck Yeager (ret.), *"The P-51 [D] carried six .50 caliber machine guns that fired around 850 rounds per minute and they were armor piercing incendiary bullets that penetrated deep into the Me109 or 190 that you were fighting, and it did a lot of internal damage to the mechanism in the airplane."*

He also notes, *"You gotta remember that the Me109 and 190s were designed as interceptors to shoot down bombers. They were very good between fighter to fighter because they were quite maneuverable. But since they were firing against bombers, they used cannon shells more than the smaller caliber shells that we used in the P-51. And those cannon shells such as the 20 mm cannon and the 30 mm cannon had a lot of explosive shrapnel when it hit the thin skin of the B-17s and B-24s. And consequently during aerial combat, I think we were at a big advantage with the P-51 by firing .50 caliber machine guns (which were armor piercing incendiary) that penetrated deep into the internal organs of the Me109 or 190, whereas if we got hit with a 20 mm shell it merely shredded the skin on your airplane and you didn't have very deep penetration into the internal organs of your P-51."*

Cannon and gun shells can be fired separately or in unison on airplanes equipped with both air-to-air weapons. To fire the primary weapon (machine guns are considered the primary weapon) press the 1 key. To fire the secondary weapon (cannon guns on aircraft with both cannons and machine guns), press the 2 key. To fire primary and secondary weapons at the same time, press the space bar or use the trigger on the joystick.

Tip: *Timed rockets will detonate at approximately 3000 yards range. Because these weapons are unguided and you can't carry a whole lot of them (they're big and heavy), you have to try and make each shot count. So if you try to fire an impact-detonated rocket at a formation of bombers, your rocket will just sail past them unless you actually hit one of them.*

On the other hand, if you fire a timed rocket into a formation of bombers and time it right, regardless of whether you actually hit your target, you'll cause it damage. Therefore, the basic rule of thumb is to use impact rockets against ground targets and timed rockets against air targets.

Rockets

The origins of the rocket can be traced all the way back to Ancient China where they were originally fired from kites. Although they're unguided weapons due to their larger size (which allows them to carry more explosives) they pack a much larger punch. This makes them suitable to use against large bombers or against ground targets.

The two types of rockets modeled in Combat Flight Simulator are:

Wgr 21 21cm/8-in. air-to-air rocket
(Bf 109G and Fw-190A)
Projectile Weight: 90 lb (41 kg)
Muzzle Velocity: 1050 ft/sec
High lethality requires:
Detonation within

5-in./12.7cm air-to-ground rocket
(P-47D and P-51D)
Projectile Weight: 50 lb (22.68 kg)
Muzzle Velocity: 1000 ft/sec
High lethality requires:
Detonation within

> **Tip:** *You can calculate detonation ranges for timed rockets by multiplying the detonation time by 1000 meters per second.*

Rockets can be fused to detonate in either one of two methods—by contact detonation or by timed detonator. To fire a contact-detonated rocket press the 3 key. To fire a timed rocket, press Ctrl + 3.

Durability

By "durability" we're referring to the amount of damage that an aircraft can sustain. In addition to this being important to your personal survival, knowing how much damage an enemy aircraft can sustain (read: *how much damage you'll have to inflict to bring it down or disable it*) also bears some tactical benefits. If you encounter an enemy aircraft that can take lots of damage and your ammo count is low, you may want to avoid taking it on. Armed with this information, you're able to make these kinds of decisions. Otherwise you might run out of ammo and still have a really angry bandit flying next to you.

Back in WWII, the way that aircraft achieved resistance to damage basically came down to three schools of thought. The first was maneuverability. The theory behind this was to build an aircraft that was small, very fast, and ultra maneuverable. This way the enemy wouldn't be able to hit it because this fighter would be either on its tail shooting at the attacker for flying away before the attacker could do anything about it.

The second school of thought relied on simple construction with light, strong materials like wood and canvas. Besides being cheaper, and easier

How the Self-Sealing Seal Themselves

The way that self-sealing fuel tanks worked is that these tanks were basically two neoprene bladders (one inside another). Filled in between these bladders was raw rubber. When the tank was punctured fuel would come in contact with the raw rubber—which caused it to swell and seal the puncture. This worked out well for small punctures of 1/4" to 1/2" size, but not for the punctures created by 20 mm or larger cannon shells.

to repair than metal skinned birds, the idea was that machine gun and cannon fire would literally fly in one end and straight out the other causing very little damage.

Then the third school believed that the only way to deal with bullets and cannon shells was to protect the pilot and critical systems with armor plating and self-sealing fuel tanks.

Aircraft Specifications

Instead of forcing you to become a "test pilot" of sorts to discover the performance numbers of each aircraft, we've done the hard work for you. All you really need to do is look up and memorize the airspeed specs presented in this chapter. The information that follows in this section contains the balance of information about the performance capabilities of the aircraft you'll fly and some that you'll fly against. Knowing the specifications and performance abilities of your aircraft will allow you to fly the aircraft at its peak abilities. It's important to know what your plane is good at so that you can adjust your flying tactics accordingly.

Focke-Wulf Fw-190A.

Focke-Wulf Fw-190A

The Fw 190 has been considered by many to be the best German propeller-

driven fighter of the war due to its speed, impressive rate of roll, excellent responsiveness, and the ability to carry a variety of extremely powerful armaments and yet provide superior performance. Its biggest shortcoming was that its performance fell off significantly above 20,000 feet—where the high altitude Allied bombers earned their pay.

Kurt Tank designed the Fw 190 "Würger" (Butcher Bird) which has been described as an "easy to fly" airplane. The Fw 190 was very stable compared to the twitchy Bf 109 and was one of the first fighters to offer a clear view canopy for good all-around visibility.

The 190 sub type's basic armament included two 13 mm machine guns and four 20 mm cannons, making it a formidable weapon and a great bomber interceptor. The Sturmbock variant brought a 30 mm cannon and 21cm rockets to bear with devastating effect.

While fast, the Fw-190A isn't as fast as the P-51D and P-47D (and is equaled by the Spit IX). Although its climb rate is unexceptional, its turn rate is poor. Given these characteristics and its excellent firepower, the Fw 190 should be flown as a BnZ aircraft exclusively.

Strengths
- Fast, easy to fly, and stable
- Responsive high-speed handling
- Excellent roll rate
- Strong and able to sustain damage
- Air-cooled radial engine can take a lot of damage
- Heavy firepower
- Large ammo load
- Strong, wide landing gear
- Excellent visibility
- Maintains good performance even when heavily loaded with weapons

Weaknesses
- Poor turner
- Unexceptional climb rate
- Severe stall characteristics with very little to no warning
- Loses energy rapidly
- Poor zoom climber
- Tends to compress at high speeds

Empty/Max Weight & Dimensions

Weight:	7055 / 10,800 lbs (3200 / 4900 kg)
Span:	34'5.5" (10.49 m)
Length:	29 ft (8.84 m)
Engine(s):	BMW 801D-2 14-cyl air-cooled, 1700 hp
Fuel Capacity:	641 liter (141 Imperial gallons) tank under cockpit floor
Armament:	Two 13 mm MG131 machine guns in top cowling & four 20 mm MG 151 cannon (two in wing roots, and two outboard of landing gear); A-8/U11 carried one 550-lb bomb or four 110-lb bombs
Max Speed @ Altitude:	408 mph (653 km/h)
Ceiling:	37,400 ft (11,410 m)
Climb Rate:	2350 ft (717 m)/min
Range:	560 mi (900 km)

Hawker Hurricane I

Constructed of wood and canvas, the Hurricane was Britain's first truly modern fighter since World War I. The Hurricane entered service a year earlier than the Spitfire so it was in greater supply during the Battle of Britain. What isn't generally known by most casual WWII trivia buffs is that the Hurricane shot down far more German aircraft than the better-known Spitfire. With 14,000 Hurricanes built during the war, three-fifths of the British squads used them.

Considered by many to be the most versatile aircraft of the war, this very well-armed, easy to fly, maneuverable, solid and forgiving airplane lacked the Spitfire's glamour, and its performance. Although its top airspeed was only around

Hawker Hurricane I.

300 MPH, its simple construction allowed it accept damage quite well and its wide landing gear made it suitable for grass field operations. The Hurricane was basically the workhorse of the RAF (Royal Air Force).

Due to its slow speed and good maneuverability, the Hurricane can only be used as a TnB fighter (you can BnZ with it, but don't expect to Zoom away). However, that doesn't mean you shouldn't try and keep your airspeed up. Stay *relatively* low and stay fast and you'll do well.

Strengths
- Very forgiving
- Gentle stall
- Stable gun platform
- Very maneuverable below 20,000 feet
- Tight turn radius
- Eight .303 machine guns
- Wide, sturdy landing gear
- Can take a lot of damage (fabric-covered frame is easy to repair)

Weaknesses
- Poor acceleration and climb
- Rifle-caliber bullets not as destructive as larger rounds
- Carburetor causes engine to cut out under negative G loads
- Loses maneuverability above 20,000 feet.
- Relatively short range

Empty/Max Weight & Dimensions

Weight:	4670 / 6600 lbs (2118 / 2994 kg)
Span:	40' ft; (12.19 m)
Length:	32' ft; (9.75 m)
Engine(s):	Rolls-Royce Merlin III 12-cyl V liquid cooled, 1030 hp
Fuel Capacity:	97 Imperial gallons in two center tanks between wing spars and gravity tank in fuselage
Armament:	Eight .303 Browning machine guns w/334 rpg (rounds per gun)
Max Speed @ Altitude:	318 mph (512 km/h) @ 20,000 ft (6100m)
Ceiling:	36000 ft (10,980 m)
Climb Rate:	2520 ft (770 m)/min
Range:	460 mi (740 km)

Messerschmitt Bf 109E.

Messerschmitt Bf 109E

It's been reported that Willy Messerschmitt basically designed the 109 in 1934 by placing the largest most powerful engine he could find and mating it to the smallest possible fuselage with a thin wing. What he ended up with at that time was considered to be an ultramodern fighter that outclassed all fighter designs up until then. Extensively used during the Spanish Civil War (1936-1939), it proved to be both fast and agile.

The big, fuel injected, water-cooled V-12 powered Bf 109 Emil was used in the Battle of Britain in 1940. But its extremely narrow landing gear and massive propeller torque made the 109 tricky to take off and land with. According to some statistics, as many as five percent of all of the 109's destroyed during the war weren't shot down. They simply crashed while taking off or landing.

When the Focke-Wulf Fw 190 made its debut, some believed it should replace the 109, but many German aces (the *experten*) preferred the superior high-altitude performance of the 109 and refused to give it up.

The 109E isn't extremely fast and it only has a very short range, but it is considered to be a good turner. Its main attributes are good climb rate, and small plan form (making it a small target to shoot at). So if you're going to TnB with this airplane, make good use of its estimable climbing ability by using vertical maneuvers. The E sub type has pretty lethal armament for fighter eradication, but it isn't as good for bomber intercepts as other airplanes in the German arsenal.

Strengths
- Highly responsive
- Excellent acceleration

- Good climb rate
- Highly maneuverable
- Fuel-injected engine does not suffer from negative G cut-off
- Excellent high-altitude performance
- 20 mm cannon

Weaknesses
- Narrow, weak landing gear makes takeoff and landing tricky
- Heavy engine torque (swings hard to left on takeoff)
- Twitchy handling
- Heavy controls at high speeds
- Thin wing and light construction make it more fragile than others
- High wing loading makes steep dives and high-G pullouts dangerous
- Adding extra wing armament; degrades speed and maneuverability
- Cannon are slower than machine guns
- Even with cannon, too lightly armed to be an effective bomber interceptor
- Short range
- Relatively poor visibility from cockpit

Empty/Max Weight & Dimensions

Weight:	4189 / 5523 lbs (1900 / 2505 kg)
Span:	32'4.5" (9.87 m)
Length:	28'4" (8.64 m)
Engine(s):	Daimler-Benz DB601D 12-cyl V liquid cooled, 1050 hp
Fuel Capacity:	400 liters (88 Imperial gallons) in fuselage tank under pilot's seat
Armament:	Two 20 mm MG FF cannon w/60 r.p.g, & two 7.9 mm MG 17 machine guns w/1000 rpg E-1/B had racks for 4 110-lb bombs or 1 550-lb bomb
Max Speed @ Altitude:	342 mph (550 km/h)
Ceiling:	34,450 ft (10,500)
Climb Rate:	3100 ft (945 m)/min
Range:	410 mi (660 km)

Bf or Me?

Although you may have heard the Bf 109 referred to as Me 109 over the years, modern historians use the Bf designation exclusively. The Bf signified the company that the 109's designer Willy Messerschmitt worked for—the Bayrische Flugzeugwerke (Bavarian FlyingWorks). That's why it is not uncommon to see "Messerschmitt Bf 109" as the designation.

But the story behind the complicated naming convention is that the Bavarian FlyingWorks restructured in 1939 and changed its name to Messerschmitt A.G.. That's when the designation of the 109 was changed to Me 109. The first production version to carry this designation was the Me 109E— with which the Luftwaffe went to war in September of that same year. Although several Messerschmitt designs officially had the prefix "Me," the 109 is usually referred to as the Bf 109 today.

Messerschmitt Bf 109G

Because of the 109's excellent high altitude performance (and probably equally due to the Fw 190's lack of it), 109's were generally assigned to fly top cover while Fw-190 attacked the bombers. There were many more Bf 109 Gustav fighters produced (which flew from late 1942 until the end of the war) than their (relatively) less impressive Emil siblings.

That's easy to understand when you consider that the 109G is an all-around better version of the Emil. It's slightly faster than the Emil, has a slightly increased range, is armed heavier, and it turns a little better as well. It also retains the Emil's qualities— good climb rate, and small plan form. So make smart use of its superior climbing ability by using vertical maneuvers. The G-6 sub type's addition of a 30 mm cannon plus the 109's excellent high altitude performance makes it a good bomber interceptor.

Messerschmitt Bf 109G.

Strengths

- Highly responsive
- Excellent acceleration
- Very good climb rate
- Highly maneuverable (better than the Emil)
- Fuel-injected engine free from negative G cut-off
- Excellent high-altitude performance
- 30 mm cannon

Weaknesses

- Narrow, weak landing gear makes takeoff and landing tricky
- Heavy engine torque (swings hard to left on takeoff)
- Twitchy handling
- Heavy controls at high speeds
- Thin wing and light construction make more fragile than others
- High wing loading makes steep dives and high-G pullouts dangerous
- Adding extra wing armament degrades speed and maneuverability
- Short range (but better than E1)
- Relatively poor visibility from cockpit

Empty/Max Weight & Dimensions

Weight:	5880 / 7496 lbs (2667 / 3400 kg)
Span:	32'6.5" (9.92 m)
Length:	29'8" (9.04 m)
Engine(s):	Daimler-Benz DB605A V-12 liquid cooled, 1475 hp
Fuel Capacity:	400 liters (88 Imperial gallons) in fuselage tank under pilot's seat
Armament:	One 30 mm Mk 108 or one 20 mm MG 151 cannon firing through prop hub; two 13 mm MG 131 machine guns w/300 rpg above engine. Optional: two 20 mm MG 151 cannon w/150 rpg in pods under wings (pods add weight & drag). G-6/R2 can mount rack for four 110-lb bombs or one 550-lb bomb; G-6/R2 carried two WGr 21-rocket tubes.

Max Speed @ Altitude:	387 mph (623 km/h)
Ceiling:	38,500 ft (11,750 m)
Climb Rate:	3300 ft (1005 m)/min
Range:	450 mi (725 km); with belly tank, max. 615 mi (990 km) (Bf 109G can carry one 300-liter tank under fuselage, or one on each wing)

Note: *It's been reported that Schmued's Mustang design was inspired by a captured Bf 109. Compare it to the 109 Emil and see if you see the similarities. The first Mk I model arrived in July 1942 to Europe. The British quickly replaced the original Packard Allison engine with the Rolls-Royce Merlin, which increased its high altitude performance (which became known as the P-51B). (Its liquid-cooled engine and low fuselage-mounted radiator made it vulnerable to ground fire for a ground-attack aircraft, so those plans were scrapped.)*

North American P-51D Mustang

Designed by a German (Edgar Schmued) and first built for the British, the Mustang had an unusual beginning but it quickly became one of the best propeller-driven American fighters of the war. In 1940, the British asked for a replacement for the P-40, but there were none available. North American offered to build another aircraft and based on the 120-day prototype stipulation imposed by the British, the first metal stressed-skin prototype was completed in 117 days.

Although it was originally used as a low-level recon and tactical aircraft (ground attack), and the US used it as a dive bomber (named the A-36 Invader dive bomber), the Mustang (so dubbed by the British Purchasing Commission) eventually produced nearly 1/2 the kills in Europe. In fact on October 12, 1944, Chuck Yeager flew

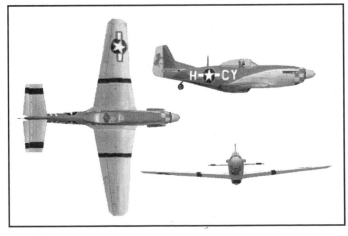

North American P-51D Mustang.

the P-51 to Bremen, Germany and made five kills in one day! The very first pilot to become an "Ace" in a day.

The P-51 was the supreme long-range fighter of the war. The combination of the highly efficient Laminar flow wing (increased efficiency, speed, and range by moving the thickest part of the airfoil shape rearward), slender fuselage, and the supercharged Rolls-Royce Merlin V-12, the Mustang was fast and agile. It had everything needed at the time—speed, maneuverability, and most importantly range. With its twin wing tanks, and auxiliary tank behind the cockpit and optional drop tanks, the P-51 could carry about 8 hours of fuel.

Up until that point P-38s and P-47s could only escort bombers part way on their raids into the heart of Germany. When Reichsmarshall Hermann Goering saw the first P-51s escorting bombers over Berlin, he realized that Germany had lost the war.

"The P-51 would do for eight hours what a Spitfire would do for 45 minutes. Range, long range—the P-51 allowed us to take the fight right into the homeland of Germany," reported Brig. General Chuck Yeager, USAF, 13 kills.

To give you an idea of the effect of the Laminar flow wing, the P-51D is 30-40 mph faster using the same engine as the Spitfire. The drawbacks to this wing design are it won't turn as well, and it's less forgiving. But due to the thickness of the wing, it allows you to carry more fuel, and it does have a combat flaps setting to minimize its turning deficit.

The P-51D will turn fairly well for short stints if you keep its speed up and make use of the combat flaps. However, if you don't make the kill right away and get stuck in a turning fight you're in for trouble. The Mustang turns terribly at low speeds. Most pilots find the P-51D to be the premiere BnZ plane; make use of the Pony's speed and you'll see why it has such a great combat record.

Strengths
- Excellent acceleration
- Very fast
- Good maneuverability (combat flaps)
- Enormous range
- Heavy firepower (six .50-caliber guns)
- Excellent pilot visibility

Weaknesses
- Very sensitive to sudden throttle application (can cause severe swing or rollover on takeoff, or induce spin)

- Treacherous handling with aft fuselage tank full
- Liquid cooling increases engine vulnerability to small arms fire
- Not as forgiving as some other planes (sudden stall)

Empty/Max Weight & Dimensions

Weight:	7125 / 11,600 lbs (3230 / 5206 kg)
Span:	37' .25" (11.29 m)
Length:	32'2.5" (9.81 m)
Engine(s):	Rolls-Royce/ Packard V-1650-7 12-cyl V liquid-cooled, 1590 hp
Fuel Capacity:	184 gallons in wing tanks and 85 gallons in fuselage behind pilot
Armament:	6 .50-cal Browning machine guns w/270 rpg (ob&ctr pairs) & 400 r.p.g (ib pair); alt config: I 4 .50s w/400 rpg and two 500 or 1000-lb bombs or six 5-in. rockets
Max Speed @ Altitude:	437 mph (703 km/h)
Ceiling:	41,900 ft (12,780 m)
Climb Rate:	17.3475 ft (1060 m)/min.
Range:	1300 mi (2092 km); with drop tanks, 2080 mi. (3347 km)

Republic P-47D Thunderbolt

Affectionately known as the "Jug" (short for Juggernaut), the P-47 Thunderbolt was the biggest, heaviest fighter of the war. First entering combat in April 1943, it bore the brunt of the USAAF's fight in Europe until the longer-range Mustang appeared. Although it was designed as a high altitude interceptor, the P-47 was used in multiple roles—which explains why it was produced in larger numbers than any other fighter in American history.

The P-47 continued to be the Allied fighter-bomber of choice due to its massive and durable air-cooled radial engine that made it less susceptible to ground fire than the P-51's lower fuselage-mounted radiator. Nothing could out-dive a Thunderbolt (it's been said that it dives like its namesake), and its less-than-stellar rate of climb improved dramatically when water injection and a massive "paddle-blade" prop was added in later models.

The Jug was fast, tough, had a phenomenal roll rate, and eight (count 'em!) .50 caliber machine guns. For all its weight, power, and performance, however

it was a forgiving airplane to fly. All of which no doubt helped its pilots achieve their outstanding combat record of only one lost for every 5 aircraft destroyed. P-47's destroyed 3700 German aircraft and ruined an additional 3300 destroyed on the ground.

Republic P-47D Thunderbolt.

The Jug has excellent high altitude performance, but you have to keep your speed up. Other aircraft will out perform it at lower altitudes in all areas except for lethality (the eight .50's are *very* deadly), speed and roll rate—in other words strictly BnZ or you're dead. While its ability to withstand damage makes it a good choice for close air-support aircraft, remember to avoid picking fights with fighters—especially at low altitude.

Besides its dismal turn performance, other drawbacks are similar to other very large-engine-equipped airplanes. They're more difficult to fly due to torque issues, and you have to adjust trim with power changes because your airspeed will change quite quickly from the massive engine.

Strengths
- Fast
- Can sustain massive damage
- Impressive roll rate
- Excellent dive rate
- Eight .50-caliber guns
- Good ammo load
- Great ground-attack fighter-bomber
- Excellent high altitude performance

Weaknesses
- Mediocre rate of climb
- Limited rearward visibility through "razorback" canopy

- Poor turner
- Poor zoom climb
- Bleeds energy like crazy
- Range not as good as the Mustang
- Mediocre low altitude performance

Empty/Max Weight & Dimensions

Weight:	10,700 / 19,400 lbs (4853 / 8800 kg)
Span:	40'9.25" (12.4 m)
Length:	36'1.25" (11.03 m)
Engine(s):	Pratt & Whitney R-2800-59 Double Wasp 18-cyl radial air-cooled, 2300 hp
Fuel Capacity:	270 gallon fuselage tank and 100 gallon auxiliary tank under pilot's seat
Armament:	6 or 8 .50 Browning machine guns w/267 or 425 rpg and one 500-lb bomb. Late config.: same guns + two 1000-lb or three 500-lb bombs or ten 5-in rockets
Max Speed @ Altitude:	428 mph (689 km/h)
Ceiling:	42,000 ft (12,810 m)
Climb Rate:	2750 ft (840 m)/min.
Range:	1000 mi (1610 km); with drop tanks, 1900 mi (3057 km)

Supermarine Spitfire Mk I

Based on Reginald Mitchell's brilliant Supermarine floatplane (Schneider Trophy Seaplane winner three consecutive years—1927, 1929, and 1931 as the world's fastest floatplanes) the Spitfire Mk I came on to the scene just in time for the Battle of Britain. Housing a powerful Rolls-Royce Merlin V-12 in its all-metal airframe with its trademark elliptical wing, the Spitfire Mk I had speed, agility, and a serious punch (from its eight machine guns) by all 1940 standards. To this day the Spit I is considered the equal of (and some say superior of) the Messerschmitt Bf 109E—its adversary in the Battle of Britain.

In June 1938, Squadron 19 was first to receive the Spitfire. By September 1939 nine squads were flying Spits. The Spitfire was developed continuously throughout the war with some 24 versions. Most pilots who flew the Spitfire described it as a machine that somehow became an extension of the pilot's

nerves and muscles. Which is perfectly understandable considering the Spits small size—pilots almost literally wore the airplane like a glove instead of merely sitting inside of it.

The light, thin ellipse shaped wing has been attributed to giving the Spitfire its excellent maneuverability, but few people realized how strong it was too. This elegant wing could sustain stresses in excess of 10 Gs. One of the biggest problems you'll encounter with the Spit's performance is not getting it to turn, but rather keeping yourself from blacking out while it preforms its turns!

Although the eight .303 caliber machine guns had fair killing power, the duration of the ammo load was quite short. The other drawback was the relatively narrow undercarriage combined with the powerful torque of the Merlin engine, which made takeoffs and landings a handful.

Note: *A little known fact is that there were a few American pilots who flew Spitfires during the early days of the war. Well, actually ex-Americans—they had to give up their U.S. citizenship in order to join the RAF.*

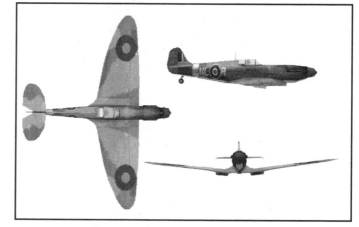

Supermarine Spitfire Mk I.

Strengths
- Pleasant to fly
- Tight turning radius
- Retains energy well
- Decent rate of climb
- Eight .303 machine guns
- Good visibility through canopy

Weaknesses
- Engine cut out under negative G's
- Rifle-caliber bullets not as destructive as larger rounds

- Small ammo load
- Limited range
- Controls very heavy at high speeds

Empty/Max Weight & Dimensions

Weight:	4810 / 5784 lbs (2182 / 2624 kg)
Span:	36' 10" (11.23 m)
Length:	29' 11" (9.12 m)
Engine(s):	Rolls-Royce Merlin III 12-cyl V liquid cooled, 1030 hp
Fuel Capacity:	85 Imperial gallons in two fuselage tanks behind pilot's seat
Armament:	Eight Browning .303 machine guns w/300 rpg
Max Speed @ Altitude:	365 mph (587 km/h)
Ceiling:	34,000 ft (10,370 m)
Climb Rate:	2530 ft (770 m)/min
Range:	395 mi (635 km)

Supermarine Spitfire Mk IX

Two major revisions of the original Spitfire were the 1440-hp Mark V, of which some 6464 were produced in 1941-1942, and the Mk IX. The Mk IX was quickly designed as a response to the newly emerging Focke-Wulf 190. The 14-cylinder Fw 190 engine outclassed the Spit V quite handily.

The high-altitude version of the Mk IX was essentially a Mk V with a 1710-hp Merlin 70 engine, capable of more than 400 mph. From 1942 to 1944, 5665 Mk IXs were built. Pilots have said that the Mk IX was the best Spitfire of all time. That's quite a compliment when you consider that with more than 40 variations in its line, the Spitfire was produced in the largest production numbers in British history and it was used in every British conflict from Dunkirk to Burma, to New Guinea.

RAF pilots adored the Spitfire and the enemy admired it as well. When Adolph Galland was asked what kind of airplanes he would like, he responded, "I should like a squadron of Spitfires."

Using the classic "big engine in light airframe" motif (as opposed to the Mustang's "heavy airframe with the right size engine" design philosophy), the Mk IX was faster with a slightly longer range, and had better armament than the Mk I. The real world Spitfire's long nose inhibited pilots' view forward

during landing. This required the pilots to side-slip it in during landing and to perform S-turns while taxiing. Overall, the Spitfire Mk IX handles as well as its siblings—it's well balanced and will do what's required of it with authority and grace.

Supermarine Spitfire Mk IX .

Strengths

- Pleasant to fly
- Tight turning radius
- Retains energy well
- Decent rate of climb
- Better armament than Mk I
- Good visibility through canopy

Weaknesses

- Small ammo load
- Limited range
- Controls very heavy at high speeds

Empty/Max Weight & Dimensions

Weight:	5800 / 7500 lbs (2636 / 3409 kg)
Span:	36' 10" (11.23 m)
Length:	31' 4" (9.55 m)
Engine(s):	Rolls-Royce Merlin 70 12-cyl V liquid cooled, 1710 hp
Fuel Capacity:	85 Imperial gallons in two fuselage tanks behind pilot's seat
Armament:	Two 20 mm Hispano cannons with 120 rpg, and four Browning .303 machine guns with 350 rpg
Max Speed @ Altitude:	408 mph (656 km/h)
Ceiling:	44,000 ft (13,420 m)
Climb Rate:	2985 ft (909 m)/min
Range:	434 mi (698 km)

Chapter Eight

Intermediate Combat Training

Now that we've covered the basics, let's move on to some intermediate concepts. In this chapter we'll begin by discussing how to navigate the Microsoft Combat Flight Simulator world. Then we'll discuss missions, mission tactics and strategies, and finish up with bombing procedures and techniques.

Navigation

Being the world's best dogfighter is worthless unless he can find his mission targets. That's why learning to navigate is very important. While you can always figure out where you are and where you're heading by using the fold-out map included in Combat Flight Simulator in conjunction with your airplane's directional gyro, this method does require some interpolation (known as *pilotage*) along with many course corrections.

As Combat Flight Simulator covers a historic time period, it models the real world like its cousin Flight Simulator 98. Because the virtual world you'll be flying within is based on historical information and atlas data, you can use real-world navigation techniques to get where you need to be. But if air combat is your main interest and learning aviation navigation isn't a main priority, Combat Flight Simulator offers some features that can relieve you of many of the more complicated duties. We'll talk more about this next.

Waypoints

A waypoint is a reference point. It can be a bridge on a river or a point in space 15,000 feet in the air. If you think of waypoints as flight path markers, you'll begin to understand their function. To

> **Note:** Combat Flight Simulator's online map (select it from the Views menu or from the pull-down menu with a right mouse click or by pressing Shift +]) for navigation is limited mainly to locating landmarks or providing general directions.

Waypnt: 6.2 km at 161

Waypoint information is displayed as text and viewed via the waypoint indicator on the Tactical Display.

simplify your workload in Combat Flight Simulator, waypoint information is presented on the Tactical Display.

Using the Tactical Display for Navigation

We covered the Tactical Display and its radarlike functions in Chapter Six. The Tactical Display also presents waypoint information in two forms—in text, and in the form of a radial line that revolves around your virtual representation (recall the yellow cross at the center of the display) and resembles clock hands.

Text waypoint information is fairly straightforward. It's presented just below the Tactical Display, and it clearly provides the heading and distance to your waypoint. Merely turn to the indicated heading and you're headed where you need to go.

Note: *When airplanes turn, they don't just rotate—they move in arcs. Because the waypoint display reflects the correct heading information at any given moment (regardless of your current heading), by the time you turn the airplane, the indicated waypoint heading may read quite differently from what it read when you first started the turn.*

This waypoint line/indicator on the Tactical Display always aims you toward your next waypoint. When the line is colored blue, it indicates that your present course is greater than +/- 10 degrees of the course that will take you directly to the next waypoint. When the line turns green, it indicates that you are within +/- 10 degrees of the waypoint heading.

The method of working with the waypoint line/indicator is simple—just turn in the direction that the line is pointing and stop turning when it centers in the 12:00 upright position. As long as you keep that line centered, you'll get to your next waypoint.

The closer you are to the waypoint, the less chance a heading correction is required. The reason: The further away you are from the waypoint, the greater the distance between directional radials.

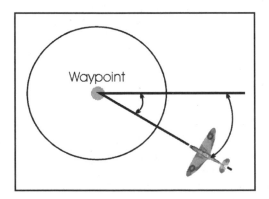

Waypoint

Because directional radials emanate from a single point, the farther you are away from the point of origin, the greater the distance between radials.

Cutting to the Chase

A fighter pilot once described the fighter jock business as "hours and hours of boredom interspersed by moments of sheer terror." It's reasonable to assume that a large part of the "hours of boredom" this insightful aviator referred to dealt with navigating and flying toward his target or rendezvous point.

Fortunately, Combat Flight Simulator offers two features that will help minimize this less interesting aspect and maximize the most exciting part—combat. And we're not talking about Quick Combat mode, but rather the Simulation Rate feature and the Skip to the Next Action feature.

Note: *In Free Flight mode, Quick Combat mode, and in other modes when enemy aircraft are nearby, waypoint text and the waypoint line/indicator is not displayed on the Tactical Display.*

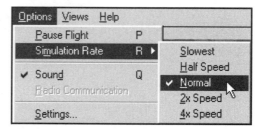

Access the Simulation Rate feature from the Options menu selection.

Simulation Rates

By increasing Combat Flight Simulator's simulation rate, you're essentially compressing time. To access this feature, use one of two methods.

1. Press the R key and then either the = (Equal Sign) or - (Hyphen) key to increase or decrease the simulation rate respectively. You have the ability to change the simulation rate to 0.25x, 0.5x, 1x, 2x and 4x the normal simulation rate.

Tip: *To view the current simulation rate setting, go to Options/Simulation Rate on the menu, a check mark indicates the current rate.*

2. Click Options on the menu bar and select Simulation Rate, and then choose the desired rate factor from the sub menu.

To return back to 1x rate without using the menu method above, you'll need to first press the R key again, if you've done anything other than change the rate, and then press the appropriate = (Equal Sign) or - (Hyphen) key to change it back to 1x. Unfortunately, you can only view the Simulation rate setting can from the menu under Options; Simulation Rate. So unless you count

> **Tip:** *While it's not of much use for navigation purposes, changing to a slower simulation rate can make air-combat maneuvering easier to learn.*

and keep track of how many times you press the = (Equal Sign) or - (Hyphen) key and press the opposite key an equal number of times, you might as well just use the menu to adjust the simulation rate back to 1x.

The rate feature allows you to cover long distances in a fraction of the time it would normally take. Some of the pitfalls of time compression are:

> **Tip:** *Keep an eye on the waypoint information on the Tactical Display. If it disappears, it means a bandit is near.*

- Your control inputs will become overexaggerated at higher time-compression rates by many times. This makes it impossible to fly with any precision.

- Keep up your detection scan. Time is passing so quickly that it won't take long for an aircraft to close in on you—so spotting "dots" in the distance becomes even more crucial. On the other hand, missing dots (read: *opportunities*) can be wasteful as well—you may miss some opportunities to increase your kill tally!

- Don't forget to return the simulation rate back to 1x when you go into combat or you may end up a statistic before you even realize it.

Skipping to the Action

If flying waypoint-to-waypoint, even with time compression enabled, is too tedious (and that's totally understandable), try using the Skip to the Next Action feature. Pressing the X key will transport you to the next waypoint or action area unless the following conditions exist:

- You currently have bandits in the vicinity.
- You've already reached your last waypoint (where it will end the mission instead).
- You are still on the ground (you must take off first).
- You are flying below 120 MPH (or 200 km/h) after takeoff.
- You are flying below 150 feet (or 50 meters) AGL.

Navigation Tips

Here are some final navigation tips that may help:

- The top of the online map always points in the same direction you are facing.

- Compass directions are 360 (north), 90 (east), 180 (south), and 270 (west).
- Use your rudder for minor course corrections.
- Climb at the best Climb Rate airspeed numbers found in the Pilot's Manual. Pitch the nose of your aircraft to control your airspeed and let your rate of climb fall where it may. The most important thing is to maintain your best rate of climb airspeed.
- Waypoints are not carved in stone. As pilot-in-command, you can fly the mission as you see fit. If the assigned altitude seems too low to you, by all means climb.
- Don't obsess with flying the waypoints. It's unlikely that the enemy is flying directly on your flight path. Keep scanning the skies (and your Tactical Display, if you use it) for bogeys.

Mission Types

Now that you know how to get to where you've been ordered, let's discuss what you're supposed to do when you get there. More specifically, let's look at the different missions you'll be flying in Combat Flight Simulator plus some tips and tactics for each.

Sweep

A fighter sweep (also known as a *Rodeo* by American pilots, *Free Chase* by British pilots, and *Freie Jagd* by German pilots in WWII) is an offensive mission where you're sent out to a certain area and are told to take out anything flying. (Anything that the enemy is flying, of course!) These missions are similar to intercept missions, the main difference being that in intercepts you know something is out there and you usually have a specific area to protect.

With fighter sweeps you have much more freedom to plan your attack path, so take advantage of this. Fight your fight, and do it in the manner that will exploit your aircraft's strong points. There's no pressing need to dive right in, so plan your attacks. As always, gain altitude and position if you can before beginning your attack.

Some fighter sweep tips: During the battle, keep an eye out for enemy reinforcements—especially over enemy territory—they can ruin your day fast. Note the way home to friendly territory (and friendly Ack) as you attack. If things get too hot in the kitchen and you have to bug out quickly, you can't rely on the kindness of the enemy to help you out—unless you want out in a parachute.

From a historical and tactical perspective, Spitfires were regularly sent on fighter sweeps over France until April 1943. They are generally characterized as ineffective. Although fighter sweeps are usually the mission of choice for fighter pilots, strategically they're problematic because they waste fuel and thin out your air power if you're covering a lot of territory.

Ironically, the concept behind the fighter sweep is to "thin out" the opposing force's aircraft. Fighter sweeps used in conjunction with escort missions are useful, but fighter sweeps alone—as the British in 1943 discovered—are ineffective. Fighter sweeps for defensive purposes are even less effective. To quote a general combat axiom, "he who attempts to protect everything, protects nothing."

When one lacks the air power to fill the sky with fighters, using fighter sweeps for defensive purposes is not only inefficient, but it also leaves huge gaps for the enemy to slip through. This is precisely what the British faced during the Battle of Britain.

Intercept

An intercept mission (or more formally, *Ground Alert Intercept*) is defensive in nature. Essentially your orders are to prevent the enemy from completing his mission or to get killed trying. But if you have an air-based asset, you sometimes have a third option—keeping the invaders busy until the air-based asset can get away, perform its mission, or until (and if) help arrives. In any case, you're now faced with time and position variables that will generally tend to complicate your mission.

Tip: *Before beginning any intercept, note your orientation to the direction of what it is you're protecting. This will not only help you keep track of where you want to be, but also where the bandits are headed. This will help you identify and locate stragglers and those aircraft that got through.*

Due to the nature of intercept missions, you have an incentive to reach your targets as soon as possible. The attackers are moving toward your asset, so you want to engage them as far away from your asset as possible, thereby creating a sort of safety cushion. If any of the invaders get through, this cushion will buy you additional time and space to recover and attack.

If you need to attack quickly (from little advance warning), there's a drawback: being forced to attack before you're really ready (stored enough E, for example). With enough advance warning, you may have a window of time to grab some E, so use it wisely.

One common mistake with intercepts is concentrating too much on gaining altitude at the expense of worrying about your airspeed. This allows you to climb high, but leaves you slow when the attack starts—you know by now you're not in a good position if the enemy is higher and faster. The solution is to reduce your climb angle as you get closer to the enemy. Although this will reduce your ultimate altitude, you'll at least have some speed to maneuver. It's not a perfect solution, but it is the lesser of two evils.

Another tip is not to take any bandits head-on if you can help it. Ideally, of course, you want to place your intercepting flight between the bandits and their target, but it isn't always the best option. Remember, you

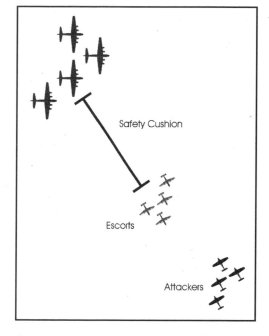

Flying out to meet all threats will create a small safety cushion between the attackers and their target.

have an advantage over your enemies—you know where they're headed. This allows you to plan your intercept point and direction.

If you intercept the incoming raiders far enough away from the assets you're protecting, one strategy is to let them fly by you and then tuck in behind them as they make a run for their target. Recall this is what's known as a *stern-conversion tactical intercept*, and it'll likely net you a tail shot at them. Not only does this work well for shooting them, but it can also help you keep track of who you got to break off the attack run. If you can get any of the raiders to break off their attack run, it will buy you more time.

There are two types of attacks that intercepts are designed to defend against. The first, the penetration attack (what's often referred to today as a *surgical strike*), occurs when a small number of aircraft (as few as a single fighter or fighter-bomber) tries to evade detection, strikes its target, and egresses as unnoticed as when it came in.

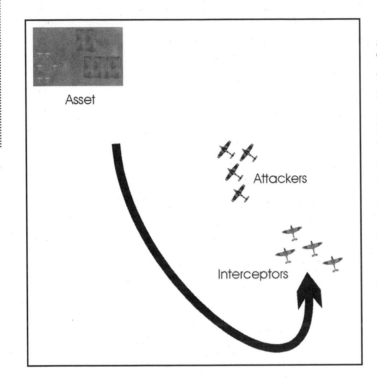

Asset

Attackers

Interceptors

Letting attackers fly by so you can then tuck in behind them will allow for tail shots.

The second type of attack is the massed attack. The classic example of this type of attack is when a large number of bombers use altitude, speed or both to help them strike their target. This brute-force attack uses active defenses such as escorts or self-defense gunners, as well as raw numbers, to overwhelm the enemy.

Naturally, if the invaders you're sent to intercept are bombers, attacking them from their stern can be a bad idca. We'll see why in a minute, but let's first take a look at the intercept from historical and tactical perspectives.

During the Battle of Britain, the British had the advantage of radar. The combination of that technological marvel and the Observer Corps (observer personnel) gave them 1 to 1-1/2 hours advance notice of approaching Luftwaffe attacks.

Although the German Luftwaffe outnumbered British aircraft during the Battle of Britain (at ratios as high as 10:1), the strategy afforded by Ground Alert Intercepts allowed the British to maximize their air power. Instead of sending out massive defensive sweeps, radar and observer position information allowed them to send fighters and pilots not only to where they were needed, but also at the last minute (which helped conserve fuel).

Attacking Bombers

Make no mistake about it—attacking bombers can be hazardous duty. Whether they're fighter-bombers or heavy/medium bombers, you may have to deal with

two forms of their defense—their escorts and their gunners. While each is equally dangerous, on another level there are ways you can reduce your risk when attacking either.

> **Tip:** *Bombers generally are large, slow, and have poor maneuvering capabilities. This affords you the time to plan your attacks better. Lumbering bombers can't employ evasive maneuvers like fighters can.*

Reducing Escorts

One way to reduce the danger when attacking bombers is by reducing their escorts. You accomplish this by shooting them down or drawing them away from their charges. While slugging it out with other fighters appeals to the fighter pilot who loves to dogfight, every minute you delay in shooting down or diverting the bombers, the closer they get to their target—which subsequently reduces the amount of time you have to execute your mission.

The decision of whether to engage the escort or the bombers first is based on the proximity of the the bombers to their target. If you have enough advanced notice and are able to meet the bombers far from their target and their escort has strategically worked its way between you and the bomber group, by all means go after the escort (but be sure you save some ammo for your mission!). Escorts generally make nuisances of themselves later on, so it's always best to get them out of the way if you have the time and ammo.

On the other hand, if you completely ignore the escorts, they can potentially ruin your afternoon. In that light, destroy the escorts if you have the opportunity, but only if it won't take too long or draw you too far away from your mission objective. Most of the time you can just dive in and shoot the bombers and you won't have to worry about their escorts unless they get on your tail.

Attacking Heavy and Medium Bombers

By now you know that a tail shot at any aircraft gives you the least number of computational problems. That's because you don't need to pull much lead (if any) to hit it. Furthermore, bombers are relatively slow compared to your sleek fighter, so lining up on a bomber's six is easy work. Unfortunately, bomber designers realized this too (although it was only after the first bombers took heavy casualties) and began adding defensive guns to bombers with the biggest and most maneuverable ones in the tail—this proportionally reduced the appeal of the stern attack.

A rear gunner can easily target a stern attacking aircraft because the attacker is moving straight into his line of fire. All of the heavy and medium bombers modeled in Combat Flight Simulator, except for the Mosquito, have tail gunners. This means you should try and attack bombers from some other angle than from directly behind. This of course causes deflection-shooting problems for you again—but on the upside, it complicates the enemy gunner's chances of making a direct hit. Although there are several ways to attack bombers, there are only a couple that are really advantageous: the side attacks and the vertical attacks. In order to understand why, we first need to take a look at the stern attack and its drawbacks.

Stern Attack

As we've noted, the simplest and yet most dangerous attack against a bomber is the stern attack. It's the simplest because it doesn't require complex deflection shooting. While the stern attack is used against fighters (because they don't have rear gunners), it's not generally recommended for use against bombers due to the extreme danger presented by the rear-gunner.

Side Attacks

A much better angle of attack is the side attack. Side attacks are generally broken down into high and low variations with front and front-and-rear bias.

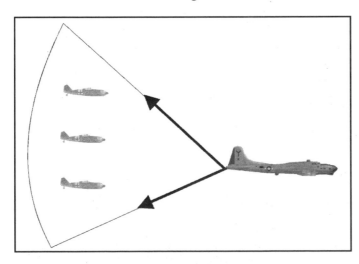

We don't recommend the stern attack against bombers due to the extreme danger presented by the rear-gunner.

The high attacks are preferable because they allow you to maintain an E advantage over your target(s), but the low side attack is advantageous (regardless of the inherent E disadvantage) if the bomber does not have a lower ball turret gunner.

The trick to each of these side attacks is proficiency with deflection shooting. To your advantage, bombers will generally fly straight and level, so all deflection problems are created by *your* relative flight path. The main problem to watch for is losing your SA. If you do, you can't maneuver your aircraft ahead to the next attack position to begin your attack run once again.

The high side attack is generally more effective simply because it begins from a high position above the target (1200 yards or more). Your E advantage over the bombers allows you

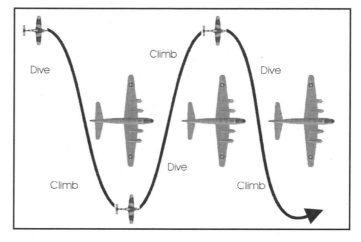

The high side attack is generally the most effective side attack against bombers.

to zoom climb after the attack so you can reposition yourself for the next attack run.

On the other hand, the low side attack doesn't require as much of an altitude advantage (only 400-600 yards). In a low side attack you first dive below the bomber and attack as you climb upwards. This attack is less desirable than its high-side cousin because your attack speed is reduced as you climb toward your target.

Either side attack will place you into firing position without you needlessly becoming target practice for the bomber's rear gunners. As previously noted, this approach gives enemy gunners deflection-shooting headaches. The side attack quickly brings you into position for a full deflection shot at the side of the enemy bomber. But as you hold your course, the deflection angle decreases to the point where a full stern attack is possible. (This is known as *homing*.) Therefore end the attack before the one-quarter deflection angle is reached by breaking away beneath the enemy.

Vertical Attack

The vertical attack is similar to the vertical BnZ attacks discussed earlier, so they share the same advantages. You shoot at your target's widest cross sections— bigger targets are easier to hit, and your target's maneuvering options are limited. But perhaps the biggest advantage with this attack is that you'll likely have to deal with only one or two of the bomber's gunners at the same time.

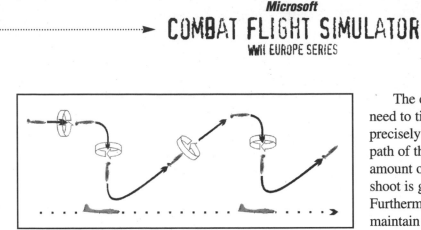

Because of its similarity to vertical BnZ fighter attacks, the vertical bomber attack shares the same advantages.

The drawbacks? You need to time your dive precisely ahead of the flight path of the bomber, and the amount of time you have to shoot is greatly reduced. Furthermore, you'll need to maintain a relatively high speed in order to reposition yourself ahead of the moving bombers for subsequent attacks. However, with the E advantage you'll start with (in combination with the slow relative speeds of bombers), it shouldn't be too much of a problem for you.

Opposite Attack

The opposite attack is made against the front end of the bomber. It often includes a vertical component. (In other words, it's a slashing head-on attack to the front of the bomber.) Like the stern attack, the advantage of the opposite attack is that it requires very little deflection shooting skill because the approach to the enemy bombers is nearly from dead ahead. But as we've seen with the stern attack, this also has its disadvantages.

First and foremost among these drawbacks are the Chin gunners and Forward gunners. Second, the high rate of closure between your aircraft and the bomber leaves very little time for lining up a shot. In addition, once you've made your pass it takes a long time to turn back and regain speed again to set up another pass. Therefore, in most cases consider using the opposite attack for an initial attack pass, and then shifting to one of the others for subsequent passes.

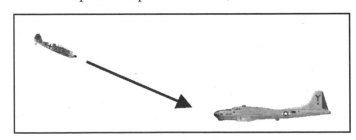

Although it requires very little deflection shooting skill, the opposite attack pits you against Chin and Forward gunners.

Attacking Fighter-Bombers

When attacking fighter-bombers, one generally uses the same tactics already outlined for heavy and medium bombers. It's important to note, however, that fighter-bombers maneuver better than their heavier cousins. On the other hand, they don't have lower ball-gun turrets, and they often go on missions without escorts. (If escorts are present, you need to draw them away or do away with them if they become pests.)

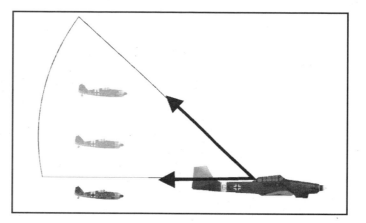

Attack fighter-bombers from below and behind because their rear gunners are generally unable to shoot below their rear stabilizers.

Once you get the escorts out of your hair (or you figure you can ignore them long enough to attack the fighter-bombers), attack from below and behind. Without a ball turret, their rear gunner is unable to shoot below the rear stabilizers (it will also conceal your position as well if you reach this prime location undetected). This means you can fire on them with a tail shot from a position of relative safety. But watch out if the enemy begins to climb or roll—this usually indicates an attempt by the rear gunner to gain a shot at you.

CAP

The CAP or Combat Air Patrol is kind of a cross between a sweep and an intercept. It's like a sweep because your mission is to shoot down as many enemy aircraft as possible, and it's also like an intercept because you're defending something on the ground. The difference is that in a CAP mission, you patrol (hence the name) a specific area of airspace and stay there as long as you have fuel, ammo, or the ability to do so.

Because of the similarities of a CAP mission to the sweep and intercept, all of the tactics covered thus far will help you achieve your goals. Nevertheless, the single most important thing to remember is that you are on patrol, so don't get drawn away from your patrol zone. The enemy will do anything and everything within its power to get you to move from the area you are protecting, so beware.

Escort

Your job as an escort is to make sure that whatever you're escorting stays in the air so it's able to complete its mission. Essentially you're a flying bodyguard. The problems you'll encounter as an escort are very similar to the intercept missions and CAP. The only differences: the area of airspace you're patrolling is moving, and the asset you're protecting is flying.

You do have the advantage of having relatively more time to prepare for an attack. And your main advantage is that you're not likely to become the enemy's primary target.

Basically, the options open to you are the same as those we've discussed for intercept missions: kill the enemy, keep them busy, or die trying. There are four general groupings from which to carry out an escort mission—close escort, detached escort, remote escort, and reception escort. As you might suspect, the difference between each is based on the proximity to your charges, but also where or more precisely *when* the escorting begins.

The basic characteristics of each are as follows. A close escort is the type that most of us visualize when hearing the term. Fighters flying side-by-side alongside a group of bombers on their way to target, for example, is one. A detached escort is similar, except that there's a greater distance from the bombers (to continue with our example). A classic example is a group of fighters ranging ahead of the group of bombers they're protecting, forming a sort of defensive screen. (Detached escorts don't need to range ahead of their charges. Their positions can be anywhere around the asset being protected.)

Resembling a fighter sweep in that they may not appear to be even associated with the escort charges, the remote escort is sent out in advance to meet the main group at a specific time and place. Their job is to clear the airspace in preparation for the arrival of the main strike force (again, using our bomber group example).

Just as with remote escorts, reception escorts are timed to meet the main group at some point during their mission. The main difference is reception escorts are assigned to meet the group during their last leg of the mission. The theory behind the need for this type of escort is that all of the escorts by this time may be low on fuel and ammo, so these *fresh* escorts can take over and help the group make it home with minimal enemy intervention.

Soon after the Japanese attack on Pearl Harbor, when the U.S. officially joined the war, the Allies began around-the-clock bombing of Germany's industrial base. The British would bomb during the night generally using penetration attack tactics, while the Americans used precision daylight bombing in massed attacks.

Tip: *Although fighter sweeps are considered ineffective by themselves, when they're integrated as part of a remote escort, they prove to be extremely effective.*

The way in which these various types of escort duty worked during the daylight massed attacks went something like this. Groups of Allied bombers would take off on missions staggered throughout the day. An individual group of bombers would leave an hour earlier than their assigned P-51 escorts. (Mustangs, being much faster, could catch up quite easily.)

Note: *In the Eighth Air Force, a heavy bomber "group" would send 18 to 36 aircraft on a mission (the larger number later in the war). A fighter group would typically send as many as 70 fighters along for escort duty (or even more aircraft for a maximum effort, but 48 was the more common number).*

The Mustangs and bombers would meet over the Dutch or German borders, where they'd relieve the strike group's P-38 and P-47 escorts—or both. The Mustangs would then take the bombers all the way in, and part way out of Germany. On the way back to England, other Allied aircraft would meet the returning (and many times damaged) bombers and escort them home.

For the most part, the biggest disadvantage with escorting is being "tied" to your flying asset. Obviously this impacts your ability to take the fight to the enemy. If you go off to meet the enemy, you leave your asset(s) unprotected and forced to fend for themselves. So how do we deal with this?

First, take up a good starting position. Let's say we are assigned to escort bombers. The best starting patrol position is above and ahead of the bombers if you have no idea where the intercepting fighters will be coming from. If you *do* know the direction of the enemy attack (such as when flying along an enemy border), place your escort flight slightly in the direction you expect an attack from.

Because attacking fighters must get close to the bombers to shoot at them, from this high vantage point you are able to see nearly every area around the bombers. Plus, by being stationed in front of the group you are able to see ahead and aren't in a disadvantageous position. The time it will take to reach the bombers is proportionately reduced by the bomber's forward-flight velocity.

One problem you'll have to tackle: fighters are much faster than the lumbering bombers. One solution is simply to fly slower, although this will impair your fighters' fighting ability. The best solution is to fly a zigzag

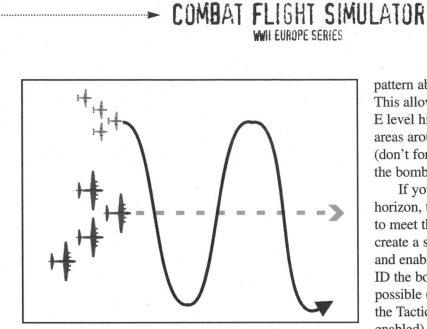

Flying a zigzag pattern is the best solution for dealing with the speed differential between fighters and bombers.

pattern above the bombers. This allows you to keep your E level high and to see all areas around the bombers (don't forget to look below the bombers in your scans).

If you detect dots on the horizon, take your flight out to meet them. This will create a small safety cushion and enable you to visually ID the bogeys as soon as possible (if you fly without the Tactical Display enabled). Just as with one-on-one combat, the enemy flight closest to your strike group is the most dangerous, so it's given top priority. Remember not to stray too far from your charges, because drawing escorts away (as we've discussed earlier) is a standard offensive tactic. If you're over enemy territory, you can be sure that any bogeys you see out there are bandits, but don't stray too far away from the bombers.

If the bogeys turn out to be bandits, begin your attack. If you're far enough away, consider using the stern-conversion—letting the interceptors start their attack run on your asset(s) so you can tail shoot them as they try. It works for protecting bombers because they can protect themselves a little, but be very cautious attempting this with unarmed charges. In fact, you're better advised not to try the stern-conversion in that situation.

Keep your eyes open for enemy fighters attacking from an unexpected direction, a common ploy used by interceptors. While sticking with a bandit until you kill him is a good general rule, it isn't always the best plan when it comes to escort missions. The decision really depends on your skill level and your aircraft's abilities, but there are two schools of thought on this. One is if you can't kill the bandit quickly, let him go and get back to the bombers. This prevents you from getting drawn away and leaving them unprotected. Conversely, the drawback is if you don't make sure that you kill the bandits one at a time, you'll very likely never get on top of the situation.

In the end the best decision depends on several factors: how good you and your wingmen are, and how much damage the enemy is inflicting on the main group. If you think you can kill the bandit, it's preferable. But weigh your decision on how good of a job your "wingies" are doing versus how badly your charges are getting beaten. Sure, it's a tough decision, but risk management is really what escort missions are all about.

Tip: *Before beginning any escort attack, note the direction of the assets you're protecting as well as their flight path towards their objectives. This will help you remain in contact with them and enable you to rejoin them again if you're delayed or lost.*

With so much action in a big air battle, it's very easy to forget the key points. To sum them up:

- Remember your mission—escort! Kills are secondary.
- Don't fixate on one bandit.
- Do not get drawn away from the asset you're protecting.
- If you can't kill the bandit quickly, don't get drawn into a long drawn-out battle. Get back to your mission.

Strike Missions

The hardest part of a strike mission is getting in and out of the target area in one piece. Hitting targets is relatively simple. We'll talk about how those procedures

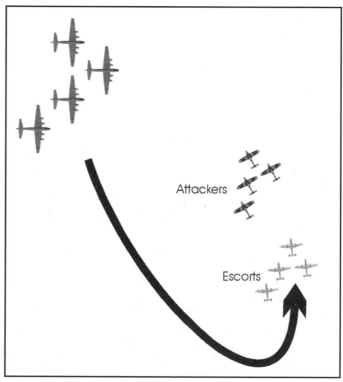

If you've got the safety cushion to allow it, using the stern-conversion can net tail shots at the attackers and can help you keep track of who has broken off their attack.

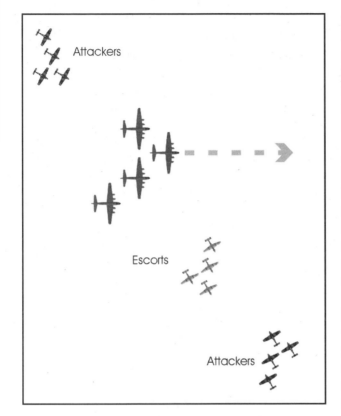

Attackers

Escorts

Attackers

Don't stray too far away from your charges—drawing escorts away is a standard offensive tactic to get you to leave the backdoor unguarded.

work in a minute, but first let's look at a couple of tips about getting you in to your target with the least hassle. These are the three defensive tactics you can use to help insure your success—stealth, altitude, and escorts.

Stealth

Basically, stealth is the art of not being seen. We've covered how to avoid visual detection during our Detection Stage discussions, and the same tactics apply. But there are a couple of other things we could add here.

Escorts will do little for helping you remain unseen. If you want to attempt a stealthy penetration attack ingress, consider doing it without an escort. Although you can't edit out or reassign who you get to fly with in Combat Flight Simulator, flying ahead of the main group and hitting the target first is the next best thing.

Stealth flying usually means flying low, and low flying isn't conducive for bombing or for evading fighter attacks once they spot you. Flying low also makes you more vulnerable to enemy Ack and decreases your ability to survive explosions created by your ordnance. If you're too low or too slow, you can literally blow yourself up. You can damage or even kill yourself with the blast of the bombs you drop.

Altitude

Altitude can be the best friend of a strike aircraft. That's because many fighters simply can't climb very high. Also, sometimes the enemy just won't bother with you or aren't able to climb up to your high altitude before you're over

your target. Still, climbing to extreme heights is less fun than watching paint dry. (Increasing the Simulation Rate can help here.)

Ground Attack Escort Considerations

If you're part of the strike group flying as a ground attack aircraft, you should base your decision to engage enemy aircraft on your ability to complete your mission and on your confidence in the escort abilities of your fellow pilots. You can forge ahead and get to your target as soon as possible, but remember that while speeding up may decrease some of the attack pressure, it will affect your ground targeting accuracy, too.

> ## Escort Tactical Errors
>
> *During the bomber attacks on England during the Battle of Britain, Goering ordered Luftwaffe escorts to stay near their charges rather than attack the climbing interceptors. Of course hindsight is 20/20, but according to many modern air-combat tacticians this is considered a tactical mistake for a couple of reasons. The first, as you probably now realize, is that this formation makes it very difficult to defend your bombers. Second, it only allows your fighters to fight defensively—which isn't their strength. As you no doubt realize by now, when it comes to fighters, the best defense is a good offense. Adolph Galland once said that the day the Allies took their fighters off the bombers and allowed them to go after the German fighters (moving from defensive to offensive duty), Germany lost the air war.*

Generally, sticking to your formation and flying your mission as planned will cause the least amount of problems for your escorts. However if you're very close to your target, it's pretty difficult to resist the temptation to veer off course when you're attacked. Nevertheless, staying on target is really the best thing you can do. Let the escorts do what they can. You just worry about taking out your target and there just may be a medal waiting when you return to base.

Ground Attacks

Reaching your target on a ground strike mission is only part of the battle. You've spent all that time and effort getting there, so you deserve to have some fun blowing something up now! The ordnance you're able to use against ground targets come in the forms of gun

> **Tip:** *200 feet AGL is the minimum, guaranteed safe altitude from which you can drop a bomb, although you can drop them from lower if your airspeed is high enough—but there are no guarantees.*

and cannon shells, unguided rockets, and unguided iron bombs. Here's how to use them and how to increase your accuracy.

Strafing

Although this technique is identical to shooting airplanes in the air, strafing is a term used for shooting things (including airplanes) on the ground. Therefore, all of the same techniques apply, such as pulling lead on moving targets like trains. Just as with shooting airborne aircraft, you can limit your deflection angle problems by attacking moving ground targets by strafing them head-on or directly from the rear. Of course, striking from the rear will provide a longer targeting/firing window due to the forward motion of the target. Also, slowing your aircraft down during your attack run will extend your strafing opportunity.

The biggest difficulty you'll encounter is estimating the range of ground targets if you play with labels disabled (all mission-creditable ground targets have labels indicating range). Gun and cannon tracers as well as shell impact-point graphics (where shells hit the ground) will provide range feedback, but as with the "hose method" gunnery, it tends to waste ammo.

Strafing approaches are fairly level, or radically vertical. The only factor that will dictate what not to use is the presence of AAA. The main concern, however, is keeping your airspeed under control. Going in low and fast is safer than high and slow, but flying too fast will affect aircraft control and your aim.

Tip: *There are anywhere from two to eight AAA batteries per asset. One bomb can disable one, as can one good strafing pass in a cannon-equipped fighter (or more than one pass, with a machine gun only-equipped fighter).*

Finally, if you use the vertical strafing attack run, be sure to time your pull-out early. If you dive with too much speed, you risk entering an accelerated stall (a high-speed stall caused by excessive AOA) and you may wind up as an unwitting kamikaze.

Firing Rockets

As we covered in earlier, there are two types of rockets modeled in Combat Flight Simulator. You can deploy both the German 8-inch rockets and the American 5-inch rockets with timed fuses or set them to explode on impact. Because neither rocket is unguided but "propelled" (unlike free falling bombs), their deployment is almost identical to strafing.

The differences between rocket deployment and strafing? Rockets don't fall off (the effects of gravity) as soon as gun and cannon shells, they have much longer range, and their destructive capabilities are much greater. (8-inch rockets have a blast radius of up to 30 yards and 5-inch rockets up to 15 yards.) This means your aim doesn't have to be as precise, but naturally you should try to land them as close as possible for maximum destructive power.

> **Tip:** *To conserve ammo during strafing attacks, fire machine-gun shells to line up your shot (press the 1 key), and then follow up with cannon shells (press the 2 key) when you're ready for the kill.*

You aim your rockets with your gun sight. Note, however, that rockets will arc like gun and cannon shells if you pull G's, so it's best to stabilize your airplane before firing them. Due to the much smaller number of rockets you can carry aboard your aircraft compared to gun and cannon shells, you have to make each one count.

Bombing

There are two techniques here: dive bombing and glide bombing. Each has its drawbacks and advantages.

Dive Bombing

The difference between dive bombing and glide bombing lies in the angle of approach. While dive bombing ise a bit less difficult, the technique you use depends (like strafing) on the enemy's defenses.

Due to the angle of approach to the target, dive bombing will net you a longer, more stable view of the target than glide bombing. The drawback, of course, is it will provide the same for enemy defenses.

You use the gun sight for bomb-targeting reference, but because a bomb's aerodynamics (more precisely the bomb's lift properties) aren't the same as your airplane's (it is, after all, meant to hit the ground), itl "flies" a different flight path from your airplane. Therefore, although the target is stationary, you need to lead the target slightly (aim beyond where you want it to land).

The exact amount of lead required depends on the dive angle (the steeper the dive, the less lead required) and the range at which you release the bomb (the farther away you release the bomb, the more lead required). With a little practice, you'll learn how much lead is required, but as with everything else in aviation, if you fly or bomb "by the numbers," you're able to recreate your

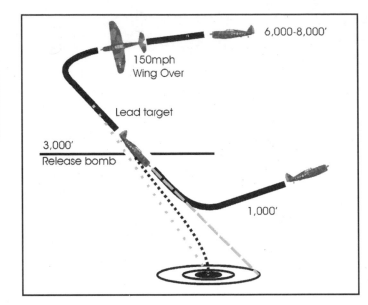

6,000-8,000'

150mph
Wing Over

Lead target

3,000'
Release bomb

1,000'

Dive Bombing.

results every time. Dive bombing procedure is:

1. Approach the target slightly to one side at about 6000-8000 feet altitude AGL.

2. Reduce throttle to achieve an airspeed of 150 MPH.

3. When the target is just about to pass under your wingtip, perform a wing-over in the direction of the target rather than pushing the nose over into a dive. (A wing-over will allow you to keep sight of the target.)

4. Dive at a 45- to 60-degree angle with your throttle pulled all the way back to keep your speed down.

5. Maneuver the aircraft so the gun sight is lined up on the target and stabilize the airplane.

6. Once stabilized, pull the proper amount of lead and release the bomb at about 3000 feet AGL.

7. After the release, advance throttle and pull out of the dive. You should be able to recover above 1000 feet AGL.

Here are some tips to help increase your dive bombing accuracy:

• Practice dive bombing in free-flight mode. Attempt to place bombs in craters produced by previous bombs.

• Excessive speed will hamper accuracy. Dropping your flaps can help you keep your airspeed under control (use your dive brakes or spoilers if you have them on imported aircraft).

- Watch out that you do not pull negative G's in your dive. For bombs to release predictably, you must be in a positive G condition.

> **Tip:** *Attempting a second bomb run on a protected target is very risky, so try and get it right on the first pass.*

- Keep your airspeed down. Speed destroys accuracy.

- Don't pull up before the bomb is released.

- Avoid using your rudder pedals to line up the target. Your bombs will drop in the direction of your flight path and yawing will not appreciably change your flight path.

Glide Bombing

As we mentioned earlier, the difference between dive bombing and glide bombing is in the angle of approach. Dive bombing is done at a 45- to 60-degree angle, while glide bombing is achieved from a 25- to 50-degree angle.

Glide bombing procedure is as follows:

1. Start at 2000-2500 feet AGL.

2. Entry speed should be below 220 MPH at a normal cruise setting when you begin your glide.

3. Pitch down to 25-30 degrees and keep your speed below 320 MPH.

4. Maneuver the aircraft so the gun sight is lined up in the target and stabilize the airplane.

5. Once stabilized, pull the proper amount of lead and release the bomb at about 500-700 feet AGL.

6. After the release, pull out of the dive. Stay above 200 feet AGL or you risk damage from the bomb explosion.

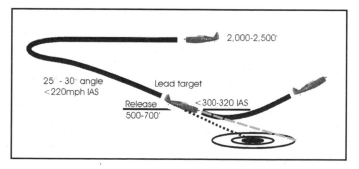

Glide Bombing.

Tip: *Never attempt a second bomb run on a protected target or you'll be destroyed by AAA.*

To help increase your glide bombing accuracy, note these tips:

- Practice glide bombing in free-flight mode. Attempt to place bombs in craters produced by previous bombs.
- Keep your speed below 300-320 IAS. Speed destroys accuracy.
- Don't make your diving run too flat or your bombs will likely land short. (In reality a bomb could even ricochet and miss the target completely as a result.)
- Watch out that you do not pull negative G's in your dive. For bombs to release predictably, you must be in a positive G condition.
- Don't pull up before the bomb is released.
- Avoid using your rudder pedals to line up the target. Your bombs will drop in the direction of your flight path, and yawing will not appreciably change your flight path.

Chapter Nine

Advanced Multiplayer Combat

Now that you've mastered the basic flight skills and know how to complete your mission, it's time we discussed advanced concepts relating to working with other pilots and honing your air combat skills. In this chapter we'll cover multiple fighter tactics as well as a few advanced combat strategies.

Multiple Fighter Tactics

The topic of Multiple Fighter Tactics encompasses several areas. We're talking about how more than one aircraft work together, of course, but also how to avoid being overwhelmed by your opponents. We also discuss the most effective ways to deploy air power, as the strategies you use to distribute an air force make a world of difference in your combat performance.

Up until this point, we've largely covered single fighter tactics. So now let's widen our tactical discussions to include the following situations: One vs. Many, Two vs. One, and Many vs. Many tactics.

One vs. Many can be pretty intimidating, but don't give up.

One vs. Many

Not surprisingly, the One vs. Many combat scenario is the most intimidating situation that combat pilots may find themselves in (especially if you're the "one" and not the "many"). Granted, this situation is hardly ideal, but if you find yourself in it, you shouldn't give up all hope.

A single pilot can successfully strike many enemies using BnZ attacks. That's because a sole BnZ'er can attack a large number of enemies of equal skill and survive to fight again—while a TnB'er can't. TnB'ing requires a numerical advantage to be successful in the long run.

As with a One vs. One scenario, a pilot with a substantial energy advantage can dictate the fight regardless of how many enemies are hunting him. Any number of low and slow fighters can do little against you if you're higher and faster. However, when you have an energy advantage (as opposed to a numerical advantage as you'll see later on in this chapter), you can only make so many passes before your advantage disappears.

As you know, each pass you make reduces your total E, and longer battles give your enemies the chance to improve their E states. The key to engaging multiple bandits is knowing when it's okay to attack and knowing when it's time to "run for the hills." Furthermore, the key to being really successful at air combat is picking your targets carefully.

Mission Goal Considerations

Two factors that'll help narrow down your target choices are your mission goals, and the locations of your goal/target and enemies. For instance, if your mission is to intercept bombers, the bombers obviously are the focus of your attack. Unfortunately, bombers are rarely dispatched without escorts. Then, as we've previously discussed, the decision whether to engage the escort or the bombers depends upon how close the bombers are to their target.

On the other hand, if you're part of an attack mission, which flight group you should attack depends on your mission role. If you're flying CAP or escort, give the enemy flight closest to your strike group your top priority. If you are part of the strike group, make the decision to engage the enemy aircraft based on your ability to complete your mission and your confidence in your escort and CAP abilities of your fellow pilots.

Pick a Victim

In any air battle (whether against humans in multiplayer mode or otherwise), your goal is to end the battle as soon as possible in the Attack stage. This is most preferable because if you allow the battle to proceed into the Maneuver stage, you increase the length of the battle and, with it, the enemy's chances to fight back.

Going round and round with a single bandit is the least complicated type of battle because you've only one target to shoot at (and, more importantly, you only have one to worry about). As you might imagine, multiple bandit battles get a bit more complicated. First and foremost, you now need to pick a target.

If you choose your target carefully (read: *correctly*), you're essentially picking a victim. That's because ideally your advantage over the target should help you create the air combat equivalent of a slaughter.

So now that you've chosen a flight group, we need to choose an individual bandit to attack—so that you can pick a target and stick with it (that is, of course, until the target is shot down or you can't stay with it any longer). The idea is if you keep switching targets before shooting any of them down, you're soon massively overwhelmed. It's far better to take out the enemy one by one, than not to score any kills at all.

So which bandit should you target first? There are three philosophies on this subject, and each is based on a quick danger assessment. Two are based on attacking the bandit that's the biggest threat, while the third is based on the least dangerous threat. The problem now becomes what exactly constitutes "the biggest threat."

Two schools of thought exist—one fears the most dangerous pilot, while the other says target the most dangerous aircraft first. In many situations, the most dangerous pilot is flying the most fiercesome aircraft. At other times, though, they are not one and the same.

Target: Best Pilot

In most cases the bandit you want to attack first is the best enemy pilot in the group. New warriors, looking for quick and easy kills, often make a common mistake of going after the worst enemy pilots. While these neophytes usually score the kill, they soon find the most experienced enemy pilot on *their* six. More often than not, these pilots wind up as another kill for the enemy!

You want to attack the best pilot when you know where he or she is (which is usually in front of you at the beginning of an attack) to maximize your chances of taking it out early. The theory at work here states that you can always sweep up the novice pilots with ease afterwards.

So let's assume you know whom you want to attack. How do you find them? Figuring out who the best pilot is isn't an exact science, but there are some rules of thumb that can guide you. Unfortunately, these rules are

somewhat less reliable when you face multiple human opponents than when you're squaring off against AI-generated opponents.

Just as in real life, the flight leader is the most experienced pilot, and he will usually occupy the most forward position in a flight formation. So, if you're able to, target the aircraft in that position first.

While this first rule of thumb is almost always correct with nearly every AI opponent you'll encounter, multiple "real life" opponents generally follow this convention too. Whether this happens by conscious decision or simply by coincidence, isn't terribly important—just know that it works out this way more often than not. Sure, there are exceptions to every rule (especially if you happen to face better pilots), but if you keep these guidelines in the back of your head, they may come in handy.

Target: Best Aircraft

If the target flight group consists of multiple aircraft models, go after the leader of the best (read: *most dangerous*) aircraft. Of course, the most dangerous aircraft can be a threat to you either by it's design or performance or by its E statc and proximity. Dcciphering which is the best (or rather, the most threatening) aircraft is determined with a quick study of aircraft specs—the most dangerous aircraft based on E state is the aircraft or group which has an E state equal or better to yours. Sometimes, however, the most dangerous opponent is the wily opportunist who casually lingers outside a furball until he or she finds a ripe victim. So beware!

Put the Weak out of Their Misery

If you're one of those pilots who's smart enough to hover over a furball, the most dangerous aircraft is the one closest to your altitude. When air battles clump into big furballs, you should target the stragglers on the outside and work your way toward the middle. Pilots on the outside tend to be either low on E or thinking about returning home. Furthermore, the chances of your getting overwhelmed are considerably reduced because the majority of the airplanes are positioned nearer the center of the furball.

Note that working your way in from the outside toward the middle means working from the top down as well. You can approach the outside of a *ball* (hence the "furball" reference) from any direction due to its shape. In any case do not, repeat, do *not* just dive in the middle of a furball looking for a target unless you're just looking to test your luck. The odds will definitely work against you in that situation.

Working with Wingmen

Just as in the real world, air combat became a lot safer when pilots began to fly with a wingman. So it shouldn't come as any surprise that it works the

Note: *The skill levels of your wingmen change with the Enemy Level setting you choose to use.*

same way in Combat Flight Simulator. Of course, when you play Combat Flight Simulator in multiplayer mode, your "wingies" are human. But when you play Combat Flight Simulator offline you're working with computerized countrymen.

Computerized AI (Artificial Intelligence—the "brains" behind computerized opponents) has typically been limited in its abilities. Although Combat Flight Simulator's efforts have taken big steps to change this, you are still the most dependable pilot you'll be flying with, despite the ability settings displayed by your wingmen. Therefore, if you absolutely must accomplish something, consider doing it yourself (or at least assisting your wingmen). The old axiom "If you need something done, do it yourself" is good advice. Although you're the most reliable pilot you're going to fly with, when you fly with a human wingman, things can be different. Regardless, let's talk about how to work with other pilots.

To minimize confusion, from this point onward we'll use the USAAF fighter organization designations. Namely, a *Flight* is composed of four aircraft, and an *Element* is one half of a flight (two aircraft) and is comprised of a leader and a wingman.

Note that the titles "leader" and "wingman" sometimes refer more to the type of attack tactics used, rather than being based on rank or combat skill. Although the roles have changed over the years, becoming equal in duties and nature, the fighter with the "leader" title generally is the attacker, and the wingman is the support fighter. You'll understand how this works later on in this chapter.

Anyway, a wingman (or rather, *your* wingman) is responsible for your safety and success just as you're responsible for his. While you can infer this definition of responsibilities to anyone on your side, a wingman remains more or less devoted to only one other pilot for a period of time.

You may think that this section of the book is only applicable to human players while playing in multiplayer mode, but that really isn't true. While you can't issue commands to your computer-generated wingmen, you're still able to work with them if you understand how wingman tactics work.

Wingman tactics are just as the name suggests—tactics you and your wingman use to beat the enemy into submission. The concept behind the basic Two-vs.-One tactic is very simple—one pilot maneuvers to force the bandit to give the other pilot a tail shot.

The advantage that two fighters have over a single opponent is that the single bandit can only defend against one problem/attacker at a time—namely E state, plane disparity, or relative vector. This leaves the bandit open to attack because the enemy pilot has to ignore one of you. The two usual ways to force a bandit into this position are by using the Drag or the Bracket.

The Drag

Basically, the way that the Drag works is that your wingman has a bandit on his tail so you slip in behind the bandit's tail and kill him. This works because the bandit fixates on shooting down your wingman and doesn't realize that you're moving in behind them for the kill. The Drag tactic has three variations:

- Drag and Bag—This variation of the drag baits and drags the enemy into a trap comprised of assorted converging friendlies so that the bandit suddenly finds himself outnumbered. The main difference between the Drag and Bag (DnB) and the Drag is that the DnB usually takes place in a long horizontal chase, whereas the Drag usually takes place during a turning fight.

Tip: *The drag is an effective defensive tactic as well. Dragging a bandit over friendly Ack can clear your six.*

- Rope-a-Dope—The concept behind the Rope-a-dope (RaD) is while you're a safe distance away, you lure the bandit into expending his E by initializing a climbing turn. Then you or your wingman kill the bandit while it's most vulnerable—when it's energy is lowest as it climbs after you. When the bandit stalls or spins, roll over and shoot him. You can also use the RaD successfully as a single pilot, but only if you have a better climbing aircraft and at least

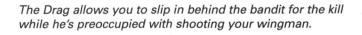

The Drag allows you to slip in behind the bandit for the kill while he's preoccupied with shooting your wingman.

a slight E advantage, or an absolute E advantage over the enemy. The same concept applies—when the bandit stalls or spins, you rack up a kill.

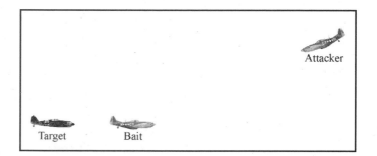

The Drag and Bag baits the enemy into a situation where he suddenly finds himself outnumbered.

- Waltz—The Waltz (also know as the *assisted waltz*) takes advantage of the bandit's preoccupation with you or your wingman while in a stalemated turn fight. This leaves the other free pilot to BnZ while the other two do their little dance among the clouds. The difference between the Waltz and the standard drag is that one pilot uses a different tactic than the TnB partner. In addition to the inherent danger borne by the pilot playing the bait (although the bait doesn't need to be purely defensive, it just has to occupy the attention of the bandit), he must keep an eye out for another enemy TnB'er showing up while E is low.

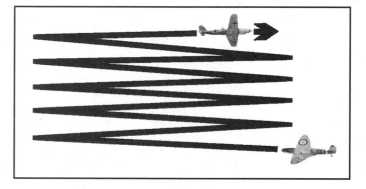

A single pilot can also use the Rope-a-Dope successfully by luring the bandit into expending his E.

Note: *Obviously the Rope-a-Dope won't work against an experienced pilot—hence the moniker "dope."*

The Bracket

The second general type of wingman tactic is called the Bracket. The Bracket (also known as the *Pincer*) places the enemy between your two attacking

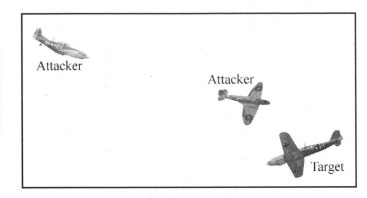

The Waltz pits the BnZ and TnB attack against the bandit.

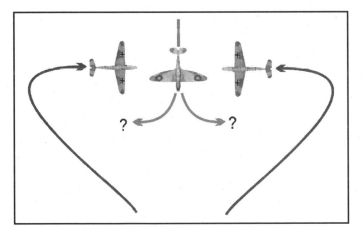

The Bracket places the bandit in a lose-lose situation because it's in between your two attacking fighters.

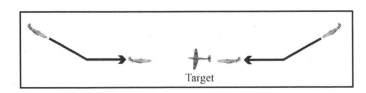

The BnZ version of the Thatch Weave employs a timed series of BnZ runs to limit the battle choices of the enemy.

fighters. The bandit either has to engage one of you (which gives the other a clear tail shot) or ignore both of you (which allows tail shots by both of your planes). What makes the Bracket so effective is this is a lose-lose situation for the bandit. The only drawback of the Bracket is that you may have to fire in the general direction of your Wingie—so be careful.

One variation of the bracket is known as the *Thatch Weave*. Named after the man who perfected the tactic during World War II, a Lt. Commander Thatch, the Weave actually exists in two forms—one is offensive, with the other being used in either offensive or defensive situations.

The first employs a series of timed BnZ runs. Two fighters (or flights of fighters as it was used during the war) take turns diving on the enemy from opposite directions. If the enemy tries to climb to meet the first flight head-on or chase the first flight after the pass, they become sitting ducks for the second flight because they lose E turning or climbing, and vice versa.

You can also perform the BnZ Thatch Weave in a manner that resembles a drag. Instead of attacking from opposite directions, two fighters begin their runs from the same direction. Timing is crucial, so the second flight has to delay their attack run until the first flight is just closing over the enemy.

The second variation of the Thatch Weave is used in TnB situations. Instead of following the attacking fighter while it chases the bandit, a series of opposite turns are employed to enable the free fighter to achieve multiple "snapshot" opportunities.

As a defensive maneuver the TnB Thatch Weave works like this: as the bandit attacks from the rear, both fighters first turn toward each other and begin the tactic's characteristic weaving. If the bandit engages one of the fighters, it'll give the free fighter multiple opportunities to shoot it, just as with the offensive TnB Thatch Weave.

Naturally, the effectiveness of this defensive maneuver depends on a number of factors—the skill of the attacker and the free fighter. Ideally your Element shouldn't have let itself get into a T2H attack situation, but if it has, the Thatch Weave is an option—not as a cure-all—but a makeshift solution.

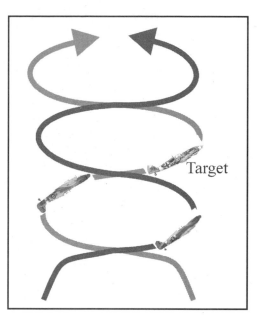

The TnB use of the Thatch Weave is very effective because it enables multiple shot opportunities for the free fighter.

Advanced Attack Concepts

We covered basic attack skills and concepts way back in Chapter Six: Air Combat Basics. We didn't have room to focus on the finer points of attack tactics then because we were more interested in providing insights into the larger overall issue of battle. So now that that stuff's out of the way, let's talk about some of these advanced attack concepts.

There's a humbling air combat adage stating that no matter how good you are (or think you are!), there's always someone better out there. Knowing all of the basics that are required to stay alive and complete your missions is enough to make it through, but for many of you that isn't enough. Air combat is very

competitive (not to mention addicting), so let's talk about some advanced concepts that can help you become a better fighter pilot—one capable of laying waste to enemy aces.

Remember, no matter how many tricks you learn, nothing can take the place of practice. A pilot with solid flight skills and good SA will win against the fanciest flying and tactics every time.

Making the BnZ Work

BnZ'ing is more than just a way to fight—it resembles an art form more than it does a science. If your BnZ kill percentage is relatively low, there isn't much advice that can help you other than choose your targets/victims better and polish up on your marksmanship skills. But if your BnZ work results in more deaths to you than enemy kills, there are a few things we can talk about to help increase your chances of staying alive.

There are three places in a BnZ attack in which you can get killed—during the attack, during the Zoom extension (or attempted extension), and if you planned really poorly, during the reversal. But the most fundamental mistakes made in BnZ attacks are made before the attack runs even begin. Of course we're talking about making the decision to attack in the first place.

In addition to judging your E state in relation to the bandit's, you should base your decision to stick around or call it a day on the same factors you used when you began your initial attack. These factors include your aircraft's condition, fuel load, and the potential for other bandits to drop in and make your life difficult. All of this should have a bearing on your decision. If you go over this short list before every attack run, it'll at least get you started off on the right foot.

Outside of getting nailed on the initial attack run, many people believe the quality of subsequent attack runs and extensions all relate back to the reversal. It's easy to understand why people believe the reversal is the key to the whole puzzle. They reason that a poor reversal will result in a poor attack run (low velocity, or too short to net a good, clean shot), and a poor attack run leads to poor extension (not enough velocity to escape harm), which subsequently leads to another poor reversal. As you can imagine, the downward cycle continues from here until you're nothing more than a smoking hole in the ground.

There are two schools of thought regarding reversals. The first school believes that you should turn back and begin your next attack run when your airspeed is about to drop below the minimum airspeed to complete a vertical reversal—without any regard to the proximity of the bandit. The theory behind the offensive reversal is that at this particular point you're too slow to extend with any great efficiency, so you're stuck fighting anyway—and fighting with your guns is better than trying to fight with the tail of your airplane.

The second school of thought believes that you should only turn back when you've achieved enough separation (usually about 2500 to 3000 yards) to safely perform your reversal. "Safely" usually means being separated far enough from the enemy so they can't shoot at you before you've turned and regained some speed to make your next attack run (the textbook BnZ we described back in Chapter Six: Air Combat Basics).

Despite the compelling argument that the reversal is the key to BnZ success, the reality is the sections that make up the BnZ are tied together so intricately that it's

Reversals of Fortune

Which is best to use—the offensive reversal or the safe reversal? We believe the best choice is to make the safe reversal. If you lack the E to perform a safe reversal, you've most likely already overstayed your welcome. You probably never should have made that last attack run in the first place.

Your Zooms should extend as far as practical to make a safe reversal—if that isn't possible, head for home or help. This doesn't sound very courageous, but this is where most inexperienced pilots make their first mistake—attacking when they're not ready, with the odds already against their success—which in this case is usually due to prolonging an attack longer than is considered "safe." While there are pilots out there who are skilled enough to come out of such situations victorious, for most mortals the decision depends on how much you value your virtual life.

BnZ'ing isn't wall-to-wall action like TnB dogfighting. It takes skill and (above all) patience to become good at BnZ'ing. According to some accounts of fighter conflicts in WWII, unless it was warranted by mission objective(s), BnZ attacks were little more than a couple passes at the enemy followed by everyone running for home regardless of whether all bandits were killed or not. (If the odds weren't in the attacker's favor, such a hasty retreat made especially good sense.)

It was very rare for pilots to hang around until the "bitter end" if there wasn't a really good reason to do that. This may sound less than thrilling in the context of playing Combat Flight Simulator, but the alternative is hanging around and getting shot down with little hope of emerging victorious.

really difficult to isolate a single factor as being the key to the whole thing. Nonetheless, due to the order of occurrence of these sections, the ultimate success of a reversal is really tied to your initial E level and how you expend it on your zoom. In other words, the real key to the BnZ is in the Zoom. So let's talk about the finer points of Zooming next.

Zoom or Go Boom

Make no mistake about it, the goal of the Zoom is to put as much separation between you and your opponent as possible. The first concept to understand is that separation between you and the bandit can be vertical as well as lateral. Although it's easy to believe that distance is distance to the bandit's bullets (while gravity does affect bullet velocity, it generally doesn't cause any great increase or decrease in lethality range), when it comes to fighter separation, there's some cause for concern in certain cases.

As we've already seen, you shouldn't take the relative E state of the enemy lightly. Let's use a couple of radical examples to illustrate these concepts. If you extend to a safe reversal distance with a fairly level Zoom (assuming you begin your BnZ attack with an E advantage), your E state in relation to the bandit at the end of the Zoom should be roughly equal. Conversely, if you Zoom-climb straight up, although you separate and you gain potential E, your airspeed will drop off proportionally. This isn't too bad of a situation to be in, unless your E advantage over the bandit's isn't very wide or the bandit can climb very well or both.

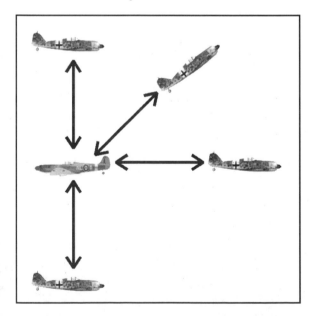

Separation is vertical as well as lateral, but not all types of separation are the same.

Now let's look at the exact opposite situation. If your separation is based on vertical positioning and you're on the bottom, although you'll gain on airspeed—you're in a worse position than either of the other two scenarios above. That's because the bandit now dictates the fight. In this position, you can only lose E. If you try to climb to gain or re-gain E, the bandit can dive on you and ruin the paint job on your airplane.

Therefore, the best choice (that is, if you have a choice) is to separate with a mixture of lateral and vertical distance. And of course (as we've illustrated), unless you're going to disengage, the preferable form of the vertical separation component is superior altitude. You may recognize this as the classic textbook Zoom we discussed way back in Chapter Six: Air Combat Basics. Now it all starts to make sense why the classics remain classic, doesn't it?

Unfortunately, the textbook Zoom (a climbing extension) is perhaps the hardest Zoom there is to perform. To be blunt, unless you have a major E advantage over your enemy, a climbing extension won't work and you'll get your tail chewed into tiny little pieces! While you may get away with such a Zoom on your first and possibly second pass (again, only if you have the E), the odds are very much against you doing it again without grabbing some serious E before-hand. The reality of the situation is that the *majority* of Zooms you execute are in level or slightly descending flight.

> **Note:** *Zoom climbs straight up are not recommended (unless you have an overwhelming E advantage) because they present two potential problems. First your separation isn't very likely to be as great as with other Zooms, and TnB aircraft generally tend to climb better than BnZ aircraft (for short stints anyway). Secondly, you're now stuck hanging in the air with mushy airplane controls (due to the loss of airspeed) with a bandit climbing to shoot at you.*

Here are some rules of thumb for Zooming. If the enemy's E state is close to yours, sacrifice altitude to increase your airspeed. This means climbing at a lower angle, or if the situation warrants it, continuing your dive. Separation is the most important factor for survival when you're going to show the enemy your tail. If your aircraft is faster, you can climb later to regain some E.

Switching from the BnZ to TnB

If you stick to BnZ attacks exclusively, they'll generally yield relatively few kills in relation to

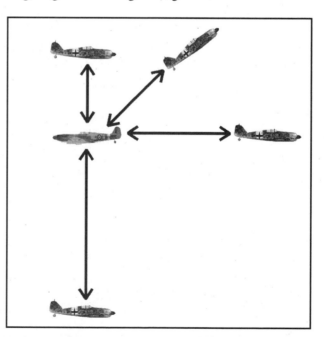

Actual separation potential varies with the direction you use. Although this would seem to favor the lower relative position, the bandit can use gravity to eat up the separation advantage in a dive just as you have.

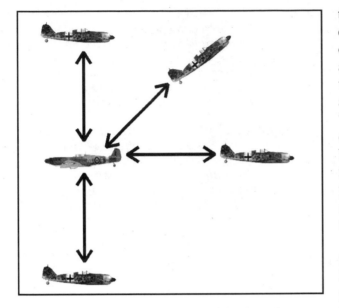

The best choice separation is a combination of lateral and vertical distance with you above the bandit.

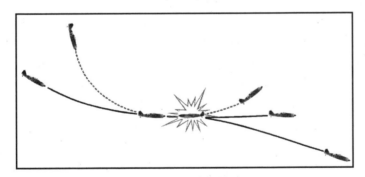

Unless you have a major E advantage over your enemy the climbing Zoom extension (dotted path) won't work. In reality the majority of Zooms you execute are in level or slightly descending flight.

the time spent in flight. It's very easy to understand why when you consider that the safety trade-offs afforded to you by the BnZ also work against you. High-speed attack runs reduce the targeting "window of opportunity" (the duration) for you as well as the bandit. So it all boils down to the fact that if you want to increase your kill-to-bullet ratio, you're going to have to slow down and turn with the bandit sometimes.

If you've ever attempted to turn with a bandit and achieved less than satisfactory results, you probably realize the secret to successfully changing attack tactics lies in knowing when it's relatively safe to do so. We already know that part of this decision is based on knowing the capabilities of your aircraft versus those of your opponent's aircraft, and that E is more valuable than gold in air combat. So let's talk a little about how to recognize what favorable turning opportunities are.

By now you know the best shot in air combat against a fighter is the H2T shot. That's because you get to shoot at the bandit and, more importantly, the bandit can't shoot at you. You also don't need to lead your target as much to shoot at it. And, you're now in position to see what the bandit is doing, so evasion becomes more difficult for him. While attacking an unsuspecting fighter from the rear is always most desirable, you'll rarely stumble across the opportunity for such attacks without effort on your part or a major blunder from your enemy. But if presented with an opportunity, take it!

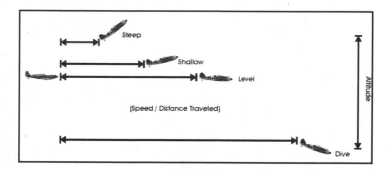

Basic Zoom choices are to sacrifice airspeed for more altitude (Zoom at a steeper angle), or sacrifice altitude for more airspeed (Zoom at a lower angle). Which you ultimately choose depends on how close the enemy is, their relative E state, and what you want to do.

The Roll Away

If you're going to switch from a BnZ attack to a TnB fight, the biggest problem is slowing down to corner speed. E conversion maneuvers like the High Yo-Yo, or Roll Away, fit the bill. Do anything it takes to slow down (deploy your spoilers or brakes, drop your landing gear, flaps, whatever)—if you don't slow down enough, you are too slow to zoom away and too fast to turn—which makes you a perfect target for getting your tail shot off.

A variation of the High Speed Yo-Yo is known as the Roll Away. It's basically performed the same way as the High Speed Yo-Yo except you literally "roll away" from the initial turn at the top of the climbing turn. This further increases the distance between you and your target compared to the High Speed Yo-Yo, but there are two drawbacks.

First, as you might imagine, it doesn't work very well if your airplane has a poor roll rate. Second, this maneuver is a little unnerving because there's a short period of time in which you lose visual contact with the bandit. One thing that can help you here is a little faith—you just have to believe that the bandit's still down there and is remaining more or less committed to turning to evade your attack.

BnZ to TnB Considerations

Having an advantageous AOT situation presented to you is good, but AOT isn't everything. In addition to weighing the situation based on your aircraft performance and E state relative to your opponent's, you will need to consider just how much E your opponent has in relation to their aircraft's flight performance as well.

The Roll Away is a variation of the High Speed Yo-Yo.

Just the fact that you're barreling down on your opponent suggests that you already have the E advantage (you shouldn't have begun a BnZ attack if you didn't have an E advantage). But if the bandit's E state places him low on the turn performance curve, this can negate any skill or aircraft-turn performance advantage he'd normally have under other conditions.

Let's give you an example of what we're talking about here. If a bandit is virtually stalled (well below his corner speed), even if due to his skill or better airplane he's able to out-turn you, he may be slow enough for you to make the kill before he can turn and do anything about it.

In addition to position opportunities, you should look for E and ammo advantages. Without getting into the philosophical arguments regarding concepts such as air combat chivalry and vulching (preying on those taking off during multiplayer games), the best and easiest place to make a kill is from a position of absolute advantage. Of course, whether or not you choose to take advantage of some of these *opportunities* is up to you, but let's talk about them anyway.

Basically what we're suggesting here is hitting the bad guys when they're down. Obviously "down" can refer to a lot of things in air combat (down on E, down on ammo, down as in relative altitude, and so forth), but in all cases when it's used in regard to your enemy it works in your favor. As we just pointed out, if the enemy is down on E you stand a good chance of outturning a better turning airplane even if it's only for a short period of time. As we've pointed out, in many cases that's all you'll need (especially if your marksmanship skills are adequate).

The biggest problem is that estimating when the enemy's E supply is down isn't an exact science. There are, however, some situations to watch for. Some of the most common scenarios are:

- If a bandit's been attempting to outturn you on each BnZ attack run with the intent of trying to get a shot at you as you zoom, the chances are pretty good that after a couple of passes his E state will be lower than when you first started the attack.
- Being down on altitude is easy to recognize. If the bandit's down on the deck, his maneuvering choices become severely limited. If the bandit's down on airspeed, he can't really dive to gain any speed due to his proximity to the ground—effectively shutting off one direction for maneuvering (down)—which makes him a riper target for picking. (Just remember not to come in too hot or you'll become a lawn dart.)
- If the enemy was just engaged in a turning fight, the chances are also pretty good that his E bank is nearly empty or is already overdrawn. The most important thing to be aware of in this situation is that the longer you wait to attack, the more time the bandit has to regroup (recover E) and return to fighting status.
- This same situation (just engaged in a turning fight) also lends itself to presuming the bandit's ammo supply isn't what it used to be. While there's no safer attack than attacking an unarmed opponent, you need to be careful. A good pilot (real or computer generated) will only fire if they can hit you, so if your opponent knows their stuff they might still have some reserve shells with your name on them. Also be aware that a bandit may not show his hand (and gamble his remaining shells right away), so don't dump your E believing you're dealing with an unarmed target without thoroughly assessing the situation first. Now, no one is suggesting that you make yourself a target to see if the bandit shoots at you, but always assume the worst and work from there. Fight the battle assuming the bandit has ammo. You'll learn soon enough whether the bandit really has something to shoot you with if the battle lasts long enough. (Hopefully it won't—and it'll end in your favor!) Just keep the enemy's ammo situation in mind and take advantage of the bandit's predicament.
- Another situation you want to look for is a bandit that Immelmans or uses some other extreme vertical maneuvers in response to each of your attack runs. If his altitude is much higher after an attack or two, you can pretty much count on the fact that his airspeed will be pretty low at the top of those maneuvers. Thus, adjust your next attack run accordingly.

Creating Opportunities

Unfortunately the biggest problem with waiting for the "proper conditions" before considering switching to a turning fight is that the chances of actually coming across such opportunities are pretty slim when you're fighting a good pilot. Fortunately, there are things you can do to increase your chances, provided you don't mind a little duplicity. What we're really talking about here is taking a pro-active role in making your enemy screw up.

When you have a bandit that Immelmans or uses some other extreme vertical maneuver in response to your attack runs, even though the bandit's altitude is much higher after an attack, his airspeed will be pretty low at the top of those maneuvers. You can use this against the bandit.

Although there are some major differences in the effects of gravity, vertical maneuvers are really just turns made on the vertical plane. Before we talk about how to lure a bandit into climbing, let's consider the general theory behind the process. Because the bandit is at a much lower airspeed at the top of a vertical maneuver, if you have the E to climb substantially higher and retain enough airspeed to maneuver, three things work in your favor:

1. The bandit won't have the E to raise his nose to shoot at you if you're relatively high enough above him after your climb (proportionate to the bandit's E state). Obviously this situation is desirable because his not begin able to shoot at you is the next best thing to having an enemy who's totally out of ammo.

2. Even if your E state is as low as the bandit's after your climb, when the bandit is below you, you generally have enough E to accomplish your goal—that is, shoot the bandit. This is because you only need to point your nose more or less downward to shoot at him, and it takes a lot less E to lower your nose than it does (as in the lower bandit's case) to raise it.

3. Because you're now more or less set up in the vertical BnZ position and the bandit has no option but to maneuver away from you due to his lack of E, this increases the likelihood of netting you a H2T shot. The only way the bandit can avoid this bad situation is for him to raise his nose to meet you head-on when you dive on him. Of course the bandit's lack of E will make this nearly impossible—but not always. (More on that soon.)

The most basic, and arguably best, bait for attracting fighter pilots is an easy kill. Fighter pilots will generally beat themselves into a feeding frenzy if they sense a quick kill (just like sharks do when they smell blood in the water). Other than having a user-operated faux smoke system to attract fighters (something not modeled in Combat Flight Simulator or done in real life, either), the only option you have left is to use yourself as bait.

What you need to do is BnZ the bandit, but always remain above your target. Do this enough times, and the chances are the bandit will try and climb to kill you. This essentially is the same concept behind the RaD, but interestingly enough, even experienced pilots tend to fall for this one. It seems that being just outside of the bandit's reach increases their desire to kill you (just like teasing someone makes them want to do you harm).

Psychological analysis aside, the way to stay above the bandit is by beginning your Zooms early (even when using level attack runs). An additional benefit to beginning your Zooms early is that this decreases the likelihood of becoming a statistic in a head-on collision. On the downside, it also reduces the amount of time you have to shoot at the bandit, but don't lose sight of your goal—make the bandit expend his E.

Climbing above a lower opponent seems pretty straightforward when you're BnZing because you have the E advantage. Even though it's pretty easy to believe that all you need to do is simply pull back on the stick, being a little more selective by using one maneuver over another can yield further advantages. Just as with everything else in air combat, your E state will dictate what maneuver is best for your situation.

Pilots with a good amount of E tend to use vertical maneuvers that are best described as a *very* High Yo-Yo or as a vertical Immelman (pulling more or less straight up). If your E state is marginal on E, using a high wing over or even a Hammerhead can work in some situations, but the latter is dangerous because you're almost stalled at the top. Which, of course, leaves you with little or no ability to maneuver other than downward.

Although vertical maneuvers like the vertical Immelman are good choices if your E state is pretty high, they can work against you if you have a lot of E. To illustrate why, let's go back to the basic concept behind this tactic.

Some pilots believe that the idea behind vertical plane maneuvering and turning is to put some distance between yourself and the bandit. Although going vertical will achieve that goal—and correspondingly reduce the ability of the bandit to shoot you, what you're actually after is a vertical angle advantage— specifically an angle disadvantage for the bandit so it can't shoot at you. This is

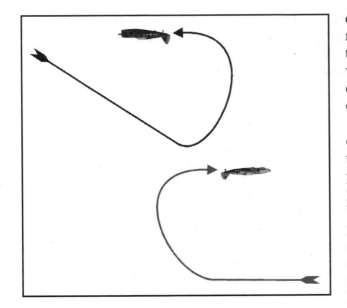

Climbing substantially higher than a bandit when he uses a vertical counter-maneuver usually leaves the bandit lacking enough E to raise his nose to shoot at you. You only need to point your nose down to shoot at him because the bandit can only go downward or maneuver away from you because of his lack of E.

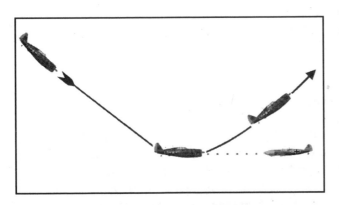

Zooming early will help you stay above the enemy.

exactly why these vertical maneuvers are classified as turning maneuvers rather than vertical Zooms (the former depends on angles and the latter on distance).

The problem with trying to convert too much E using one of these maneuvers occurs when you put too much distance between yourself and a bandit who's well beyond gun range. Although you'll decrease the bandit's ability to shoot you, you'll actually reduce the disparity of E states that we're trying to gain. Ideally we want to shoot at the bandit when his E state is the lowest, so every second your attack is delayed when you have an advantage (excessive separation distances increase the delay) turns into time the bandit can use to recover E. If you allow this to happen, what you're likely to find yourself facing is a H2H vertical pass rather than the much more desirable H2T shot.

Getting back to our example, if you use a vertical Immelman when you have extra amounts of E, you'll end up increasing your separation because you're merely trading airspeed for altitude (more altitude produces more separation distance). A better choice for this situation is a maneuver known by some as a *Vertical 8* or *Double Immelman*. Whatever you call it, it's basically an Immelman immediately followed by another Immelman (which explains the name).

Rather than just trading airspeed for altitude, you're further able to bleed E by turning vertically in the half loop portions of the maneuver. This is because every time you move the nose of the airplane (more specifically, change your angle of attack or *yaw*—which you may recall is really very similar to AOA but on the airplane's vertical axis, so the drag penalty is lower due to the relative effect of gravity in normal orientation and size of the vertical stabilizer) it costs you E.

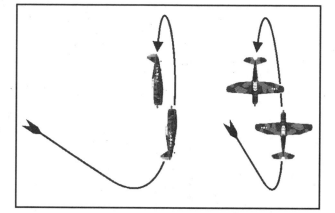

The Hammerhead uses the rudder to make the turn at the top as you near stall. This makes it a relatively dangerous maneuver because your airspeed is very low on E top—making regaining airspeed for turning tough, and zoom escapes nearly impossible.

Although the main advantage to these maneuvers is that they allow you to bleed E and subsequently reduce your separation compared to more basic vertical maneuvers, they also have one additional benefit. By reversing direction twice, you'll end up flying more or less on the original heading you began your attack at. This can further help keep the enemy off balance if the bandit believes that you're going to fly straight over.

Finally, a few last thoughts when you're switching to a TnB fight:

- Pulling back hard on the stick for the vertical section of a maneuver may help you bleed E, but (depending on the Flight Model Realism Setting you fly with), you may need to watch for some pitfalls. Blacking out from g forces, or getting into an accelerated stall (where your *climb* resembles a descent more than a climb) are all telltale signs that you've pulled too hard.
- Although E discussions tend to treat altitude and airspeed as equals, they really aren't. In a turning battle it doesn't matter how much altitude you have if you're well below corner speed. If you don't have the airspeed to maneuver, you can be killed regardless of your altitude.

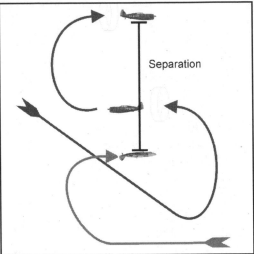

The Vertical 8 or Double Immelman bleeds more E because every time you move the nose of the airplane it costs you E. An additional benefit is you end up flying more or less on your original heading because you reverse direction twice.

Using a vertical Immelman (or other highly vertical maneuver) when you have an abundance of E increases separation because you're trading airspeed for altitude (more altitude means more separation distance).

- Finally, timing your pull up to position your plane directly above the bandit will net the greatest angular disadvantage for the bandit.

Advanced Defensive Concepts

When you're learning the ropes of air combat, you're going to spend a lot more time defending yourself, and getting shot down, than you'd like to admit. Still, it's important to realize that being the best offensive pilot in the world will not guarantee that you'll never end up in defensive situations. So it shouldn't come as any surprise that the best pilots are the ones that can turn bad situations into good kills.

Note: *Half rolls (or rolls in general) do not significantly alter your E state.*

Learning to make kills safely and efficiently is only part of the equation. That's why we need to talk a little more about how to stay alive in bad situations and how to turn them around if at all possible.

Moving from Defense to Offense

Regardless of the tactics you ultimately use, let's not forget that the ultimate goal of fighter air combat is to destroy the other pilot. Whether you're attempting to kill a BnZ opponent while flying a TnB fighter or trying to down the enemy in an equal or lesser aircraft, the job becomes more difficult if the attacker has a big E advantage over you. In these situations the next best thing you can do is to deprive the attacker of anything you can in the hopes of moving yourself closer to a new addition to your kill list.

The items we're talking about whittling down for your attacker(s) are a clean shot (at you!), any E advantage, their ammo supply, their fuel, and their airplane parts. The basic strategy is if you can't kill 'em right away, bleed 'em dry until you can. Of the items we've just listed, besides denying shots at yourself, the only one that you have any semblance of control over is airplane parts and fuel (if you happen to create a fuel leak in your opponent's tanks).

Of course, the best way to remove airplane parts from the enemy is to shoot them off, but even though the other items are not under your direct control, there are many things you can do to lure the enemy into yielding his advantages to you. And the more advantages you have, the easier it is to target the enemy.

One thing to keep in mind: just because an opponent is flying a TnB aircraft doesn't mean the bandit won't BnZ you during his initial pass or passes. An attacker will either BnZ you, try to out-turn you, or fake the BnZ to lure you into climbing up to meet him—all with the intent of turning your airplane into little pieces of flaming scrap metal.

Regardless of the type of attack brought against you, in most cases the solution is the early turn. That's because it provides the best chance of shooting airplane parts off your attacker's craft despite your lack of control over any of the other items.

The first order of business is to avoid being shot during the attack. Most *traditional* TnB airplanes either have thin armor (if any at all), or smaller caliber guns with correspondingly lighter ammo loads to minimize weight.

The concept behind the weight loss program for an aircraft generally has the same net affect as increasing lift performance which, as we've discussed, directly relates to increased turn performance. Avoiding H2H encounters is usually a smart idea while flying a TnB aircraft—you probably aren't as durable as the traditional BnZer and you're probably outgunned as well. On the other hand, if your attacker is in a TnB craft, you could risk the head-on with better odds, although there's still a risk of being shot down.

Whether the bandit wants to zoom on by or wants to turn with you, the early turn is still the key. If you recall, gravity has a profound effect on aircraft performance, so it shouldn't come as any surprise that defending against a vertical BnZ attack requires some different tactics.

The process is basically the same (avoid the head-on followed by an early turn maneuver while coaxing the bandit to bleed E), but due to angular disadvantages and the effects of gravity, different tactics are required. You need to consider the consequences and benefits of the direction of your turn as well as the maneuvering plane in which the turn is made.

As always, which direction you turn depends on your E state and condition (lack of ammo, fuel, and airplane parts). Of course being low on E is the second worst situation—being damaged when low on E and ammo is the worst! Fortunately, if your aircraft control technique is adequate, E is the one factor that you have direct control over.

If you're low on E, although you may be tempted, don't climb to meet the vertical attack. That'll just make you a slower target. On the other hand, horizontal turns are also bad in the low E condition because you won't maximize your situation to your advantage. Before talking about what to do, let's determine what our goals are.

The most important thing to do is keep your air speed up. Next, you want to bleed as much of the bandit's E advantage as possible. The ways to do this are by getting the bandit to dive below you, or getting the bandit to turn.

As we discussed earlier, turning away from the attacker on the horizontal plane to avoid the head-on is a bad idea. That's because in a vertical attack—from the attacker's point of view—any turn nets a low deflection T2H at yourself. This limits your options to turning on the vertical or oblique planes with the critical factor being timing (in relation to gun range).

What you need to do is make a downward turn (dive). This increases your airspeed (which increases your ability to maneuver plus reduces closure rate), and presents your attacker with a reason to dive lower than he may have originally intended. You may even entice the bandit to turn (maneuver) with you. Next, climb using a vertical maneuver to capitalize on the early turn.

Turning upward accomplishes two things: you gain E, and because you are slower than the high-speed attacker, you can turn (by using a loop or half-reverse Cuban 8) inside the bandit and get the kill if he decides to follow you around. If the bandit chooses to buzz on through, at least you've gained E and the bandit has expended E. So even if you don't net a kill or ping the bandit as he extends, you're making progress. Whatever you do, do not continue your original turn downward (in a Split-S, for example) because it'll eliminate any possible gains you may have made.

Out of Plane Maneuvering

No, even though it may be what you're wishing you could do when you're in a bad situation, "out of plane maneuvering" is not getting out of your airplane and running for the latrine. The plane that "out of plane maneuvering" refers to is the maneuvering plane of the attacker. Although this tactic is used when everything has gone wrong and you've suddenly got a bandit parked on your six showing you his tracers, it's usually the only tactical option left when you're out of E in this situation. You'll see why in a minute.

The concept behind the tactic is based on the fact that unless you're flying straight and level, a bandit on your six must pull lead to hit you. For example, if you're turning in a 30-degree bank, the bandit must turn tighter to shoot you. This usually manifests itself as a turn at a greater bank (greater than 30 degrees in our example) in order to pull lead on you. This principle also applies to pitch as well. If you're climbing at 15 degrees of pitch, the bandit must climb at a higher pitch to shoot you.

There's no way to determine what the bandit's bank and pitch angles are in degrees while looking out your rear view without performing a lot of analysis, but you can, pretty readily, determine when the bandit is matching your bank. (Besides, if you're down on E with a bandit on your six, the last thing in the world you want to do—and it would probably be the last thing you do in this world—is climb.) The fact is, whether you're climbing or turning, the bandit must more or less match your bank in order to pull lead on you.

You can use these facts to your advantage because they produce three benefits. First, you're able to determine when you might be shot, which will enable you to do something about it. Second, by reducing your defensive maneuvering to what's absolutely necessary (as opposed to blindly banking and yanking), you're allowed to conserve E—which, if you can gather enough of it, you can use to escape. And finally, it may coax the bandit into expending his

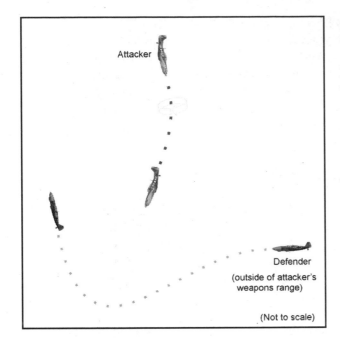

You can use the Early Turn tactic (avoid the head-on followed by an early turn) against vertical attacks.

ammo by firing wildly because he thinks he's still got you.

Although the basic drill is to look out your rear view and roll your airplane to a different bank angle as soon as the bandit rolls to match your bank, there's a little more to it. First, you'll find that you'll need to apply a bit of elevator after each roll change to move out of the bullet stream the bandit may have fired at you. Second, you need to maneuver (roll and pitch) in a direction that will not place you in the bandit's previously fired bullet stream.

For example, if you're in a left-hand turn and the bandit moves to match your left-hand bank, roll further to the left to more or less descend. If you roll to the right, you risk running into the bandit's bullet stream as the bandit rolls to the left. The only time that reversing roll direction is even somewhat safe is when it won't put you directly in the lethal path of the bandit's bullet stream that's trying to catch up to you.

Defense Against the Bracket

We know that the goal of Bracket tactics is to surround the enemy, severely limiting his options. Fortunately the solution to foil the Bracket is quite simple (even if the execution of it isn't). If you remain outside of the Bracket forming around you, you can at least reduce the danger of being attacked from two fronts. Do this by maneuvering so that all attackers remain on the same side of your aircraft.

Squadron Tactics

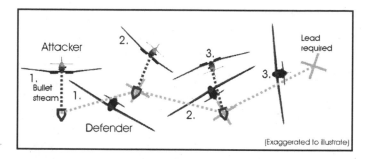

Used correctly, out of plane maneuvering could save your bacon.

Besides the speed and lethality of the aircraft used, one of the things that separated WWII air combat from the air combat of other eras was the large numbers of aircraft utilized. As you've probably gathered by now, large numbers of aircraft didn't go out in a group with the intent of fighting as individuals (known as "gaggle doctrine"). However, that's exactly what did happen, although there were some greater plans involved.

The term Squadron Tactics doesn't actually refer to tactics limited to use by designated squadrons, but rather tactics employed by "groups" of aircraft from the same force. Another distinction can be made. Squadron tactics can be force-wide tactical plans that nearly overlap doctrine level descriptions, or tactics that are used for groups of aircraft. Force-wide tactics are tactics that are more or less mission oriented, while group level tactics are more specific to the maneuver or action level.

We discussed one example of the former when we covered the topic of escort missions and mentioned how groups of aircraft are deployed on bomber missions. Basically, you should have gathered from that section that the best aircraft was used in duty best suited to their capabilities (although some might argue that certain aircraft were created for specific duty).

Another good example of how squadron tactics were used is illustrated by how the RAF utilized their air power. When air defense radar or Observer Corps sightings detected Luftwaffe attacks, forward-positioned Spitfires were scrambled to intercept. Spitfires were better suited for this type of duty over the Hurricane due to their climb rate.

Meanwhile, Hurricanes stationed further inland were brought in to fly CAP over forward assets such as airfields. Their job was to catch and destroy Luftwaffe raiders that filtered through the Spitfires dispatched to meet them. Hurricanes were well suited for this defensive duty due to their favorable performance at low altitudes.

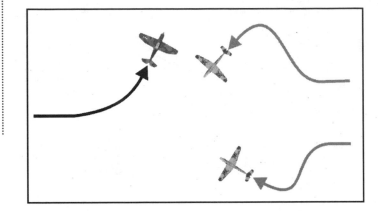

Avoid the Bracket by maneuvering to keep all attackers on the same side of your aircraft.

Offensive Squadron Tactics

As we've discussed, force-wide tactics are mission-oriented and are usually pretty general. On the other hand, squadron or group level tactics are a bit more specific in nature. Generally, most tactics that can be employed by two aircraft can be utilized by groups of aircraft, although some tactics are unique.

Here are a couple of notable examples that will help you understand the concepts. Once you understand how they work, you should be able to adapt other tactics for your own use, as situations suggest.

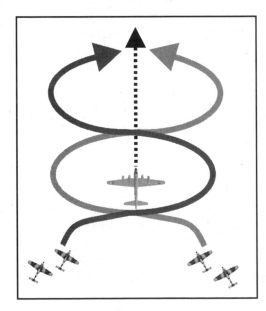

You can use another variation of the Thatch Weave against bombers.

Thatch Weave—Bomber Style

You can use a variation of the Thatch Weave with groups of fighters against bombers. If you break it down, it's actually just a combination of side attacks employed by two groups of fighters using the Bracket. As one group of fighters attack, the second group attacks from the opposite end, sandwiching the bomber/target in between.

Hit and Split

The Hit and Split technically begins as a "group BnZ," but the "Split" marks the difference. After the attack, the group splits into two or more parts. Basically, one group extends as usual, while the second group changes tactics. What you really end up with is a group level Assisted Waltz (where one group TnB's while the other group BnZ's).

Defensive Squadron Tactics

Although there are squadron tactics used for offensive purposes, there really aren't many defensive squadron tactics (other than the Lufbery Circle invented during WWI by American Ace Raoul Lufbery), and flying in formation. Let's look at these one at a time.

Luftwaffe aircraft are detected by radar (A). Spitfires scramble (B) to intercept them—due to their better climb performance. Hurricanes from inland airfields fly CAP over Spitfire bases (C) to catch enemy aircraft that filter through.

A Lufbery Circle is created when a group of aircraft fly head-to-tail in a level turn, like the connected cars of a train. This essentially enables each aircraft to cover the aircraft flying the circle directly ahead of it. For example, when an attacker enters the circle with the intent of getting on the six of an aircraft to shoot it down, the next aircraft in the sequence could shoot the attacker without much trouble.

While the Lufbery Circle worked relatively well in WWI (and it was used to some extent in WWII), the BnZ (especially the vertical BnZ) rendered it more or less suicidal. High-speed attacks allowed the attacker to hit and extend before the fighter covering the target could do anything about it. (If you recall, this is precisely the technique used to beat the loop fight—circles are horizontal loops.)

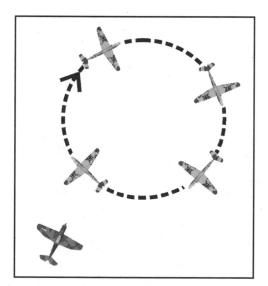

The Lufbery Circle offered mutual protection for TnB attacks, but was worthless against the BnZ.

Formation Flying Issues

Although it's widely known that military aircraft fly in formation, what isn't always obvious is why they do it. There are actually a couple of reasons. One is that it helps newer pilots keep their cockpit workload down—only one aircraft

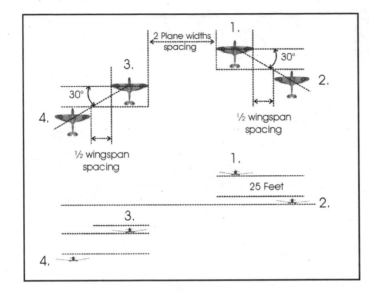

This is the spacing of a typical Finger Four formation.

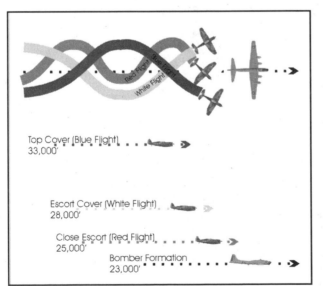

The typical escort formation provides mutual support for everyone involved.

needs to navigate—everyone else can simply follow the leader. A second reason is that by placing aircraft close together, their offensive potential increases—due to the concentrated firepower the aircraft have.

Perhaps the most compelling reason for flying in formation is the mutual defensive support the tactic offers. Although bombers flew in tight formations in order to concentrate their mutual defensive firepower, the concept of mutual defensive support stretches into detection and maneuvering benefits as well.

Formation flying is designed to overcome, or at least reduce, blind spots. Even in today's world of airborne radar, blind spots still exist, so flying in formation continues to have a place in air combat. Anyway, as we now know, detecting bandits as soon as possible will grant you the most options, and having the most options helps you win fights.

In reality, one of the problems with formations is that some are better for actual defensive purposes (maneuvering access) than others. However, because Combat Flight Simulator is a simulation, certain formations are more conducive to simulated flight than others. The root of these simulation-based formation flight problems comes from the view limitations inherent to simulations.

For example, flying in a Vic formation or Finger Four formation, in any position other than as flight leader, requires you to fly while looking out at a 45-degree view (in other words 10 o'clock or 2 o'clock). This is very difficult to do because the view of the aircraft you're supposed to match flight with is delivered at an angle that's difficult to judge on a computer monitor.

While the Inline formation (also known as the Line-astern formation) is much easier to fly within, the mutual support is rather one-sided. Although the

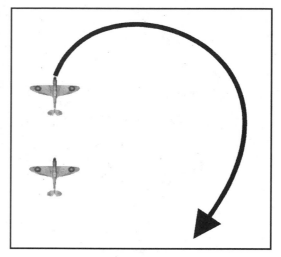

Although flying Inline makes the flying part easy, covering the rear wingman is difficult.

rear aircraft can protect the flight leader quite readily, the reverse isn't true. If a bandit attacks the rear aircraft, by the time the leader circles around to help, the wingman is most likely a smoldering hunk of metal spiraling toward the ground.

The Combat-Spread formation (also known as the Line-abreast) is tactically one of the best formations around for both offensive and defensive situations. When flown at a distance of one turn radius from each other, mutual defensive support is very good. But the Combat-Spread formation's real advantage comes as an offensive unit. That's because it allows either fighter to be utilized in attack capacity and the increased distance allows for more abrupt maneuvering without fear of crashing into one of the good guys.

The Combat-Spread formation also has the added benefit of being harder to decipher for real-life enemy opponents. Because neither pilot takes an easy to recognize lead position, either fighter can (and should) assume the role of attacker. This attack doctrine has become known as the "loose deuce" over the years and you'll find that it's very effective when employed by two good pilots.

Before the loose deuce, the flight leader was the offensive unit while the wingman took up the defensive duties. Once the leader was engaged and on the six of a bandit, the wingman would more or less become a cheerleader. In the

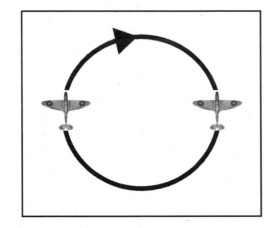

The Combat-Spread formation is slightly hard to fly compared to the Inline formation, but its mutual support is much better.

loose deuce both fighters carry out the attack. Many of the tactics in this chapter illustrate the philosophy behind the loose deuce, so it's quite easy to recognize how it all began.

Multiplayer Scoring

Within Multiplayer mode, Kills are scored as a +1, Death scores a -1, and a collision with another player is scored as 1 Kill and 1 Death. Scores are displayed when you're killed, and at the end of the session—but pressing the D key will display the score board during multiplayer games with Victory requirements that track scores.

Chapter Ten

CAMPAIGNS AND MISSIONS

Congratulations! You've now reached the end of our little combat training course. Let's continue by talking about how Microsoft Combat Flight Simulator will *test* what you've learned with its Missions and Campaigns. Because we're dealing with a simulation that covers history, we'll cover game specifics and details, in addition to some historical background related to the air battles that were fought. This is, after all, Combat Flight Simulator!

The Campaigns

Combat Flight Simulator WWII Europe Series features two campaigns—the Battle of Britain, and the Battle for Europe. You can play each campaign from either the Allied or Axis perspective.

A single campaign consists of 18 scripted missions (for a grand total of 72 missions across both campaigns and possible perspectives) that feature various random elements. If you've never heard the term scripted missions before, we'll tell you that the elements of a scripted mission (targets, waypoints, friendly and enemy types, numbers and placements, etc.) are predetermined by the mission designer (as opposed to "random missions" that are created on the fly or "dynamic missions" based on the outcome of previous missions).

Although scripted missions are generally more interesting and reflect real life better than randomly-generated or dynamic missions, their replay value tends to be low. That's because once you've played it, you know exactly when and where things will happen. Fortunately to keep things fresh, Combat Flight Simulator has implemented random mission features, as well.

While mission targets, waypoints, and scoring goals remain fixed, the position at which enemy aircraft show up in a given mission will change. In some missions, positions are randomly selected from two to three pre-defined locations.

> **Note:** *Although you can win any campaign, you cannot alter history.*

Tip: *To play any of the campaign missions as individual missions, copy the campaign mission files from the Campaigns folder into the Missions folder.*

For example in one battle, enemy interceptors might show up on your 4 o'clock position, and the next time you play they might show up at 10 o'clock.

These random elements are not limited to enemy positions. Some of the missions feature random points for friendlies too. As you might imagine, it can get pretty interesting!

The Campaign itself is linear—missions are performed one after another. You cannot alter a mission path or the next mission with your performance.

Battle of Britain (July-October 1940)

> *"The Battle of Britain is about to begin.*
> *Let us therefore brace ourselves to our duty.*
> *So bare ourselves that if the British Empire and*
> *its commonwealth lasts for a thousand years men will*
> *still say this was their finest hour."*

—Winston Churchill, Prime Minister

The Battle of Britain was different from any of the other battles and campaigns in WWII because it was a struggle between air forces. No ground troops or Navy forces were involved. Many argue that the Battle of Britain was the most important air battle in history. So, it shouldn't come as a surprise that it figures prominently in Combat Flight Simulator.

Combat Flight Simulator's Battle of Britain campaign covers three acts: Kanalkampf, the war over the English Channel; Eagle Attack, in which the Luftwaffe attacks British airfields and factories; and The Blitz, when the Luftwaffe bombs London.

To give you some history, here is a short historical timeline, which leads up to the Battle of Britain:

June 10, 1940—Italy declared war on Britain and France.
June 14, 1940—Germany entered Paris, France.
June 22, 1940—France signs armistice agreement with Germany.

After the swift conquest of France, Hitler proposed "Operation Sea Lion"—a sea-borne assault on Britain. Historians are at odds as to the reasons for invading Britain. One speculation was that Hitler knew that the British would pose a strong resistance to his plans to conquer Europe. The other was that the United States would officially enter the war to aid Britain (they were already supplying aircraft and other war essentials—but on a much smaller scale than what was to come), and England would become the staging point. So if England was under German control, the American's invasion of Europe would be much more difficult.

Regardless of the reasons behind the goal, time was critical. Autumn storms would make sea invasion impossible.

"The English Air Force must be so reduced morally and physically that it is unable to deliver any significant attack against the German crossing."
—Adolph Hitler, Directive No. 16

In a nutshell, control of the air was the key. On July 10, 1940 when the Battle of Britain began, the Luftwaffe outnumbered British aircraft 3:1 (comprised of roughly 1/3 fighters). Luftwaffe fighters outnumbered the British by a 2:1 advantage. The Germans had 1290 Bf-109s and Bf-110s, and the RAF had a mere 591 Hurricanes and Spitfires. So sure of the air superiority of the Luftwaffe, Reichsmaschall Hermann Göering assured Hitler of success. Hitler believed victory would be secured within two weeks.

Obviously the German plan was to destroy the RAF. At first their strategy was to lure the British Fighter Command into combat and destroy it plane by plane in the air. The Luftwaffe pilots tried to lure the RAF pilots away from England so if they were shot down or damaged, they'd be lost in the English Channel. But the Germans didn't know that English code breakers had broken the German codes and knew what their plans were.

RAF Fighter Command Air Chief Marshall Sir Hugh Dowding (age 60) split his forces into four groups. 10 Group covered Southwest England, 11 Group, commanded by Vice-Marshal Keith Park, covered the Southeast (notably the corner closest to France), 12 Group the covered Midlands, and 13 Group covered the Northern areas of Scotland and North Ireland. By keeping their fighters over England when pilots were shot down, they were often able to get back in the air the same day. Although there were shortages of airplanes and fuel, pilots were in the shortest supply of all.

August 13, 1940 "Adlertag" (Eagle Day) marked an all out attack by the Luftwaffe. 1485 German sorties launched that day. Using the tactics we've discussed earlier in the book, the RAF kept their loses down to a mere 13

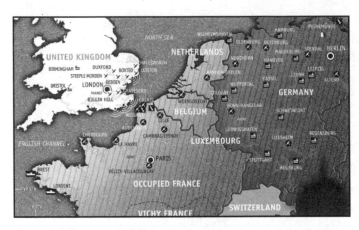

The European Theater of Operations (ETO) during WWII.

aircraft in the air, with another 47 lost on the ground. The Nazi's lost 34.

August 15, 1940 was the last day the Germans attacked Observer Corps radar installations. The Germans lost 70 aircraft compared to 29 lost by the British. Oddly enough (and truth is often stranger than fiction), the Germans believed that the destruction of radar installations was not making a difference, so they abandoned the idea. In reality, they were making great progress and, years later, RAF officers admitted that if the Germans had persisted with their attacks, they would have left Britain helpless.

Analysts today blame the high German losses on Göering's orders that Luftwaffe fighters remain attached to the bombers. This has been criticized as being a critical tactical error.

"These escort missions were very unpopular because we had to fly at the same altitude and speed as the bomber formations—which meant that we couldn't make use of the tactical superiority of our fighter aircraft—the speed, the climbing capability, and the maneuverability—and as a result, we suffered great losses at the hands of the British."

—Lieutenant Colonel Dietrich Hrabak
Luftwaffe 125 kills

The Nazi's biggest raid of the Battle of Britain was launched on August 18, 1940 against the Kenley RAF installations in Southern England. Nine military personnel were killed and 10 were seriously wounded. Other casualties included six civilians dead and 21 wounded. Aircraft losses included five fighters destroyed on the ground and 3 damaged. Of the nine Dornier Do 17s aircraft sent by the Nazi's, five were shot down and four were damaged.

During the weeks of August 24 through September 6, 1940, the Luftwaffe committed nearly 1000 airplanes a day to Britain. Few historians disagree that the tide of the war began to change for Germany, from a seemingly random mistake, on the night of August 24, 1940.

On this night a Luftwaffe bombing crew mistakenly dropped their bombs on a residential section of London. Until that point only military targets were hit. In order for Operation Sea Lion to succeed, the RAF had to be crushed. Attacking airfields, aircraft on the ground, and aircraft factories would get that job done, and by most accounts the Luftwaffe's war of attrition was succeeding.

In retaliation for the bombs dropped on London, Churchill ordered an RAF Bomber Command raid on Berlin on August 26, 1940. Thoroughly humiliated by the bombing of Germany's capital city, Hitler changed tactics. Beginning on September 7, 1940 Hitler diverted the Luftwaffe to a bombing campaign of London that lasted 9 weeks.

During the summer of 1940, the Luftwaffe bombed English cities every day. On September 15, 1940 the Luftwaffe launched a maximum strength attack on London and other targets south.

"The mastery of the sky [over England] was lost by the Germans at that point. There was no strategic concept, there was only a tactical concept. There were no fighters with a great range. They were planned to defend the Reich, to defend the cities. There were no refueling tanks. And in addition to that there was this amateurish leadership. Well, they should have known from the very beginning this was something they could not win."

—Colonel Johannes "Macki" Steinhoff,
Luftwaffe, 170 kills

Hitler abandoned Operation Sea Lion on September 17, 1940 and "postponed" the conquest of Britain—which was, of course, later abandoned altogether. By October the dogfighting over England dwindled.

"Never in the field of human conflict was so much owed by so many to so few."

—Winston Churchill

If the Luftwaffe had succeeded in achieving air superiority, few doubt that Operation Sea Lion would have worked and Europe would have been under German control. This would have greatly helped the Nazi invasion of Russia and given it a much better chance of succeeding. But because of the failure of invading Britain, a two-front war remained necessary.

In the end, Air Chief Marshal Dowding and Vice-Marshal Park were criticized for their tactics of disrupting enemy bomber formations before they unloaded their bombs. Their critics said that instead they should have gone up and shot down as many aircraft as possible. They were both eventually censured for proceeding too cautiously against the Luftwaffe—Dowding was relieved, and Park was transferred to Training Command.

There is no doubt that the RAF had tactical and technological advantages over the Luftwaffe. The most important were the Early Warning System (EWS) Observer Corps tracking stations which stretched from Orkney Islands in the North to Severn Estuary in the South West. Luck (weather) also played a factor. The English fog helped hide ground targets, and storms grounded attacking aircraft.

In the final analysis the British advantages included several key factors:

- Dowding understood aerial warfare while Göering didn't have large air unit deployment experience.
- British pilots flew over friendly territory. This allowed them to fly four to five sorties daily and bail out over friendly territory.
- Radar enabled the RAF to save fuel by scrambling aircraft to the right areas at the right time.

German disadvantages were:

- Limited range of Luftwaffe escorts.
- Most attacks were against Southeast England and the main brunt of the action was borne by Air Vice Marshall Keith Park's 11 Group.
- Luftwaffe pilots flew missions for as long as they were physically capable. 1000 sortie tours of duty were not uncommon. By contrast, British pilots flew 80-100 sorties before being rotated out.

"If you ask what were the mistakes that caused the loss of the Battle of Britain, you have to cast a wider net and ask yourself was the Luftwaffe suited or built for and armed for such a purpose—were the airplanes suited, where the tactics suited? And then you come up against all sorts of hurdles, and you realize that the Luftwaffe was never meant to fight Britain."

—General Major Adolph Galland, Luftwaffe, 104 kills

The final tally—the British started with slightly more than 1000 pilots and ultimately lost 451 of them and 915 aircraft. Germany lost a total of 1733 bombers and fighters.

Battle for Europe (June 1943-April 1945)

On December 7, 1941 "a day that will live in infamy" as U.S. President Franklin Delano Roosevelt so aptly stated it, the Japanese Empire attacked Pearl Harbor, Hawaii. Soon afterwards, the United States officially joined the war. Until then, the U.S. was providing supplies, materials, and aircraft to Britain, China, and later Russia through the Lend-Lease Act (March 1941).

By the Summer of 1942, the United States 8th Air Force set up shop in England. As Hitler feared, England would be used as a launch point for the invasion of the European continent. The Allied plan was markedly different from the Nazi plan to conquer Britain. The concept was to thrust air power deep into enemy territory and to cripple the enemy's war machine, so that the enemy would surrender without the intervention of a land army.

To accomplish this goal, Allied air power was give two tasks in Operation Point Blank, adopted on May 14, 1943:

1. Destroy the German supply lines. Without vital supplies such as ammunition, fuel, and food the German army couldn't be effective.

2. Destroy Germany's industry—in particular, Germany's aircraft factories. Again, air superiority had to be obtained before any sea crossing.

To facilitate the second goal, the Allies employed "around the clock bombing." The U.S. used daylight precision bombing while the RAF used night bombing. RAF bombers were designed for range and distance rather than speed and firepower—and as a rule, the RAF offered no fighter escorts for their bombers.

While darkness offered protection from detection, it also worked against the bombers. During this stage of the war, bomb targeting was still done optically. So the darkness of night made the identification of ground targets more difficult. As a result the technique was named area bombing.

The American 8th Air Force used massed, precision daylight bombing raids. The deployment of the Boeing B-17 bomber with its excellent high altitude performance made daylight bombing acceptable. Not only was the B-17 tough and capable of carrying lots of bombs, it had the range to reach Germany. The ability to fly high and fast meant that intercepting fighters and AAA would have a harder time shooting it down, but the high altitudes also made the targeting necessary for precision bombing more difficult.

During the opening months of the bombing campaign, Colonel Tooey Spaatz and American Fighter Projects Officer Benjamin S. Kelsey saw no need for fighter escorts for the B-17. They believed the B-17 Flying Fortress could mount an effective self-defense with onboard gunners (at least 10 were on the B-17F). As a result, the 8th Air Force was torn apart on the notorious Schweinfurt mission of October 24, 1943. Key ball-bearing factories in Schweinfurt were the targets and—although damage to them was recorded as "substantial"—60 American bombers were shot down and another 138 were damaged, out of the 291 sent on the mission.

At that point, those in charge realized the daylight offensive would have to be halted unless fighter cover could be maintained all the way to target and back. Fortunately the development and deployment of the P-51 allowed that to happen. (Göering once admitted privately that he realized that Germany would lose the war when he first saw the P-51's over Germany.)

"When we finally got the B-17F's and started going deep penetration, we didn't have fighter escorts to go very far. We had P-47's, but they'd only go in a short ways and then they'd have to leave us—and then the Germans would take over and uh, it scared us to death."

—Lieutenant Colonel Boardman C. Reed, USAAF B-17 pilot

In 1943, the RAF Bomber Command had considerably more heavy bombers available than the USAAF and actually dropped more strategic tonnage from July 1943 through March 1944. To counter the night raids, the elite Luftwaffe nachtjager (night fighters) were put into action.

To counter the American bombing raids, the Germans began moving some of their fighter units from the Russian front to protect Germany. Because American aircraft factories were out of reach of Luftwaffe aircraft, there was little the Nazi's could do to end the war, other than to make the American campaign so costly that the Allies would cease their attacks (much like what happened to Germany in the Battle of Britain). At this point, Germany pretty much had its back to the wall.

"Considering the distances we had to cover, we were like a fire brigade putting out fires. This meant being transferred every three to four days. We had tremendous logistical problems, so on a daily basis we had to perform our missions and already think about the next airfield we were going to use."

—Major Gunther Rall, Luftwaffe 275 Kills

From the end of 1943 into early 1944, the Americans experimented with radar targeting to allow bombing through cloud cover. Although accuracy was reported to be no better than RAF night bombing, bombing in bad weather often meant that German interceptors would remain grounded.

In January 1944, General "Jimmy" Doolittle took command of the 8th Air Force. In addition to leading the famous bomber raids on Tokyo later in the war, another of his contributions was the approval of new tactics allowing fighters to range ahead of bombers on sweeps. Then, if they were able, on the way back they could "hit the deck" (fly at tree-top level) and strafe anything that looked German. This further facilitated the destruction of the Nazi supply lines and Luftwaffe aircraft.

During the third week of February 1944 the weather cleared enough for the Americans to launch "Operation Argument." The battles that ensued from this operation from February 20th through February 25th have become known as "Big Week." The heavy bombing during Big Week also resulted in heavy losses to the Allies and the Nazis. The 8th and 15th Air Forces lost 294 aircraft (which included 266 heavy bombers) while destroying 355 German aircraft.

March 4 through March 8, 1944 brought the first daylight bombing raids on Berlin. Soon after came D-Day in June 1944—the Allied invasion that landed in Normandy, France from across the English Channel. Although this wasn't "the beginning of the land war" by any means, it was the beginning of the big push towards Germany.

Although not a participant modeled in Combat Flight Simulator, the aid of the Russians toward the destruction of the Third Reich should not go unnoticed. Germany was being attacked from the Russians on the East, the Allies on the west, and bombarded day and night from the air.

The Battle of the Bulge (December 1944 to January 1945) marked the Allies ground forces reaching the doorstep of Germany. By this time, the largest Luftwaffe unit was the anti-aircraft component, which was comprised of 1-1.5 million individuals. The combination of Allied bombing, and the Luftwaffe policy of sending up the same pilots until they were wounded or killed, began to take its toll. The once mighty Luftwaffe, an offensive weapon instrumental in conquering Poland and France, became an almost exclusively defensive force.

Despite the creation of the elite all-ace jet fighter wing JV 44 (headed by General Galland), the Allies entered Berlin in April 1945. On May 7, 1945, Germany signed an unconditional surrender—the war in Europe was over.

Many factors were poised against the Luftwaffe from the start. The Luftwaffe was built for concentrated attacks on a small area and it had no

power to reach an enemy's industrial base and communications centers unless they were within a few hundred miles. The Luftwaffe was essentially a tactical air weapon put together for a small, local war. With the multiple-front war and the vast distances it had to cover, the Luftwaffe found itself so unprepared and overwhelmed that neither its cutting-edge technological brilliance nor extraordinary determination could save it from eventual destruction. Because the United States wasn't under constant bombing attacks as was Germany, the Americans remained able to produce an unending supply of war materials.

Advantages of the Allies:
- Allies could attack from more than one direction.
- Industrial base not accessible to the enemy.
- Had strategic plan.
- Developed long range weapons to implement plan.

Disadvantages of the Luftwaffe:
- Poor leadership.
- No long range aircraft.
- Industrial base vulnerable to attack.
- Super-aircraft came too late or were misused.

Being There: An Interview With a B-17 Pilot

Although we've covered many of the details of the air war over Europe, there's nothing quite like getting some perspective from someone that was actually there—Captain Carl E. Hellerich, 100th Bomb Group, USAAF. We were fortunate to discuss his experiences with him.

Captain Hellerich was a USAAF B-17 pilot who served in the 8th Air Force from 1943 to 1946. He was stationed at the Air Base at Thorpe Abbots, England when he arrived there in January 1945. By the way, Captain Hellerich commented, in an aside to our comments, that "Bob Blair (Waist Gunner) was the one who leaned over to recover something and, while in that position, a piece of metal went *through* the plane. If Bob had been in an upright position, it would have been 'good-bye!'"

Here are a few excerpts from our conversations with Captain Hellerich:

PC Press: How many missions did you fly?

Hellerich: 17 missions total. After six missions, I was asked to fly Lead Crew, which changed the structure of our crew. Lead crews included

Navigators, Bombardiers, and Radar Operators. *[Note: The war ended before Captain Hellerich could complete the usual 25-mission tour. The Lead Crew aircraft directed the rest of the bombers to target.]*

PC Press: What was the nickname of the B-17 you flew?

Hellerich: The Aircraft used in Lead Crew positions were equipped with radar equipment so we used whatever unit was available. Consequently, we didn't have a plane with a descriptive name.

PC Press: How many bombers flew with you in a typical mission?

Hellerich: A typical mission would involve 48 planes from each bomber base. Depending on the target, planes from other bases would line up behind leading planes. A typical formation would be 480 planes [bombers]. I think the maximum I remember seeing was 1400 planes.

PC Press: Which fighters escorted you on your missions?

Hellerich: Fighter escorts that were provided us were crafts that Fighter Command had available. Fortunately, they were P-51 Mustangs. Less frequently used were P-47's.

PC Press: When enemy fighters confronted you, did you ever change course to try and evade them, or did you just fly straight through?

Hellerich: We had German fighters headed towards us several times but we also had American escorts. If we altered our course, it was to take advantage of a change in wind currents. We had some German passes, but .50 caliber firepower from the B-17's and eager P-51's in the area helped us meet that challenge.

PC Press: Did you ever take a second pass at a target (as depicted in the movie Memphis Belle) or is that all fiction?

Hellerich: I don't recall ever trying to make a second pass at a target. I can understand what the Memphis Belle had to go through when there was heavy cloud coverage. Earlier in the war, [bomber] radar was not available and that made a big difference. Having radar to read your location, even through clouds, was a significant development in favor of the Allies.

PC Press: In your opinion, what was the most vulnerable section of a B-17 to enemy fighters?

Captain Carl E. Hellerich, USAAF.

Hellerich: I would say that the section containing the fuel tanks would be the most vulnerable section of the B-17.

PC Press: In your opinion, how does a B-17 handle?

Hellerich: I found the B-17 to respond very well and was easy to fly in formation where it was necessary to slide smoothly, keeping the squadrons and groups real tight. Getting our planes off the ground and into formation with other squadrons was usually accomplished over England. This was normally a trouble-free function. If we had weather conditions to cope with, we would fly above the clouds single file and then slide into proper positions.

PC Press: What was your most memorable mission?

Hellerich: Here's the summary of a mission that I wrote in a journal that I kept back during the war.

"It was an early wake-up call on March 30, 1945. We all know this is another 'big' one, so even our most routine motions have a little more zip. We do what needs to be done at the barracks and the next move is to eat breakfast. Some do and some don't.

By now it's 4:00 in the morning and time for the mission briefing. The weather is 6/10 coverage*, which is not good, but the forecast is worse. The curtain is pulled** and the briefing starts. We learn the target, for us, is Hamburg. This is a major operation and includes the 1400 B-17's and 24's, and 900 Mustang and Thunderbolt fighters. We learn the weather forecast is still undesirable, but with radar our risks are reduced substantially. It takes three to four hours to reach our target and all crews are moving well. Along the way, some of the bombers and fighters turn off to other targets. I'm not sure how many planes will unload bombs on the town of Hamburg today.

When we reach target the flak is extremely heavy but we're barely aware that we are being hit. Bob Blair become extremely aware, however, when he drops something, bends to pick it up and a piece of flak tears through the wall of his ammunition box. He knows he would have been hit had he not bent over at that instant.

No bombers or fighter are lost on this mission that I'm aware of. Our plane has 20 flak holes, all deemed repairable by the ground crew."

[*6/10ths of the sky overcast]
[**Mission details and maps were kept behind a curtain in the briefing room.]

From left to right, back row first: Sgt. Bob Blair (Waist Gunner), Capt. Carl Hellerich (Pilot), Lt. Eddie Whitney (Co-Pilot), Lt. Leroy Duncan (Navigator), Staff Sgt. Jim Finn (Radio Operator), Staff Sgt. Eddie "Pete" Miller (Engineer), Flight Officer John Clinto (Radio Operator), and Lt. Tony "A.J." Shuirba (Bombardier).

Enemy Levels

What the Enemy Level settings (also sometimes referred to as *mission difficulty levels* for Campaign mode although it's labeled as such) change varies according the mode you play. In Quick Combat mode, the Enemy Level setting only changes the skill level of the enemy forces you fly against. In Single Missions and Campaign modes this setting adjusts the skill level and in some cases the number of enemy forces you'll face.

There are three Enemy Level settings. Each setting specifies the range of possible AI skill levels allowed in the mission (which include friendlies).

New pilot

Enter pilot name

Ben

○ Rookie

○ Veteran

◉ Ace

? Cancel OK

Quick Combat scores are affected by the Enemy Level selected.

They are as follows:

Rookie: AI levels 1, 2, or 3
Veteran: AI levels 2, 3, or 4
Ace: AI levels 3, 4, or 5

As you can see, Combat Flight Simulator features five AI levels. Each AI level beginning with Level 1 (for lack of a better term, the "dumbest" level) increases in difficulty until you reach Level 5 (the best pilots). The higher the level, the greater the AI pilot accuracy is in fighting.

Regardless of level, the missions in Combat Flight Simulator were designed so that there's always a realistic mix of good pilots, fair pilots, and inexperienced newbies—who inevitably get shot down. All of the differences between AI pilots (remember AI impacts friendly as well as enemy pilots) lead to interesting situations. If you observe carefully, you'll often see advanced pilots taking advantage of the novice pilots.

Mission Briefings

Although you're tempted to bypass the mission briefings (that's what we like to see—enthusiastic pilots!)—read the mission briefings. Note the five "W"s; the Who, What, Where, When, and Why of your mission. If you fail to read them, you may end up wandering around in the middle of the mission trying to figure out what you're supposed to do.

Here are some pointers on the mission briefings:

- **Who** is who you're flying with. Note which airplane you're flying as well as all of the other aircraft involved in your mission. Knowing your aircraft will help you plan tactics based on its limitations and strengths.
- **What** is what your mission is. Your mission will dictate the basic strategy you want to use. The briefing will also outline what your mission goals are.
- **Where** refers to the mission waypoints you're flying. Roughly note on the map where your route will take you and how many waypoints

Meet the AI

One old combat axiom advises "know thy enemy." This advice is true when we look at the differences between aircraft, but we should also point out that it's the pilot, and not the airplane, that has the greatest ability to ultimately change the course of an air battle.

In Combat Flight Simulator, AI (Artificial Intelligence) refers to the "brains" behind the computer generated pilots, gunners, drivers, and engineers that control the vehicles in the Combat Flight Simulator world. Here are some excerpts from an interview with the Combat Flight Simulator Team that will provide some insights into the AI enemy you'll be facing.

PC Press: How does the Artificial Intelligence of the enemy aircraft work?

CFST: The artificial intelligence is based on a sophisticated sighting system. Enemy planes have to "see" you to be able to attack you. The system takes into account the visual range of the enemy pilots, realistic visual arc, and the relative distance and position of the target plane. Just like in real war, if an enemy plane "sneaks" behind your back, you are probably dead. We are modeling what so many WWII pilots say: "Most times you did not know that an enemy plane was around until you got hit". Experience level of the enemy plane matters. Aces are better at "seeing" enemy planes than "rookies". Users are expected to face a mix of aces, average pilots, and novices in battle.

Another realistic feature of the AI is target fixation. If you see a plane pursuing another target, it's going to be a lot easier to sneak up and get some good shots off while they are preoccupied.

AI pilots will also prioritize targets through a points system. If they settle on a target and something else comes along that looks more promising, they'll change their minds—just like real fighter pilots would. They will also try to run away in some cases when they are severely damaged.

All the computer piloted bombers have individual gun stations that in turn have their own set of ranges and visibility. Bring your Bf-109 in fast and strafe across the side of a B-24 and you might just take out the gunners. Fly in between two bombers and they might accidentally shoot each other.

PC Press: Do the enemy planes have any advantage over players?

CFST: We run our AI planes through the same physics engines as players so you won't see the AI pilot pulling off any impossible stunts. What we do is choose a flight stick position, and then have the plane react accordingly based on the same flight model. So we are calculating flight stick positions for every artificial intelligence-governed plane. You'll see very realistic maneuvers from the AI pilots. You can hit the pilot and kill him and the plane will react as if the pilot died and lost control of his flight stick.

you're flying. Also note the direction of enemy territory and the direction home.

- **When** is self explanatory. For example, if you're sent on an escort mission and don't show up when you're supposed to, you've missed *when*.

- **Why** explains your mission goal. If your mission is to escort bombers to Frankfurt, you need to keep the bombers from being shot down until they reach Frankfurt. On the other hand, if you're out to intercept bombers headed inbound toward London, you'll know you need to stop them before they can drop their bomb loads on London.

Scoring

There are three areas where scores are tallied in Combat Flight Simulator—Quick Combat, Campaign Missions, and Multiplayer mode.

Quick Combat Scoring

Your score in quick combat is cumulative. In other words, it tallies until you end your flight by exiting (pressing the X key), bailing out (pressing the O key three times), or getting killed. If your score is high enough, you're prompted to enter your name into the top-ten score list.

Quick Combat scores are affected by the Realism Setting used at the time of the kill and factor in the level of the AI. For example, if you are flying at 80 Percent Realism Setting and you are flying with the enemy level set to Veteran (which means AI skill levels of 2, 3, or 4) then every time you shoot someone it multiplies their skill level (for example, two) times a percentage factor—which is then added to your cumulative score up to that point.

Mission Scoring

The Mission scoring system has five possible outcomes: high success, partial success, neutral (bare minimum success), partial failure, and total failure. The term "scoring system" is a bit of a misnomer—missions do not receive a numerical score. A numerical score is calculated in Campaign missions, but it's used to award promotions—which we'll get to in a minute. Let's continue with Mission scoring.

Success in a mission is based on the percentage of the mission objectives that you were able to obtain. For example, in a bomber escort mission, 40 percent of the bombers have to survive for the mission to be deemed neutral. A 50-70 percent survival rate is counted as a partial success, and anything above 70 percent is total success. These percentages vary from mission to mission according to the wishes of the mission designer or the individual player's Mission Difficulty Setting. (Naturally, the more successful you are, the more points you'll score.)

> **Tip:** *If you forget what your mission targets are during your flight, remember that mission targets have * (asterisks) displayed in their labels.*

Conversely, on a bridge destruction mission you may only have to destroy one out of 10 bridges for the mission to be called a success. Therefore, the neutral outcome value is set to 10 percent. 12-14 percent is partial success, and anything higher is total success. Again these percentages will vary. Some events remain constant regardless of the skill level you set. If you are killed, your mission will always end as a total failure, and if you ditch or bail out, your mission is incomplete.

Promotions

As we just mentioned, Promotions are based on your score (although they're unseen in Campaign mode), and scores are tallied in the same way Quick Combat scores are calculated (your score is based on the Realism Setting factoring in the skill level of the enemy killed). The only differences are:

1. Mission targets and goals are worth more points than other targets.

2. If you "warp" to finish a mission instead of landing your aircraft, you'll lose 10 percent of your "internal" point score (the score on which promotions are based).

Just as in the real world, the different air forces had different ranks. The various promotions and their scoring requirements are as follows. Note that the Rookie and Veteran Enemy Level settings will limit your promotions.

Promotion Scoring

Luftwaffe Promotions	Score Requirements
Oberst	40,000
Oberstleutnant	20,000
Major	10,000
Hauptmann (maximum rank at Veteran level)	5000
Oberleutnant	2500
Leutnant (maximum rank at Rookie level)	1000

RAF Promotions	Score Requirements
Group Captain	40,000
Wing Commander	20,000
Squadron Leader	10,000
Flight Lieutenant (maximum rank at Veteran level)	5000
Flying Officer	2500
Pilot Officer (maximum rank at Rookie level)	1000

USAAF Promotions	Score Requirements
Colonel	40,000
Lieutenant Colonel	20,000
Major	10,000
Captain (maximum rank at Veteran level)	5000
First Lieutenant	2500
Second Lieutenant (maximum rank obtainable at the Rookie level)	1000

Medals

Medals are awarded based solely on the number of enemy planes you shoot down. These include fighters or bombers, but not ground objects.

Wound badges are given when your pilot (or more accurately, your pilot/cockpit hit box) receives damage.

The number of kills or hits required for earning the various medals are as follows:

Kills Required for Medals

RAF Medals	Kills required
Victoria Cross	200
Distinguished Service Order	50, 100
Distinguished Flying Cross	5, 20

Luftwaffe Medals	
Knight's Cross with Oak Leaves, Swords and Diamonds (Battle for Europe)	200 kills
Knight's Cross with Oak Leaves and Swords (Battle for Europe)	80 kills
Knight's Cross with Oak Leaves	20 kills
Iron Cross	5 kills
Gold wound badge (very severe injuries) (<75% damage to pilot hit box)	hits to pilot hit box
Silver wound badge (more serious injuries)(<50% damage to pilot hit box)	hits to pilot hit box
Black wound badge (minor injuries in the line of duty) (<25% damage to hit box)	hits to pilot hit box

USAAF Medals	
Medal of Honor	300 kills
Distinguished Service Cross	155, 250 kills
Silver Star	75 kills
Distinguished Flying Cross	15, 35 kills
Air Medal	5 kills
Purple Heart (wound badge)	Any hit to the pilot hit box

Medals awarded by the RAF

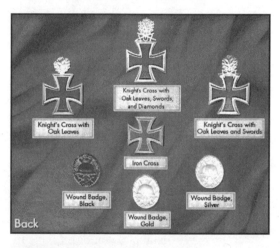

Medals awarded by the Luftwaffe.

Medals awarded by the USAAF.

Mission Tips and Insights

A mission editor will be available soon after release on the Combat Flight Simulator Web site at http://www.microsoft.com/games/combatfs. Of course once that becomes available, you'll be able to "look under the hood" and see the details of a mission. That's why we'll just leave you with a few tips and insights into Combat Flight Simulator's Mission engine. The following tips may help you to take advantage of the situation, or at the very least, help keep you alive. You should also understand what's possible when you try your hand at designing your own missions.

- You can always end a mission from the Flights menu selection by clicking End Flight.
- If you fly out of the range of enemy aircraft, you'll be able to warp to the next action using the X key command.
- Some of the AI aircraft are proximity activated. In other words, they remain "dormant" until you fly within 12 km of their position. Once you do, they'll "wake-up" and begin their mission. You can use this to your advantage. If you remain outside of their area, you won't have to mess with them.
- Every aircraft has a primary directive or target type assignment. Possible target types are fighters, bombers, or ground objects. If the primary target type is eliminated, the AI will direct the aircraft to destroy the next available target. So if you have Fw-190's going after bombers for example, you don't have to worry about them coming after you as long as there are bombers flying.
- The selected Enemy Level setting not only changes the AI setting, but it can also change the number of aircraft.
- Although the numbers of AI units can vary with the Enemy Level settings, and their positions can be randomly assigned, the number of units will remain the same with each Enemy Level setting.
- Mission targets have * (asterisks) displayed in their labels.
- AI aircraft have three flight plans. They can are assigned to either take off and land, start in the air and land, or take off and not land.
- While AI aircraft have fuel limitations, they are not limited on ammo. Watch out!

Index

Register Today!

Return this
Microsoft® Combat Flight Simulator: Inside Moves
registration card today

mspress.microsoft.com

1-57231-592-X

MICROSOFT® COMBAT FLIGHT SIMULATOR: INSIDE MOVES

FIRST NAME   MIDDLE INITIAL   LAST NAME

INSTITUTION OR COMPANY NAME

ADDRESS

CITY   STATE   ZIP

( )

E-MAIL ADDRESS   PHONE NUMBER

U.S. and Canada addresses only. Fill in information above and mail postage-free.
Please mail only the bottom half of this page.

start faster **go** farther

**For information about Microsoft Press®
products, visit our Web site at
mspress.microsoft.com**

Microsoft Press